APPLIED
HOSPITALITY
Human Resource Management

Allen Z. Reich, PH.D.
Northern Arizona University

Kendall Hunt
publishing company

Cover image © Shutterstock, Inc.

www.kendallhunt.com
Send all inquiries to:
4050 Westmark Drive
Dubuque, IA 52004-1840

Brief Contents

Chapter One: Making Human Resources Decisions   **1**

Chapter Two: Values, Morale, and Motivation   **26**

Chapter Three: Compensation, Benefits, and Incentives   **42**

Chapter Four: Employment Laws   **52**

Chapter Five: The Job Creation Process   **69**

Chapter Six: Recruitment   **91**

Chapter Seven: Selective Hiring   **103**

Chapter Eight: Orientation   **125**

Chapter Nine: Training   **142**

Chapter Ten: Performance Appraisals and Discipline   **158**

Appendix: Human Resources Functional Plan Guidelines   **174**

References: **194**

Contents

Chapter One: Making Human Resources Decisions   1

Understanding Human Resources Management   1
Major Functional Departments   2
Human Resources Impact Model   4
Who Makes Human Resources Decisions?   6
The Four Generic Responsibilities of Managers   6
Human Resources Planning   11
The Six-Step (Traditional) Problem-Solving Model   13
Functional Planning (An HR Plan)   13
Three Levels of Strategy   15
Strategic Aggression   16
Sustainable Competitive Advantage (SCA)   17
Decision-making Skills   17
Case Study 1.1: The Good and the Bad; The Symptom and the Cause   19
Case Study 1.2: Do You Have What It Takes to Be a Hospitality Manager?   20
Case Study 1.3: What Skills Are Companies Looking For?   22
Case Study 1.4 Human Resources Planning Exercise   23
Strategy Reviews (SR)   24

Chapter Two: Values, Morale, and Motivation   26

Values   26
Four Seasons Hotels and Resorts Corporate Values   27
Values and Their Influence on Beliefs, Attitudes, and Behavior   28
Mission Statement and Values   29
Four Seasons Hotels and Resorts Mission Statement   30
Social Responsibility and Values   31
Strategies Supportive of Corporate Values/Ethics   31
Questions for Resolving Ethical Dilemmas   32
Friendship and the Employee-Supervisor Relationship   32
Philosophies from the Office of Trammel Crow   33
Morale and Motivation   33
Concepts Associated with Motivation   34
Morale and Motivation Factors   36
Classic Motivation Theories   39
Case Study 2.1: Personal Problems of Hourly Employees   41

Chapter Three: Compensation, Benefits, and Incentives   42

Compensation Package   42
Base Compensation   43
Benefits   45
Incentives   48
Case 3.1: Developing a Compensation Package   51

Chapter Four: Employment Laws   52

Discrimination   52
The Civil Rights Acts of 1866, 1875, 1957, and 1960   54
The Fair Labor Standards Act (FLSA) of 1938   55
The Equal Pay Act of 1963   57

The Civil Rights Act of 1964   57
Sexual Harassment   59
Major Employment Laws Following the Civil Rights Act of 1964   60
Proving Discrimination and Defenses for Discrimination Charges   62
Affirmative Action   63
Diversity in the Workplace   64
Americans with Disabilities Act (ADA)   64
Case Study 4.1: Chef Williams Is Pregnant   66
Case Study 4.2: Sexual Harassment Role–Play   67
Case Study 4.3: Dealing with Diversity   68

Chapter Five: The Job Creation Process   69

The Job Creation Process   69
Job Analysis   70
Job Design   81
Job Description   81
Job Specifications   84
Work Flow   86
Case Study 5.1: Management Problems at the Mount Aspen Resort   88
Case Study 5.2: Duties and Tasks—Be Specific   89
Case Study 5.3: Poor Service at the Abby Rose Hotel   90

Chapter Six: Recruitment   91

Recruitment   91
Turnover   91
Recruitment Planning Decisions   93
Sources of Recruits   93
Selecting Recruiters   97
Evaluation of Recruiting Methods (Control)   97
Creating an Employee Schedule   97
Case Study 6.1: Recruitment Planning   101
Case Study 6.2: Recruitment Efforts for Potential Employers   102
Case Study 6.3: Creating a Schedule for the Front Desk   102

Chapter Seven: Selective Hiring   103

Selective Hiring   103
Selection Strategies   105
The Application   105
Background Checks   108
Interviews—First/Screening and Second/Final   108
Questions Not to Ask   111
Questions to Ask   111
Employment Tests   113
Ranking Applicants   114
Second/Final Interviews for Hourly and Management   115
Probation Period   115
Case Study 7.1: Managers' Favorite Interviewing Tactics   116
Case Study 7.2: Assessing Job Description Criteria   117
Case Study 7.3: Assessing Job Specification Criteria   118
Case Study 7.4: Interviewing Hourly Employees   119
Case Study 7.5: Good Question/Bad Question   121

Chapter Eight: Orientation   125

Overview of the Orientation Process   125
Orientation Program   126
Problems with Orientations   128
New Employee Paperwork   129
Orientation Checklist   130
Sample Employee Handbook   131
Welcome for New Employees   131
The Goals of the Business   131
The Five Responsibilities of an Employee   132
General Employee Policies   133
Optional Policies   138
Disclaimer   139
Case Study 8.1: Developing an Orientation Program   140
Case Study 8.2: Giving an Orientation   141

Chapter Nine: Training   142

The Basics of Training   142
Benefits of Training   143
Types of Training   144
Training Needs Assessment   144
Developing a Training Program   145
Job Analysis (what employees need to trained to do)   145
Training Methods   145
Schedule   149
Assessing Competence   152
Selecting a Trainer   155
Evaluate the Training Program (Control)   156
Case Study 9.1: Designing a Training Program   157

Chapter Ten: Performance Appraisals and Discipline   158

Performance Appraisals and Discipline   158
Reasons for Performance Appraisals   159
What Is Measured in a Performance Appraisal?   160
General Guidelines for Appraisals and Discipline   160
Bias in Performance Appraisals   161
Informal Performance Appraisal Basics   162
Formal Performance Appraisal Basics   162
Discipline   166
Basic Disciplinary Procedures   166
The Three (or Four) Tiered Disciplinary System   169
Case Study 10.1: Role-Play: Performance Appraisal   170
Case Study 10.2: Designing a Performance Appraisal System   171
Case Study 10.3: Compassionate Conservatism   173

Appendix   174

Human Resources Functional Plan Guidelines
(Course Project)

References   194

Foreword

As former President and CEO of Best Western International, Inc. for eighteen years, I directed the chain's growth from 1800 hotels in 7 countries to almost 4,000 hotels in 80 countries to become the world's largest lodging brand. This was accomplished by a remarkable team of people that dedicated themselves to a big dream and worked together to make that dream come true.

The hospitality business is a people business. Our people make all of the wheels turn from human resources to marketing and operations, and subsequently to achieving financial success. To do this, they must be carefully selected, trained, nurtured and developed to their full potential. Allen Reich's book helps in that effort.

In this book, Allen lays the foundation that allows future and current managers to effectively and efficiently help their businesses to succeed, and thus, themselves. He does so in a well-organized, straightforward style and language that provides exactly what the reader needs to know—without unnecessary verbiage.

I like Allen's philosophy in this book; principles, practice, and application with minimal, but pertinent examples. With all of the readily available current information from the Internet today, and the many research data bases available at most universities and colleges, why charge students extra for extraneous and soon to be outdated examples? His concept of strategy reviews to have students do their own research to find examples of human resources practices is a good one. An additional benefit of these strategies was bringing the cost of the book down to about one third of the cost of most current textbooks.

As Allen's former Dean and colleague at the School of Hotel and Restaurant Management at Northern Arizona University I have had the privilege of working with him for over a dozen years. In addition to being one of the top researchers in the hospitality industry and a dedicated and inspiring teacher, I've seen him put into practice the principles he discusses in this book. He has successfully led the School's Strategic Planning and Accreditation efforts and he helps guide University policy through his efforts on the University Leadership Council, as a member of the University President's Cabinet and as President of the Faculty Senate. He is also a much sought after hospitality consultant and expert witness.

His efforts in bringing to students proven principles and information they need to be successful will be critical for their development as they launch their careers. And in the future, I know there will be many times when human resource questions will come up that can be answered by researching them in this book.

Ronald A. Evans
2011

Introduction

The guiding principles in writing this book were to find a way to lower the cost of a Human Resources textbook, and to do so in a way that increased the effectiveness of the instructor's efforts and the student's education. Having written three others books, being a professor, and of course having been a student myself through undergraduate and graduate programs, I found one thing to be true of most textbooks. Less than half the book consisted of the principles, practices and application techniques of a subject, the rest were examples and various attempts at providing unique ways to present the information a second time in a different way. Though there is nothing inherently wrong with examples and additional methods of presenting the information, they more than double the cost of the book and both can be provided by the instructor and through the student's own research efforts.

The first goal of lowering the cost of the book was achieved through a focus on the principles, practices and application without the many examples and extra features. Minimizing examples required a clear explanation of various concepts and how they are applied. This philosophy and this book's content have been successfully tested in the classroom over several years. In essence, clarifying a concept or topic through examples is one of the main responsibilities of instructors. To help instructors provide a platform for students' research efforts, that is to find examples for important topics, I've included guidelines for preparing Strategy Reviews. These are essentially the summary of an article related to a chapter topic, along with the student's opinion of what was written (See end of Chapter One). I must also thank Acquisitions Editor Angela Lampe and Project Coordinator, Suzanne Dodd for their help and foresight in making this cost reduction effort possible.

The second challenge was to make a shorter textbook more effective. A major benefit of presenting just the principles and practices and how they are applied is that the average chapter is reduced by about half—from 40+ pages to about 20 pages. With students' tight schedules, they are certainly more likely to read 20 than 40 pages. Additionally, the brain can more effectively absorb 20 pages of information than 40 and since all the information is important, looking for specific information can be done with less wasted effort and time. Students taking my Hospitality Human Resource Management course have appreciated this aspect of the textbook.

Another concept that makes this textbook effective is that it provides the basic concepts that make individuals and businesses successful. Essentially, every firm will succeed, fail, or simply exist based on how it does three things: 1) develop an operable plan for assuring a compatible fit between each department's capabilities and the environment each operates in; 2) manage the business with strong, never wavering values; and 3) understand how each aspect of a department is best implemented (e.g., orientation, selection, training, performance appraisals, etc.).

Chapter One, Making Human Resource Decisions, not only provides students with a fundamental understanding of Human Resource Management, but also covers critical management and planning concepts. To help students understand how Human Resource planning is accomplished in the real world, I have included an HR planning project (See Appendix) that guides them in detail through the steps required to produce an operable HR functional plan. Chapter Two, Values, Morale, and Motivation, provides students with an understanding of values; how they are ingrained in the firm, how values influence behavior—both for the firm and for individuals, and how lasting morale and motivation cannot be achieved without solid core values. The remainder of the book focuses on key principles, practices of human resources and how Human Resource managers apply them. Each chapter includes at least one case study to support the chapter's contents. The vast majority of the case studies can be completed in class and presented by groups of students for feedback from the instructor and from other students.

Having spent my career in the hospitality industry, I consider it an honor to help people. Therefore, any instructor who adopts this book will receive my email address so I can respond to questions about certain topics in the book or about how to best teach a certain topic.

Thank You,
Allen Z. Reich, Ph.D.

About The Author

Allen Reich is a Professor at the School and Hotel and Restaurant Management (HRM) in the W. A. Franke College of Business at Northern Arizona University (NAU). NAU's School of HRM has consistently been ranked as one of the top hospitality programs in the United States, both for quality and research production. Allen holds a B.B.A. in Management from Texas State University, an M.H.M. (Master of Hospitality Management) from the Conrad N. Hilton College of Hotel and Restaurant Management at the University of Houston, and a Ph.D. in Hospitality and Tourism Management from Virginia Tech. Allen's teaching history, which has focused on Hospitality Human Resource Management and Marketing, includes twelve years at NAU and a five-year stint at the Hilton College. During his private sector career, he held positions from cook to corporate Vice-President. Allen owned, managed, cheffed, and consulted for restaurants and has experience in both independent and chain food-and-beverage operations. From being sous chef at Green Pastures (a James Beard top 100 restaurant for the U.S.) to manager at the Night Hawk Steakhouse (the highest volume steakhouse in Texas), founding partner of Purdy's Hamburger Market and Bakery, and responsible for company owned restaurants for Schlotzsky's Corporate Headquarters during its fast growth period of late 1970s and early 80s, he knows what it takes to please the most discerning customers and clients.

There are few restaurant consultants in the country with Allen's breadth of experience. His consulting assignments have included preparation of employee and operations policies, pre-opening training, creating marketing plans, layout, design, construction, menu development, and solving operations, human resources, marketing and cost control problems. Allen is a frequent expert witness on topics such as restaurant operations, Equal Employment Opportunity law, Americans with Disabilities Act, cost controls, financial decisions, marketing, human resources, sanitation, safety, and security. As the lead restaurant expert witness, he helped successfully settle a $1.6 billion Boston Market lawsuit for the investment firms of Morgan Stanley, Deutsche Banc and Merrill Lynch. In another recent case, he successfully helped defend the Maricopa County (Phoenix, AZ) Health Department in a case that was awarded a top-ten defense verdict. He has been recognized by the Journal of Hospitality and Tourism Education as its seventh most prolific author and has twice been ranked as one of the 100 most influential authors in hospitality journals (based on the number of his articles cited). He was twice recognized in Who's Who of University Educators.

Allen is chair of the NAU School of Hotel and Restaurant Management Strategic Planning and Accreditation Committee, President of the NAU Faculty Senate, and serves on the University Leadership Council and is a member of the University President's Cabinet. He has held the positions of President, Vice-President, and Secretary/Treasurer of Rocky Mountain CHRIE (Council of Hotel, Restaurant, and Institutional Educators) and many other industry and university positions.

A special thanks and acknowledgement is extended to reviewers Sarah Vergin of Paradise Bakery & Cafe and to Tammy Ledyard of Pappas Restaurants. Their comments were invaluable in completing this revised edition.

Chapter One: Making Human Resource Decisions

Course Project Introduction: Read the Human Resource Functional Plan Guidelines.
Begin thinking about a company for your project.
The draft of the plan and final project are due as specified in the syllabus.

Strategy Review: There are no strategy reviews for Chapter One and Chapter Five. Guidelines for preparing Strategy Reviews are included at the end of this chapter.

Case Study 1.1: The Good and the Bad

Case Study 1.2: Do You Have What It Takes to Be a Hospitality Manager?

Case Study 1.3: What Skills Are Companies Looking For?

Case Study 1.4: Human Resources Planning Exercise. This is a brief assignment to familiarize you with the planning process. Once you have completed it and understand it, the semester human resources planning project is simply a longer version.

Chapter Objectives: After reading this chapter you should understand and be able to do the following:

1. Define Human Resources.
2. Define the terms *effective* and *efficient* as each relates to managerial decisions.
3. Differentiate between a *symptom* and a *cause*.
4. Describe the major functional departments of a business.
5. Describe the Human Resources Impact Model: (a) how a business's environment influences business decisions; (b) how human resource strategies influence employee satisfaction, retention and productivity; and (c) how employees impact customer satisfaction and profit.
6. Explain who makes human resource decisions.
7. List the four generic responsibilities of managers. (Also, be able to explain each of the responsibilities and know how they collectively influence everything that occurs in each functional department and the entire business.)
8. Describe organization charts—simple, functional, divisional and matrix.
9. Differentiate between organization charts for individual restaurants and hotels.
10. Explain the importance of effective planning to the human resources function.
11. Describe some changes in the environment that impact human resources.
12. Describe the Six-Step or Traditional Problem-Solving Model.
13. List and describe the components of the HR functional plan (Internal Analysis, Environmental Analysis, SWOT Analysis, Key Factor Analysis, Objectives, Strategies, Tactics—action plans and policies and Controls).
14. Explain how to prepare a brief HR plan.
15. Describe the Three Levels of Strategy (three major types of strategy decisions).
16. Explain the Strategic Aggression concept.
17. List the three requirements for a Sustainable Competitive Advantage and be able to identify possible SCAs for a Human Resources department.
18. Describe the four decision-making skills of HR managers (Information, Technical, Conceptual and Inferential).
19. Identify your personal strengths and weaknesses relative to success as a hospitality manager.

Understanding Human Resource Management

Human Resource Management is the recruiting, training and retaining of productive employees with high morale who are motivated to satisfy customers and help the business make a profit. Another definition is the process an organization uses to make sure it has the proper amount of employees with the appropriate skills to deliver its desired products and services (i.e., finding people who can fulfill the requirements specified in job descriptions). Carrying out either of these definitions is not a simple task and at no time should a manager assume that everything will take care of itself. Historically the HR function has not been given as much attention as other areas, such as marketing, operations and finance. Today, however, it is getting recognition for a very important reason—the realization that successful businesses cannot exist without good employees (Enz, 2009).

Human Resources management is more than keeping employees happy. Employees need to feel they are an integral part of a solid organization and have a better future because of it. Most employees want to do a good job, but because of mismanagement in the form poor training, a lack of enforced standards, little or no recognition, respect, or rewards, they cannot justify their efforts or fully understand what is expected of them (Collins, 2007). Management must have a thorough understanding of the foundations of Human Resources if the business is to succeed in acquiring, retaining and getting the best effort from its employees.

Effective and Efficient

The terms *effective* and *efficient* are extremely important business terms that will be used throughout this book and in each manager's career. It is therefore critical to understand what they mean. *Effective* refers to doing things in a way that produces the desired result (i.e., effective execution). In this case, it means in a manner that pleases the customer and follows company policies. In other words, if customers are not happy, then management has to change something. If the policies were effectively set and effectively followed, then the result should be happy customers. *Efficient* refers to keeping costs at the lowest reasonable level. Providing excellent service is wonderful, but doing so when labor costs are 5% too high is a problem. Additionally, when a business is both ineffective and inefficient, employee morale quickly drops, as do customer satisfaction, sales and profit. Management has the responsibility to run both an effective and efficient operation. In the vast majority of cases, one's success as a manager is based on the ability to run an effective and efficient organization.

Symptom versus Cause

Another business concept that is critical to management is understanding the difference between a *symptom* and a *cause* (Schneier, Shaw & Beatty, 1992). The first view of a problem is normally the *symptom* of the problem. For example, the manager sees that an employee is not doing his or her job properly—the symptom. One indicator of the *micro-manager* is that they like to solve symptoms because it gives them something to do so they feel they're needed. What this micro-manager or any manager needs to be able to do is to find the *cause* of the problem. Possible causes could be poor training, low morale, minimal teamwork, more customers than normal, unusual requests, related departments are underperforming and so forth. Management can solve a symptom a hundred times, but it can solve the cause of the problem once and the symptoms should go away. Obviously, not all causes of problems can be eliminated, but good managers can take care of most of them.

Major Functional Departments

A functional department is any entity within a business that has a unique responsibility (Wang & He, 2008). **Human resources** is one of five main functional departments within a business. The others are Operations, Finance/Accounting, Marketing and Administrative Management. **Figure 1.1, Basic Organization Chart**, shows the five major functional departments and how they related to each other. Notice that most departments have *staff responsibilities*, which support the production and sales of the business's products and services, while others focus on *line responsibilities*, which sell, produce and deliver the business's products and services. Examples of staff management positions include the General Manager and Managers, Human Resources Manager (the HR department), Marketing Manager and the Financial Manager (finance/accounting department, sometimes referred to as the Comptroller's or Controller's office). Line management positions include Sales Managers, Front Desk Manager, Housekeeping Manager, Director of Food and Beverage, Chef, Bar Manager and Dining Room Manager. Functionally, with the exception of sales, line positions are referred to as operations. Operations used to be referred to as production management, but since the majority of U.S. business is now service-oriented, the term became outdated.

Figure 1.2, Historical Progression of Functional Importance, shows how the focus of business for each functional department has changed over the past decades. Prior to the 1950s there was minimal competition, so rather than spending time developing new products (marketing), heavily promoting them (sales), or making sure that quality was superior (operations), the firm could set its budgets for the year (finance), stick to them and do pretty much what it did the last year. Between the 1950s and 1970s, a few more hospitality competitors entered the market. Rather than concentrate primarily on marketing, firms focused on product quality and sales. Beginning in the 1970s, there was a significant increase in competition, which led to greater product differentiation. Concurrently, the availability of computers, more mass media and promotional expertise led to a focus on marketing. Since the late 1990s most firms have realized that while finance, product quality and marketing areas were important, the most significant means of differentiation was the firm's employees who produced and sold the firm's products and services and those that supported them.

Larger businesses will often have other functional departments based on their specific needs, such as Legal, Real Estate and Acquisitions, Quality, Facilities Design/Architecture and Equipment Design. Most managers of functional departments at the corporate level have the title of Vice-President. The following is a brief overview of what occurs in the other main functional departments.

<u>Operations</u>

This department is responsible for the creation of the product or service. In a restaurant this would generally include the kitchen, dining room and restrooms, bar and host area. In a hotel this would generally include the front desk and housekeeping, often referred to simply as rooms division or simply, rooms. The kitchens, dining rooms and catering are also part of Operations and are usually referred to as the Food & Beverage Department (commonly referred to as F&B or the F&B Department).

Figure 1.1:   Basic Organizational Chart

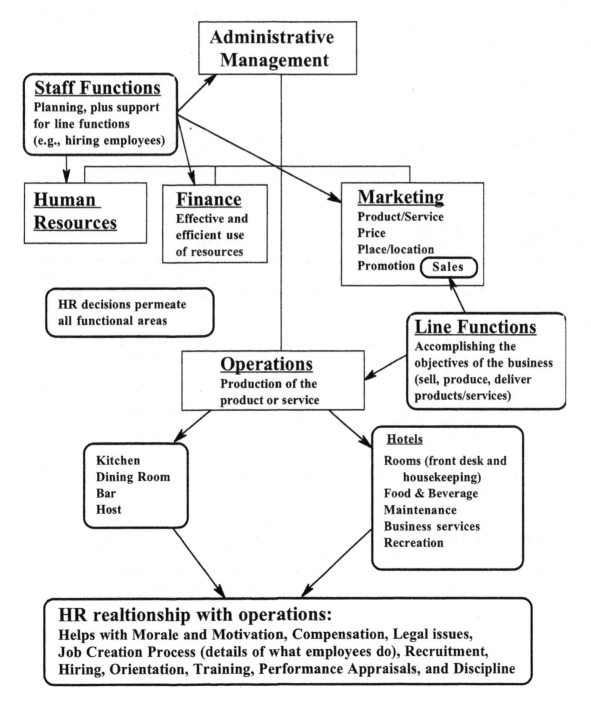

Figure 1.2:   Historical Progression of Functional Importance

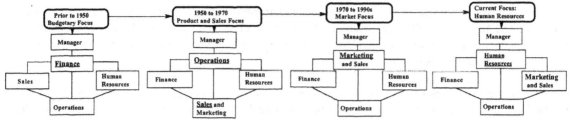

adapted from: Reich, A.Z. (1997). Marketing management for the hosptiality industry. John Wiley, New York. p. 477.

Finance/Accounting

Simplistically, these areas are responsible for the effective and efficient acquisition and use of capital (money, equipment, inventory, buildings and land). Usually the portion of financial/accounting work carried out inside the restaurant is termed *bookkeeping* and is carried out by a bookkeeper. In a hotel, many bookkeeping duties are generally carried out by a night auditor that is also responsible for the front desk. Most major restaurant finance and accounting duties are carried out off premise. In hotels, the majority of accounting and some financial duties are carried out on premise by the Controller or Comptroller (a term generally encompassing accounting and financial responsibilities).

Marketing

The functional area of marketing is responsible for the maintenance and improvement of the firm's image, sales and profit. The main strategies of marketing (also known as marketing mix variables or the Four Ps of marketing) are Product, Price, Place (location and distribution) and Promotion.

Administrative Management

This consists of the General Manager, other unit managers and corporate level management. Its primary responsibility is the effective and efficient functioning of the business. Profit, the most important measure of the success of the business, is the responsibility of all departments, but first rests with the General Manager of the unit and ultimately with corporate management (e.g., Vice-President of Operations, President, etc.).

Human Resources Impact Model

The general purpose of the model is to graphically show how human resources and other functional areas impact the business and to provide an overview of the course. More specifically, it sequentially shows: the impact of the firm's environment on the business; the impact of the business's strategies on employees; the impact of the employees on customers; and finally, the impact of customers on profit and profit on the business (**see Figure 1.3, The Human Resources Impact Model**).

Environmental Impact

The different factors in the business's environment (those outside of the business) impact managerial decisions (e.g., HR strategies) and employees in a variety of ways. For example, when the economy is very good and unemployment is low (about 4% or less), most people who want jobs have jobs. Therefore, there are fewer people looking for work and companies may need to pay higher wages. Fortunately, for the business, since most people have jobs, they have money to spend so sales should be higher, which will allow firms to pay the higher wages. If there are several excellent businesses that are competing for the same market with a similar product, these companies will not only be competing for customers, but also for quality employees. Actually, any other places that a potential or actual employee could work would be considered as competitors from an HR perspective. The human resources planning project at the end of the book has significantly more details on the interaction of the environment and the business.

HR Strategies Impact

The most important aspect of the model is the concept that higher-quality Human Resources strategies (the ten terms in the large circle) and their implementation have a significant impact (positive, neutral, or negative) on employee satisfaction, retention and productivity. Some have said that the goal of HR is to have happy employees. The problem with this statement is that employees could stay with the business a long time and be very happy, but not very productive. That is why satisfaction, retention and productivity are each major goals of HR. The ten main

strategies for Human Resources (those covered in this book) include: 1. Human Resource Planning (introduction to HR); 2. Values, Morale and Motivation; 3. Compensation, Benefits and Incentives;
4. Employment Laws; 5. Job Creation Process; 6. Recruiting; 7. Selection; 8. Orientation; 9. Training; and
10. Performance Appraisals and Discipline.

Figure 1.3:   The Human Resources Impact Model
The Impact of the Environment on the Firm; the Firm on the Employee; and the Impact of the Employee on Customers and Profit

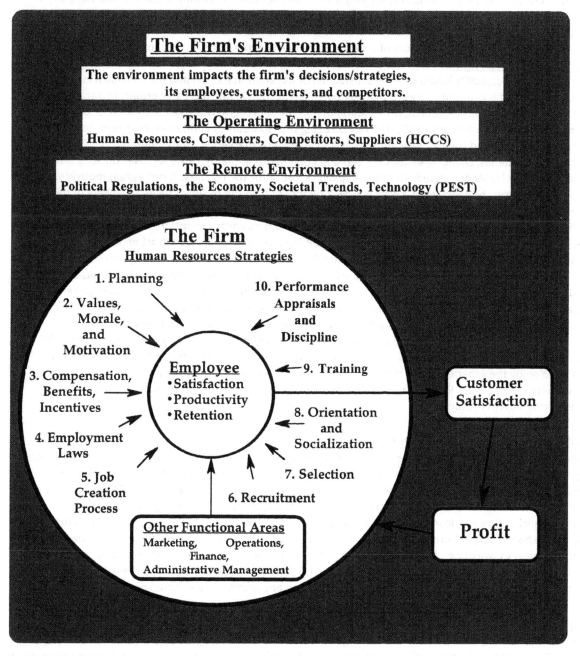

Cross-Functional Impact
Not only will HR strategies impact the efforts of employees, so will actions of other functional departments (Craig & Silverstone, 2010). For example, an effective Marketing department will help promote a strong image for the company, which will in turn make it easier to hire employees. Though it is a marketing concept,

it is important for HR students to understand that there are three key ways to increase sales— increase the number of new customers, increase the frequency of visits of existing customers and increase the amount spent by each customer. This knowledge is important because, ultimately, HR strategies are created not only to help the business operate more effectively and more efficiently, but also to increase sales. If the firm is profitable, the Finance department will be able to provide better pay and benefits for employees. Great HR policies detailing how everything is done will be wasted without an effective Operations effort that carries out the majority of HR policies.

Employees' Impact

Happy and productive employees who stay for longer than average periods of time are one of the company's greatest assets. Excellent employees assist management in meeting and exceeding both the standards of the business and the expectations of customers. One of the greatest pleasures of management is seeing enthused employees happily going about their work of creating a wonderful experience for customers.

Impact of Customers and Profit

A major goal of any hospitality business is the satisfaction of its target market(s) and the individual customers within it. Intuitively, it is commonly argued that customer satisfaction leads to greater profits. In a study by Bernhardt, Donthu, and Kennett (2000), it was found that in the short term there is a tenuous relationship between customer satisfaction and profit. The reason being that sometimes additional short-term costs may be incurred (e.g., hiring and training new employees and managers, marketing promotions, remodeling facilities, changing menus, changing various policies and implementing them). However, over the long term the relationship was highly correlated. To some employees, profit for the business is not a great motivator; in fact, profit to them may be considered a dirty word—a symbol of how the business takes advantage of them. If the concept is presented from the perspective of the opportunities it creates for employees through higher pay, benefits, incentives (e.g., profit sharing) and promotions from business expansion, their attitudes should change. Another goal for the business is to keep its current loyal customers and to attract enough of its competitors' customers or new customers to increase sales and replace customers who are lost. Saying that the loyal customer is the most valuable asset of any business is somewhat elementary, but this is based on the fundamental concept that customers are the entity that provides the business with the money necessary for success and growth. What is not always made clear is the secondary effect of dealing with loyal, rather than new customers (Reich, 1997; Reich, in-press). Because the loyal customer is familiar with how the business operates, less time is required to explain ordering or check-in procedures, how long something will take, or where something is located. This customer also feels more at home and relaxed, so he or she will be more likely to enjoy the experience and to pass on their opinions via word-of-mouth advertising. Regular and loyal customers are also more likely to overlook occasional lapses in service that might make a first-time customer decide never to return.

Who Makes Human Resources Decisions?

Everyone in management positions makes Human Resources decisions. While a Human Resources manager may be responsible for many of the decisions related to recruiting, training and retaining employees, all other *functional departments* (Marketing, Finance, Operations and Administrative Management) will help in varying degrees with these duties. For example, Human Resources department at a hotel will generally focus on recruitment, making sure employment laws are followed and providing new employees with an orientation focused on the history and culture of the hotel, plus information on its general policies. The specific departments where the employees work (e.g., kitchen, front desk of the hotel, etc.) will continue the orientation with more specific information related to the new employees' job. The department will also be where much of the basic human resources strategies, such as training and performance appraisals will be carried out.

The Four Generic Responsibilities of Managers (Plan, Organize, Direct and Control)

Managers do many things, but they can all be categorized under the topics of planning, organizing, directing and controlling. These responsibilities apply to managers of functional areas, such as marketing or human resources, as well as managers of the entire business. Frenchman Henry Fayol introduced this concept in 1916. Since then, virtually every management textbook has been based on his farsighted managerial philosophy (Parker & Ritson, 2005).   Simplistically, managers Plan what they want to do, then Organize and hire the employees to do it, Direct them to do it and finally, the managers develop a system of Controls to make sure objectives are met and that strategies are implemented correctly. This process is sequential (**see Figure 1.4, How HR Managers Manage**).

For this course, the main education into how managers Plan, Organize, Direct and Control is the HR Functional Planning Project. Additionally, each time a chapter is read, realize that the firm's efforts in that area (e.g., selection, orientation, etc.) must be effectively planned, organized, directed and controlled.

Plan

Planning consists of assessing the business's situation—factors both inside and outside the business, establishing objectives (or goals), then determining how the business will achieve its objectives. Objectives are achieved through strategies (what will be done—e.g., add benefits) and tactics (details of how the strategy will be accomplished—e.g., add life insurance benefits). There are two types of tactics—action plans that are relatively short-term and policies that are relatively long-term. This plan then becomes the basis for how the business will be operated. That is, the tactics for various functional areas, such as Human Resources, will become the policy manual detailing how each activity will be accomplished. An unfortunate common practice is for managers to set policies without adequate consultation with the employees who will implement them. This is referred to as top-down or autocratic planning or management.

Not all plans are formally written down. Much of the planning a hospitality manager does is done informally through minor tactical or supervisory changes to the formal plan. That is, if a customer has a certain dietary requirement, there may be nothing in the formal plan (no policy) that directs management on exactly what to do. Therefore the manager must be able to assess situations on a minute-by-minute basis, then determine if the solution is somewhere in the formal plan, or if a unique solution must be developed.

From *Alice in Wonderland*:

>   Alice: Which road should I take?
>   Cheshire Cat: Where do you want to go?
>   Alice: I don't know.
>   Cat: Then any road will take you there.

Lessons:
- If you don't have a plan, you are leaving the decisions to others.
- If your competitors have a plan, they will outperform you the vast majority of the time.
- If you do not have objectives, you will never know if you accomplished what you set out to do.
- If no one is assigned responsibility, little or nothing will get done.

Organize

A famous phrase in business planning is, "structure follows strategy" (Drucker, 1974). After managers determine what must be done (planning), they need to make sure they have the appropriate organizational structure to carry out the strategy (i.e., the appropriate positions, how they relate to each other and any necessary hiring). Hence, the firm's current organizational chart is examined to determine if it will effectively and efficiently support the new strategies. If not, it may need to be modified to adapt to new strategies. Subsequently, employees with the appropriate skills are hired.

There are several different types of structures. The most common are the Simple Structure (management and employees), Functional Structure (different functional positions), Divisional Structure (generally several functional structures in different geographic areas, such as East and West Coast Divisions or different brands) and Matrix (overall corporate headquarters to help different business units with functional expertise) (**see Figure 1.5, Forms of Organizational Structure**). The objective of each form is included in the figure. **Figures 1.6 and 1.7 show typical organization charts for a full-service hotel and for a casual-dining restaurant.** The restaurant organizational chart includes the structure for both the company headquarters and individual restaurant.

By analyzing the difference between the organizational structure for the individual restaurant and the hotel, one can quickly see a significant difference. While the hotel General Manager will have functional experts in each department, General Managers of the restaurants will need to rely more heavily on their own ability in each of the functional areas. Obviously, there will be help from others (e.g., corporate headquarters), but restaurant GMs need to make significantly more decisions in areas outside their area of expertise than hotel GMs. Of course, along with the advantage of greater levels of functional expertise for the hotel GM is the fact that management is generally much more complex.

Figure 1.4:   How HR Managers Manage

Managerial Tasks	Managerial Activities	Example
Planning →	**1. Current Situation** (Situational Analysis)	Selection/Hiring Performance 3.5 (5 = excellent)
	2. Desired Future Situation (Objectives)	Objective for Selection/hiring - 4.4
	3. Method of Achieving Objectives (Strategies)	Strategies: 1. Improve interviewing techniques, 2. Improve benefits and compensation
	4. Method of achieving the strategies (Tactics) (action plans--temporary actions; and policies--relatively permanent actions)	Tactics: Action Plans--Research and creation of new methods. Policies--The new means of interviewing and the new benefits and compensation package.
Organizing →	Analysis and modification of the organizational chart and staffing needs	Examine organization chart and hire new employees as needed
Directing →	Implementation of Strategies and Tactics	Acting on the new strategies and tactics
Controlling →	Measure, monitor, and correct implementation of strategies/tactics and achievement of objectives	Did we meet our objectives? If not, should we modify them? Did we achieve our strategies? Did we not implement current strategies effectively or do we need new strategies?

Bureaucracy is a generic term used to describe an organizational structure. However, it generally refers to an organizational structure that impedes effective and efficient performance of employees of the business and the business itself. The common indicators of a bureaucracy are:
- Many levels
- Often top-down decision-making
- Excessive functional division of labor
- Tends to perpetuate itself, increases its size in relation to bureaucratic power, rather than needs of the business.

Figure 1.5: Forms of Organizational Structure

(There are many variations of each form.)

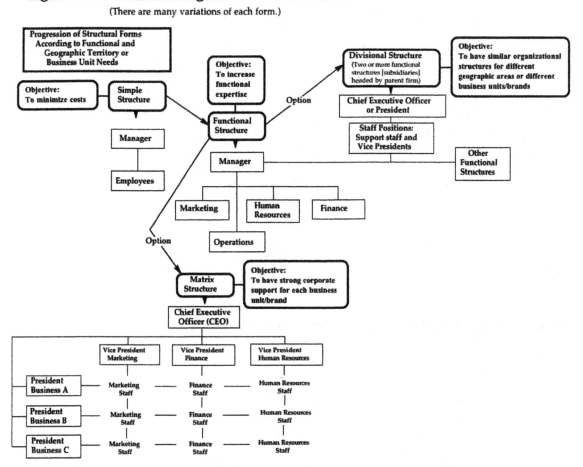

adapted from: Reich, A.Z. (1997). Marketing management for the hosptiality industry. John Wiley, New York. p. 477.

• Organizational Decision-Making Philosophies.

There are several types of *organizational decision-making philosophies*. The primary types are centralized and decentralized. Firms will vary from being highly centralized to highly decentralized and somewhere in between.

• Centralized decision making (autocratic, command and control)—Simpler levels of service (e.g., quick-service, budget hotels) utilize centralized decision making because consistency is the primary goal and low pay generally means that employees without significant business skills are hired.

• Decentralized decision making (democratic, participatory)—Because of greater customization, higher levels of service require decentralization. This is more commonly found in luxury hotels and fine-dining restaurants. This philosophy generally requires employees with significant business skills and who consequently deserve higher pay than employees in centralized environments. Mid-scale hotels and casual-dining restaurants normally function somewhere between the centralized and decentralized philosophies.

• Staffing.

Hiring employees is either included under Organizing, or under a separate title, "Staffing" (e.g., plan, organize, staff, direct and control). This book will consider it as part of Organizing.

Direct

Sometimes referred to as managing or leadership, directing is the training, supervision and motivating of employees to achieve objectives and carry out the strategies and tactics (action plans and policies) of the business. This could also include the supervising/directing of contract workers, such as a food supply company, an ad agency, or a repair service.

Figure 1.6: Typical Organization Chart for Full-Service Hotels

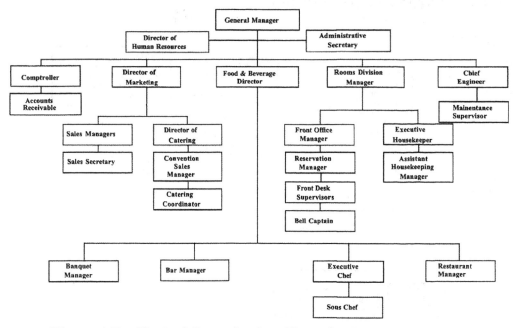

Figure 1.7: Typical Organization Chart for Restaurants

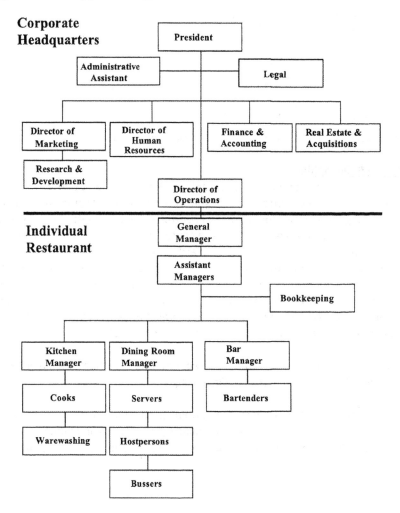

• Leadership issues, culture, rewards and motivation.

An organization or manager that does not consider leadership, culture, rewards and motivation will have problems with implementing most plans. For example, without the right leader in place, the likelihood of effective implementation is low. A corporate culture that does not accept change or is not motivated to help the firm achieve its potential will limit its success. Finally, most of our employees are at or near minimum wage. We need to give them a reason to work hard and do their best. Since we cannot make all employees wealthy, we need to offer them something. What we can provide are lessons on how to succeed in their own lives and how their current efforts with the firm will help them on that path. As the parable goes, give a man a fish and you feed him for one day, teach a man to fish and you've fed him for a lifetime.

Control

In business there are two primary levels of controls—strategic controls and operational controls. Strategic controls focus on guiding the strategic direction of the company by attempting to assure an effective match between the present internal abilities of the firm and the opportunities and threats in the environment. Therefore, strategic controls require managers to monitor changes in both the firm's abilities and in the environment it operates in. Operational controls are the systematic evaluation of the organization's overall and departmental performance to determine whether it is accomplishing its objectives and effectively implementing its strategies. While both types of controls are important, the focus of this book is primarily on operational controls.

Without control, there is a natural tendency for group endeavors to lead to chaos. Another way of expressing this is that managers need to measure, monitor and correct deviations from objectives, strategies and tactics. Objectives may be appropriate, the wrong ones were set, or they may have been set too high or too low. Strategies and tactics may be good, but not implemented effectively, or the wrong strategy or tactic may have been selected and implementation is all but doomed. Recognizing and correcting the deviations can be complex and this is one reason why both unit and corporate managers deserve to be paid well. Much of this book is concerned with teaching students (also managers and aspiring managers) how to do this.

Human Resource Planning

Human resource strategies and tactics are the deliberate use of an organization's people to help it gain or maintain an edge against its marketplace competitors (i.e., accomplish its mission and objectives). In HR planning or any type of planning, problems will surface, such as a strong competitor being the preferred employer—employer-of-choice. This is one of the main points of planning—the business cannot deal with problems unless it knows about them. Two famous quotes related to this concept are "Please give us problems so we may learn" (Japanese proverb) and "A pessimist sees the difficulty in every opportunity; an optimist sees the opportunity in every difficulty" (Sir Winston Churchill). Once problems, in planning terms these are generally weaknesses and threats, are noticed, it is managements' responsibility to effectively deal with them. The management team that deals with them most effectively and creatively will generally find the greatest success. Since most of the problems that firms face are quite similar, such as mostly the same environment and very similar internal challenges, few managers are facing impossible situations.

The primary components of the overall human resource planning process, as previously discussed, include the analysis of the firm's current situation (the business and its environment), setting objectives that support the firm's mission, designing strategies and tactics that will help the firm achieve its objectives and finally, having a control system to monitor and correct undesirable outcomes. This will be discussed further in this chapter in Functional Planning. What students will see in the next few pages is that these concepts form the basis of managerial responsibilities for any type of business.

Clichés about Planning

• Plan your work, work your plan.

• Poor planning (or poor preparation) leads to poor performance (known as the 4 Ps Rule).

Philosophies of Plan Preparation

• Top Down—The complete or nearly complete plan is presented to those who will carry it out (autocratic management).

• Bottom Up—All levels of personnel with applicable knowledge are asked their opinion of possible changes that could improve performance (participative or democratic management).

Justification for a Planning Approach to Human Resources Management

• What are the strategies for marketing? Product, Price, Place and Promotion.

• In marketing, do managers begin by setting strategies or by analyzing their current situation? First, they analyze their current situation.

• What would likely happen if marketing managers simply set strategies without any form of analysis of internal and environmental factors? The strategies would fail (poor planning leads to poor performance).

• The same process is used before Human Resource strategies are set.

Managerial Decision-Making

The vast majority of managerial decisions are supervisory or tactical in nature and do not require a written plan.

Reasons for Preparing a Written Plan

• Simplifies complicated situations;

• Assists in locating key information that has a bearing on decisions (strategic and tactical);

• Helps to view options in objective manner;

> You establish a logical relationship between your information/facts and your decision.

> There are generally several paths (options) to the same destination (a successful decision).

• Helps gain support from subordinates, peers and upper management;

• If something goes wrong, it will take less time to develop an alternative solution/strategy;

• If something goes wrong, since upper management bought into the idea based on the logic of your written plan, they should be understanding of the situation.

Changes in the Environment

Management should be aware of certain changes that have occurred in the workforce. The majority of these changes have resulted from social and economic realities that have had a major influence on the availability of workers. The following are some significant trends:

• **Increased competition for hiring service workers**. The proliferation of service firms has created a labor crisis in many areas. Managers and owners need to reassess recruitment practices, pay scales, benefits and other inducements for employees to alleviate the problem.

• **Minorities make up a significant percentage of the hospitality workforce**. In some areas, this percentage is well over 70%. About forty years ago, African-Americans were the primary minority in the hospitality industry. After the passing of Civil Rights laws, African-Americans were given more opportunities for jobs and education, so as a group, they have had more choices for employment. Today, those of Hispanic backgrounds make up the majority of minority employees. Hospitality firms must learn to accommodate the needs of all minorities and to respect and understand their cultures. Additionally, minorities must be considered for managerial positions.

• **Women are applying for a greater variety of jobs**. This has given managers a new employee base from which to hire. Women must be considered for all positions in the hospitality industry, even those that in the past were associated with men, such as kitchen manager, chef, busser, dishwasher and management. Unfortunately, women are often discriminated against for many hospitality jobs, especially that of manager, because some people still believe they cannot stand the pressure as well as men or will leave to have babies. Genetically, women have as much or more perseverance and emotional strength as men. For most of the human history, women took care of the family and therefore required better communication skills than men and they were responsible for 70% of the caloric intake of the family. Men were out hunting, being quiet while doing so and often their hunting efforts were not very successful.

• **Hiring those with special needs**. Hiring the elderly, mentally or physically handicapped, long-term unemployed, ex-convicts and other disadvantaged groups has become accepted and is providing restaurants and hotels with new sources of recruitment. Of course, care must be taken to avoid hiring people who could hurt themselves or others. Hiring those with a criminal record is discussed in Chapter Seven, Selective Hiring.

• **Immigration laws**. Because of the Immigration and Control Act of 1986, illegal aliens who were willing to work for low pay and perform menial work are theoretically no longer available.

• **Public perception of hospitality**. The public's general perception of the hospitality industry varies, but some think that it offers employment to individuals who cannot succeed at regular jobs or to students until they finish their education. The National Restaurant Association and the American Hotel & Lodging Association, along with other hospitality associations, are working to improve this image. No single manager or hospitality business can change the entire country's perception, but each manager can change the way its customers and employees view the industry by professionally managing their business and by doing whatever possible to improve working conditions and compensation. The reality is that when compared to non-hospitality counterparts, hospitality managers have excellent salaries. Managers of casual-dining restaurants generally make in the $90,000 range, while managers of full-service hotels (300+ room hotels with food service) generally make in the $120,000 to 150,000 range.

• **Low pay**. For many years, most hospitality employees received at or near minimum wages, causing high employee turnover. In the past, this was not a serious problem because there were plenty of applicants willing to take their place and customers were not as educated about quality service and food as they have become. Today, retention of quality employees at a reasonable labor cost is one of the primary concerns of management. If the business is to succeed, employees must be viewed as long-term investments and treated as such. The hospitality industry must find a way of providing better compensation for its employees if it expects them to stay with our firms and be motivated to satisfy customers.

The Six-Step (Traditional) Problem-Solving Model

Before scientific management principles became widely adopted in the 1950s, most businesses used this simple model to make many decisions. The reason it was popular is because it was effective and efficient—there were few competitors and few product offerings, so there was minimal need for information and complex decision processes. After the 50s, strategic and functional planning became popular because they provided managers with a means of simplifying complex competitive situations. Strategic planning focuses on long-term decisions (more than one year and/or on very important decisions) for the entire business. The functional plan focuses on short-term or annual decisions for functional departments (e.g., human resources, marketing, operations, finance and administrative management) that support the strategic plan. Except for the time period involved, the general format of the two plans is the same. The six-step problem-solving model still has a major role in business decisions, primarily in supervisory situations when there is no time to develop a written plan. As you read the six steps, you will also realize that this is essentially the way the people make routine decisions in their daily lives.

     1. Identify current problems or situations.
     2. Gather information (primary and secondary data) to help in finding a solution.
     3. Seek possible solutions.
     4. Decide on best solution.
     5. Implement best solution.
     6. Have a control mechanism in place to measure and monitor results of implementation and to modify the initial solution as necessary.

Functional Planning (An HR Plan)

Because the Six-Step Problem-Solving Model was inadequate for the complexity of modern business decision-making, a more complex and comprehensive solution was sought. For HR, **Figure 1.8: The Human Resources Planning Model** is used. Though there are quite a few boxes in the model, the actual concept is very simple. Since the semester project for this course will be an HR Plan, there is a much more detailed explanation in the Appendix of this book. Here, we will include a simple overview.

     The first four boxes, the Internal Analysis, Environmental Analysis, SWOT Analysis and Key Factor Analysis are all directly related. They are to help assess what is going on inside the business, what is going on outside the business and of that, what is important enough to act on. The next box—Objectives—are where management writes what it hopes to achieve. The next two boxes—Strategies and Tactics—specify how management wants to achieve the objectives. The last box—Controls—is to have a mechanism to make sure the objectives are reached. The reason the lines that join the components of the model have arrows on each end is that the model is iterative, meaning that as decisions are made in one step, managers may need to go back to a previous step to change something. A slightly more extensive explanation follows:

• In the **Internal Analysis** all key aspects of the business are examined. Since this is an HR plan, the focus will be on the ten HR strategies covered in this course—those inside the circle of the Human Resources Impact Model (**Figure 1.3**). Also, as is shown in the model (i.e., Cross-functional Approach), you need to know what is going on in other functional departments, because what is done there will impact HR and employees.

• The **Environmental Analysis** examines factors outside the business that can have an impact on it. There are two areas for the environmental analysis, the remote environment—factors that management generally does not have

Figure 1.8:   Human Resources Planning Model
(Functional-level Strategy Model)

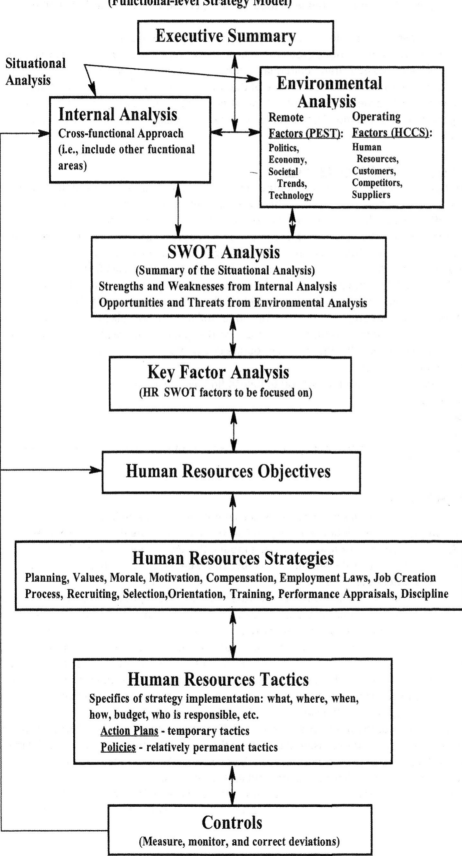

much control over (political regulation, the economy, societal trends and technology—PEST [acronym] and the operating environment—factors that management has some control over (human resources or potential employees, customers, competitors and suppliers—HCCS [acronym is pronounced, hecks]).

• The **SWOT Analysis** is simply a summary of the strengths and weaknesses from the Internal Analysis and the opportunities and threats from the Environmental Analysis. Strengths are areas where the firm does better than its competitors and meets or exceeds the expectations of employees, customers and other stakeholder groups (e.g., owners, local communities, governmental entities, suppliers to the business, etc.). Weaknesses are the opposite of strengths. Opportunities are factors in the environment that represent a chance to increase sales and/or improve the business's image (e.g., potential employees at a local university, potential employees think our business would be great place to work, customers like our food, customers think competitors' food is not very good, etc.). Threats are the opposite of opportunities—anything in the external environment that represents an obstacle to success or could reduce sales or the image of the business (e.g., potential employees expect $1.00 more per hour than what we can pay, competitors can afford to pay what employees expect, new major competitor opening in our trade area, etc.).

• The **Key Factor Analysis** is a listing of the SWOT factors that the firm will act on. If the firm had 200+ SWOT factors, it would be difficult to focus on all of them. Therefore, management would prioritize them, specifying the ones that are *key* to the firm's success.

• **Objectives** state what the business expects to achieve. They are directly or indirectly related to the Key Factors. For example, an objective related to the key factor of "potential employees expect more benefits" might be, "begin allowing employees in each department to make their own schedules by January 10, 20XX" and "allow employees to dine at the restaurant with one friend at 50% off (alcohol is full price)." Good/proper objectives state what will be accomplished, how it will be measured and by when it will be accomplished.

• **Strategies** are what will be done. They are generally short and to the point. In modern practice, some firms are not specifying strategies, since all related information will be included in the tactics anyway.

• **Tactics** are how the strategies, or objectives, in the absence of strategies, will be achieved. There are two types of tactics: *Action Plans* are relatively temporary tactics (e.g., research new methods of training employees, find out what other firms are doing to train employees, prepare a new training program and test the new training program on current employees) that would generally not be performed each planning period. Action plans are often the first step in preparing a new policy. *Policies* are relatively permanent tactics (e.g., general employee policies—dress-code or vacation policies, job descriptions, training program/manual, performance appraisals policies, disciplinary policies, etc.).

• **Controls** are the details of how management will measure, monitor and correct deviations from the plan. Management keeps an eye on whether the firm is meeting its objectives, whether factors inside (internal analysis) or outside (environmental analysis) have changed and monitors implementation of strategies and tactics to determine if the right (or wrong) actions were pursued or if the right action was pursued, but poorly implemented.

Three Levels of Strategy

Corporate-level: These are made for multi-business corporations. They focus on major decisions, such as businesses to be in and the allocation of resources between the businesses. This particular title is only remotely related to the term *corporation* as a form of business organization. The four main options for corporate forms of business are sole proprietorship, general partnership, corporation and limited liability corporation (LLC).

Business-level: These are made for an individual business or strategic business unit (i.e., an SBU—a unique business with one or multiple locations) and focus on how to compete in the business's market. A business competes through the products and services it sells and the markets it targets (consumer markets and geographic markets). Both Corporate- and Business-level strategies are referred to as strategic because they include major decisions that impact the firm over the long-term.

Functional-level: Strategies for each functional area/department of the business—Human Resources, Marketing, Finance, Operations (selling, producing and delivering the product or service) and Administrative Management are the major functional areas of business. Functional-level plans are generally prepared for the short term—a time horizon of one-year or less and modified as needed. (Some businesses will divide Functional-level strategies into two parts, *functional-level*, referring to the strategies for the department and *operational-level*, referring to the tactics for carrying out the functional-level strategies. This book uses only the functional term.)

Strategic Aggression

When determining how aggressive firms will be in changing their HR strategies, there are four options: proactive, reactive, adaptive and passive. A fifth category, discordant, is the outcome when any of the four options go awry.

Proactive

Being *proactive* can be defined as: accessing future opportunities and threats; deciding which could provide avenues or hindrances to growth and profit; then acting on the assessment before competitors. A proactive stance can come from the development of an entirely new or innovative strategy (e.g., personalized benefit and incentive package for hourly employees); capitalizing on an existing trend by incorporating more of its elements into the business than competitors (e.g., a combined college tuition along with management training); or reviving a strategy from the past (e.g., hiring a large number of 40+-year-old servers). In the ideal case early innovators will accrue advantages of increased sales, profit and improvements in image that can lead to sustainable competitive advantages (see Sustainable Competitive Strategies that follows Strategic Aggression). Important to the selection of proactive strategies is the firm's ability to carry them out. The need for an accurate assessment of the firm's ability increases with the degree of risk involved.

One of the reasons that entrepreneurial firms frequently outperform conservative firms is because of an increased propensity toward risk. They are usually smaller, less bureaucratic and in need of strategies that help differentiate themselves from larger competitors. This allows the entrepreneurial firm to take a more proactive stance when it comes to taking advantage of potential opportunities. Conservative firms, on the other hand, tend to be risk-averse, non-innovative and adaptive or passive.

Reactive

This is probably the largest category for hospitality firms. There are firms that react to or pursue proactive firms' HR and other strategies with a positive outcome. The primary advantage is that risk is minimized because the strategy has been tested by someone else. The problem is that because of being just a little late in recognizing the trend, the firm's full potential was not realized. The quicker a business can identify and begin posturing towards an opportunity-producing trend, the greater its lead time, the stronger its applicable skills and therefore, the greater its competitive advantage over rivals. Also, being known as a firm that utilizes "copy-cat strategies," rather than "innovative strategies," does little for a business's image.

Adaptive

This strategy is generally chosen by successful firms that want to continue with current HR strategies, but remain open to change if the right opportunity presents itself. These firms will generally be in relatively stable employment markets. This works because the firm has acquired the image of being a leader and can rest on its current reputation until it is begins to weaken. This does not mean that the firm ignores HR trends; it simply chooses to limit or put off major strategy decisions.

Passive

Passive firms simply do what they have been doing with little or no focus on changes in their competitive environment. The focus of strategic effort is generally efficiencies through cost minimization in HR and all functional areas, plus standardized, high-volume products and services. Proactive or even reactive strategies are discouraged because this would be counterproductive to current efforts. Passive firms will follow the lead of reactive firms, but only after the need for strategic change is unquestionable, employee morale is on the decline and employee turnover is high. Occasionally, there will be a market for passive HR strategies— for example, changing HR policies may not be necessary when the majority of employees are older, do a great job and they do not want or need change.

The following prose describes what happens to firms that attempt to stay with outdated strategies:

> Upon the plains of hesitation, bleached
> the bones of countless millions who, on
> the threshold of victory, sat down to wait,
> and waiting they died. Unknown

Discordant

The discordant firm will achieve this position through unsuccessful attempts at any of the other types of strategic aggression. Generally, the more aggressive the strategy, the greater the potential benefit to the firm—assuming it was implemented successfully. On the other hand, when more aggressive strategies are unsuccessfully implemented, there is also generally a positive correlation between the aggressiveness of the strategy and the degree of harm it causes the firm. These firms usually have a poor image as a place to work, have had problems with past strategic decisions and are therefore hesitant about what to do. This strategy is not selected, but acquired through poor performance. The specific causes vary, but include disagreements between managers and employees, doing too many things at once and misperceptions about what employees want and need. Discordant firms are generally in need of a turnaround, but unfortunately may not realize it until it is too late.

Sustainable Competitive Advantage (SCA)

Ideally, some of the selected HR strategies should give the firm an advantage over its competitors that can be maintained long enough for the firm to benefit. This is referred to as a *sustainable competitive advantage* (SCA) (Reich, 1997). One of the goals of HR planning is to find one or more SCAs. While this is desirable, it is not always possible. As more and more firms are doing a better job of catering to employees' needs and wants, it is becoming more challenging to develop employee-related SCAs. Sometimes, rather than being one thing, such as an employee stock ownership plan (ESOP), it could be a combination of things, such as great benefits—the ESOP, opportunities for advancement and offering a good quality-of-life. The best means of locating SCAs is generally having brain-storming sessions with employees.

There are three requirements for an SCA:

1. It must be valued by employees/customers—adequate demand. Even if a strategy is focused on customers, as long as it increases their satisfaction, it will hopefully lead to increases in employee satisfaction. The reasoning is that happy customers lead to increases in sales and profits, which means more work for employees, more opportunities and ideally higher pay.

2. It must represent an advantage over competitors. It must be something that one firm does better for employees than competing firms, for example, great incentives and benefits, significant opportunities created by rapid expansion, custom schedules, a training program that allows all capable employees the chance to train to become managers and so forth.

3. The advantage must last for a reasonable period of time, or at least be defendable until a true advantage is realized. Adding a new benefit that other firms can immediately copy is not an SCA.

The following quote expresses the importance of finding an SCA:

> Where absolute superiority is not attainable,
> you must find a relative one at the decisive point,
> by making skillful use of what you have.
> Karl Von Clausewitz, "On War," 1832

The logic behind this quote is that every firm cannot be the strongest financially or strongest in all other key success indicators (e.g., employee morale, sales, profits, number of locations, best locations, etc.). However, each firm can find something that can be done for employees that will lead to an SCA.

Decision-making Skills

There are four basic decision-making skills of excellent managers—information gathering, technical expertise, conceptual skills and inferential skills. Each is relatively simple; however, when combined, they can become the key to maximizing each manager's abilities and the performance of the business.

Information Gathering

It has been said many times, "I made the best decision I could with the information I had at the time." Making good business decisions requires an appropriate quantity and quality of information. To minimize surprises and be ready for changes in the business's environment, managers should make it a daily habit to keep up with global, national, regional and local trends in the industry. Generally, the quickest way to do this is to review key trade magazines and to keep up with national news. It is also important to gather information from employees. They often know as much or more about many aspects of the business as managers (e.g., front desk agents hear what guests are complaining about or complimenting, a dishwasher knows that customers are not finishing the meat loaf). It also makes employees feel respected when managers ask their opinion.

Technical Expertise

Managers responsible for operating a hospitality firm need to know how things work before they can determine what needs to be changed. Opinions can vary, but it is probably less important for a Chief Executive Officer at a corporate headquarters to understand all the details of running the business, because he or she will have help from others with appropriate skills (e.g., a Human Resources department, Marketing and Operations department, etc.).

Conceptual Skills

This is the ability to see how all the parts fit together to form the whole. For example, managers can understand front desk operations, reservations and human resource management, but if they do not know how they work together (cross-functionally), it would be difficult to make the best decisions. Highly related to conceptual skills is the concept of *symptom* versus *cause*. In the following example, the problem of a long line for checkout is the symptom. The manager must find and attempt to eliminate the cause.

Conceptual Skills Example:

Human Resources/Operational problem (symptom)—Long line for checkout.

> Objective or standard: 60-second average per guest check-in.
>
> Current performance: 90-second average.
>
> What are the potential reasons (causes) for not achieving the objective?

- Old, slow, or inadequate equipment
- Ineffective hiring practices
- Poorly trained workers
- Poorly supervised employees
- Low wages, few benefits
- Too few workers
- Unusual requests slowing service
- New marketing strategy/promotion (e.g., frequent guest program) resulting in increased time for each check-in
- Unusual number of checkouts at once

Inferential Skills

This is the ability to identify relevant issues and recognize the degree of their importance. Inferential skills are the crucible of business planning—the million-dollar answer to questions like: what are my options? What opportunities or threats are there in the environment that I should be aware of? Which opportunities and threats that do not now exist today will be important in the future? What strategies should I select and, what do employees or customers really want? One of the key reasons people study the science of management is to answer the question, what does it take to be successful? Why do some succeed and others fail? While there are many managers who do a wonderful job of motivating employees to meet and exceed customer expectations, very few have refined inferential skills. There are literally tens of thousands of things occurring in any business's environment. Someone with good inferential skills can determine what is important enough for the firm to act on. Some say that this is simply intuition and to a certain extent this is true. But well-honed inferential skills also require a vast knowledge of the business's environment so that intuition can be appropriately directed.

Case Study 1.1: The Good and the Bad; The Symptom and the Cause

Identify memorable positive and negative experiences you have had as an employee. Some lessons here are that you often learn as much from bad experiences as from good ones and that you should think about how your actions affect others before implementing them (i.e., think before you act).

Required:

1. Provide one positive experience and one negative experience. It is important to understand that this experience was the symptom of a problem.

2. After locating the symptom, management's goal is to find the cause. The concept is that you can solve the symptom a hundred times, but if you find and take care of the cause of the problem/symptom, it should not happen again.

     What do you feel was cause for these experiences? (Why did this happen?) Try to find it in any of the ten human resources strategies. Note: For performance appraisals you have formal (written appraisal) and informal appraisals (general supervision that a manager does on a routine basis).

3. What policy should have been followed (or needs to be added to keep the incident from occurring again)?

4. How would you solve or have dealt with that specific problem or incident?

_____

_____

_____

_____

_____

_____

_____

_____

_____

_____

_____

_____

_____

Case Study 1.2: Do You Have What It Takes to Be a Hospitality Manager?

First of all, *everyone* who has a good attitude and is willing to work hard has what it takes to be a hospitality manager. It could be the manager of a restaurant with ten employees or a luxury hotel with a thousand employees. Hospitality managers must have a variety of skills to be successful. This list is organized according to the manager's four major responsibilities (plan, organize, direct and control) and the various personal characteristics necessary to carry them out. A good test of whether you are currently prepared for management in this industry would be to review the list and determine whether you have strengths or weaknesses in each area. The key here is to be objective. We all have weaknesses. Whether in business or our personal lives, we try to maximize our strengths and minimize or correct our weaknesses. The next step is to determine how you can maximize your strengths and either correct your weaknesses or find a business with managers that have strengths in your weaker areas and conversely, you have strengths in areas where others are weaker. You maximize your strengths by selecting challenges for which you are prepared. An important note here is that we are all prepared to do more than we have ever done before. If an opportunity comes up that you do not have a great deal of experience with, but you feel that through clear thinking and hard work you can accomplish, go for it. Additionally, rarely will a supervisor ask a manager to do something they do not think they are ready to do.

Sometimes you can compensate for your weaknesses by focusing on your strengths. For example, all managers are not inspiring leaders who can motivate employees to walk through walls. A non-charismatic manager can make up for this deficiency by having an honest and caring attitude toward employees and being supportive of the hospitality firm's standards. This compensatory strategy can often succeed better than charisma, because it is more likely to influence employees over the long-term.

Required:

1. Review the following list of management skills, then select between five and ten of what you consider to be your best strengths. Do the same for areas of average ability.

2. List what you feel are your weaker areas, then put together a brief plan of how you feel you could improve them before you graduate. This could be through college courses, participation in various student or professional organizations, community service, special assignments at work and so forth.

3. How could you improve upon them after you graduate and throughout your career?

Plans

- Change-oriented (seeks change) and willing to change (is flexible)
- Forecasts needs
- Analyzes, sees the big picture, understands trends, knows the competition
- Has ability to understand and interpret financial data, primarily Profit and Loss Statements
- Can understand sequential math problems (e.g., If the 30% food cost is lowered by 10% and the 25% labor cost is lowered by 5%, how much will profit increase?)
- Sets standards
- Thorough in all assignments
- Vision for future (clear vision, direction for company)

Organizes

- Hiring (recruiting, interviewing and orientation) skills
- Organized (manages time efficiently, prioritizes)
- Places the right people in the right positions
- Schedules appropriately

Directs

- Collective (has a calming influence)
- Consistency in managerial style
- Consistency in product/services offered (quality control)
- Delegates (directs, shows leadership, delegates authority/not responsibility, empowers others)
- Leads by setting a positive example
- Morale (keeps morale high)
- Motivator of others
- Safety conscious

- Self-motivated
- Standards (maintains them at a high level)
- Trainer

Controls

- Ability (i.e., oral, written and math comprehension; decisiveness) to control all areas of responsibility (e.g., human resources, marketing, finance/accounting, operations, administrative management)
- Disciplinary skills
- Performance appraisal skills (informal/daily and formal/periodic)

Personal Characteristics

- Appearance (appropriate dress and neatness)
- Attention to details
- Communications (oral and written)
- Conceptual skills (knows how the various functional areas work together)
- Confident in ability
- Conflict negotiation
- Considerate, tactful
- Creative (innovative, thinks outside the box)
- Criticism (takes it well)
- Customer oriented (meets or exceeds customer expectations)
- Decision-maker (good decision-maker, common sense)
- Determined/Drive
- Empathy/sympathetic to the needs of others
- Energetic
- Ethical (Honest, Integrity, Fair—treats people equally)
- Helpful
- High expectations
- Humility
- Humor (sense of humor)
- Listens
- Loyal
- Manners, courteous
- Networks with industry leaders and other hospitality managers
- Outgoing
- Outspoken in a tactful manner
- Personal responsibility (your personal life affects your business life)
- Personality (appropriate)
- Positive outlook
- Problem solver
- Punctual
- Responsible for anything related to the business—money, people, image, facilities, customers, etc.
- Risk taker
- Role model
- Sacrifices as needed
- Sincere
- Socially responsible
- Stress management
- Success oriented (driven, focused, passionate)
- Technical competency (knows how all hospitality duties are performed)
- Thinks on feet (makes effective decisions quickly in the heat of the battle)
- Works well with others (gets along with others, respectful, patient)

Case Study 1.3: What Skills Are Companies Looking For?

Required:

1. Through any means, such as the firm's website or a phone number, contact a company from the segment of the industry you are considering working in. Ask them for information on the desired characteristics of the managers they are hiring. In HR terms, these characteristics are called *job specifications*. Examples would include experience, education and various personal characteristics, such as problem-solving skills, attitude and personality.

2. Prepare a brief list of these skills.

3. Rate yourself on a 5-point scale for each of the skills in this list (1 = I do not come close to meeting the criteria; 2 = I have some ability in the area, but I do not fully meet the criteria; 3 = I have some ability in the area and I meet most of the criteria; 4 = I have a reasonably good ability in the area; 5 = I have an excellent ability in the area.

4. Between now and the time you graduate, how can you improve your ability in areas where you gave yourself a four or lower?

_____

_____

_____

_____

_____

_____

_____

_____

_____

_____

_____

_____

_____

Case Study 1.4 Human Resources Planning Exercise

Business_____**Name**_____

Read through the HR Planning Guidelines before you start this assignment. Assume that you have prepared a situational analysis (internal and environmental analyses) for a firm you have worked for and therefore know something about the firm. Prepare the rest of this HR plan based on your assumed information. To help in understanding each section below, take a look at the examples in the HR Planning Guidelines in the Appendix.

SWOT Analysis—Include a minimum of three factors for each SWOT category.

Strengths_____

Weaknesses_____

Opportunities_____

Threats_____

Key Factor Analysis—Include at least two SWOT factors that you feel are important to deal with in the planning process (2 total, not for each heading).

1._____

2._____

Objectives—Include an objective based on each of your Key Factors.

1._____

2._____

Strategy—Include a strategy for each of your objectives.

1._____

2._____

Tactics—Set tactics for one of your strategies (at least one action plan and one policy; label each).

_____

_____

_____

_____

Strategy Reviews (SR)

These are brief reviews of articles on human resources strategies (topics) with your opinion of what was written and a reference for the source. You will prepare an SR for all strategies (i.e., Chapters) covered in the course, except Chapters #1 and #5. The minimum length is about one page of double-spaced text (a minimum of about 250 words), the maximum is about one and a half pages of text. Unless your instructor says otherwise, the sources for each set of SRs must be from academic, peer-reviewed (also known as refereed) journals (e.g., *Cornell Quarterly*, *Journal of Hospitality and Tourism Research*, *Journal of Hospitality and Tourism Education*, etc.).

  A. General selection criteria: Find an article that is of interest to you. The article could be focused on hospitality businesses or any other industry (ask your instructor if non-hospitality articles are acceptable). To limit the likelihood of students submitting SRs on the same article, please try to select an article whose author(s) has one of your initials (first, middle, or last name) as the initials in their name (e.g., Jane Abby Smith could look for an author with a first, middle, or last name that begins with J, A, or S). The purpose of this is to minimize the chances of several students selecting the one of the first few articles that come up on a database search.

  B. Oral presentations of your strategy reviews: Once the class is discussing each strategy, you can be called upon at any time to briefly discuss your strategy review on that topic (e.g., "My article focused on the idea of allowing employees in each department of a hotel to prepare their own schedules," plus a little background from the article and your thoughts/opinion on the strategy).

  After the strategy reviews have been graded and passed back, please keep them with your book so you will have them for each class.

  C. Strategy reviews are not required for Chapters #1, HR Planning and #5, Job Creation Process.

  D. Due dates—Strategy Reviews will be submitted as follows:

    1. Topics #2, 3, 4 and 6 will be turned in as a set as assigned by your instructor, as close to the beginning of the course as reasonably possible. At least before Chapter Two is discussed.

    2. The remaining four strategy reviews (Chapter #7 through #10) will be turned in as a set as assigned by your instructor. At least before Chapter Seven is discussed.

  E. Contents and Format for Strategy Review:

1. Format for **heading** of Strategy Review (general memo style):

Course Name

Strategy Review

To: Mary Wilson   (anyone)
                         Title: Director of Human Resources
From: Your name
Date: Due date
Subject: Values, Moral and Motivation (the chapter's title)

  2. A one or more paragraph **review** of what was written (what the company is doing, what the author researched and found, etc.). Someone reading it must feel that the main points of the article have been communicated. If you use a quote from the article, please cite it "the most important …" (Smith, 2001, p. 45). If you state there are four important points, at least list them, if not explain them. Make sure you proofread your work to make sure you have clearly communicated the main points of the article and have used proper grammar.

  3. One or more paragraphs of your **opinion** of the relevance or logic of what the author has discussed or what the firm is doing. Basically, what do you think can be learned from the information in the article--both pros and cons, from the firm's actions or the author's ideas (e.g., good idea, bad idea, might be successful if done in a different way, could work in luxury hotels—not in budget properties, etc.)? If you were reporting this information back to your manager, what would you write that might help him or her to change the firm's strategies and tactics?

  4. Your source must be properly **referenced**. You do not need to use a separate sheet of paper for the reference. Do not include the article with your assignment.

Sample references [This reference format is from American Psychological Association (APA) and is the most common format for business writing.]:

Book:

Woods, R. H. (2000). *Managing hospitality human resources* (3rd ed.). Lansing, MI:
    Educational Institute of the American Hotel & Motel Association.

Periodical (trade magazine, academic journal):
Kanji, G. K., & Chopra, P. K., (2010). Corporate social responsibility in a global economy. *Total Quality Management & Business Excellence, 21*(2), 119-143.
 "21" refers to the Volume and "(2)" refers to the Number of the issue for that volume.
Internet:
Barsky, J. (2010). Luxury Hotels and recession: A view from around the world. www.lhw.com/download_s/230.pdf

250 words

Chapter Two: Values, Morale, and Motivation

Strategy Review: Prepare a strategy review for this chapter (See back of Chapter One).
Case Study 2.1: Personal Problems of Hourly Employees
Chapter Objectives: After reading this chapter you should understand and be able to do the following:
1. Explain the importance of values (i.e., organizational values) to business. Provide some examples of common organizational values.
2. Explain the relationship between values, beliefs, attitudes, and behavior and how they influence organizational and employee behavior.
3. Describe what mission statements are and explain why they are important.
4. Describe the stakeholder approach to values and explain how there could be differing opinions about what actions represent appropriate values and what you can or should do for the various stakeholders, in particular employees and managers.
5. Describe the concept of social responsibility.
6. Describe the conflict between profit maximization and social responsibility.
7. List the benefits of having good values (i.e., ethics and social responsibility).
8. Explain what a business can do to promote social responsibility.
9. Describe Aristotelian friendship and explain how it can or should impact the manager/employee relationship.
10. Define employee morale and employee motivation.
11. Describe motivation concepts: (a) manipulation versus ethical inducement, (b) positive motivation versus negative motivation, and (c) internal motivation versus external motivation.
12. Explain how you could measure the morale of your employees (conceptual measurement and empirical measurement).
13. Define management style and differentiate between autocratic management and democratic management styles.
14. Explain how money motivates.
15. Evaluate fear of punishment as a motivator.
16. List seven or more morale and motivation factors.
17. Describe motivation theories provided in the chapter (Maslow, Equity, and Reinforcement, being the most important).
18. Comment on the major problem with Herzberg's Two-Factor Theory.

Values
Values are general beliefs concerning what is good or bad, desirable or not desirable, that are shared by individuals and organizations in societies (firms are organizations). They are not directed toward any specific element, but are used to assess a broad range of objects and situations. For example, firms that have strong values related to respect for others will generally do whatever is in their power to make sure that employees' and customers' feelings are considered when they make decisions. Ideally, firms should have a sincere respect for the people that do the work—some firms do, many do not. Why do some firms treat employees in a less than respectful manner? Because respect is either not one of their core values or, if it is, the firm does not live up to its core values. Similarly, if a firm or individuals believe that honesty is important, they will likely act honestly in most situations (i.e., do the right thing). Firms that value an employee's sense of accomplishment will find ways of maximizing their employees' personal growth. Employees who value a sense of accomplishment will generally try to do their best for each task for which they are responsible. Firms that value quality-of-life issues will be considerate of employees' desires to have an effective balance between their work and personal lives (Malik, McKie, Beattie, & Hogg, 2010). Firms without solid core values will generally have employees with low morale and little motivation.

Perhaps the core value at the heart of the values discussion of recent years has been ethics. In one sense, ethics, and to a somewhat lesser degree, social responsibility, are *global values* because if a firm is truly ethical or socially responsible, they will likely make appropriate decisions with everything else. In support of this statement, Noland and Phillips (2010) stated that ethical concerns must be included in all strategy discussions because capitalism should ideally be based, not only on what is good for the firm, but good for society as well. The process of making ethical business decisions is simplistically two-fold. First, is the morality of the person making the decision. This could be the President of the company or an hourly employee, for example, front desk agent. Managers and experienced employees (i.e., informal leaders) must lead by example. A firm can have the best value system in the world, but without moral people carrying them out, corporate values will at best be inconsistently supported. Unfortunately, even small lapses in ethical behavior can ruin a business. Second, the firm must have a set of core values that are consistent with high ethical standards and cultural norms (Vitell, Ramos, & Nishihara, 2009). While most firms simply use a mission statement to express their values, some firms also have corporate values statements, such as the following from the Four Seasons Hotels and Resorts (**See Figure 2.1**).

Figure 2.1:   Four Seasons Hotels and Resorts Corporate Values

At Four Seasons, corporate values are much more than a programme or a policy – they define who we are and inform the decisions we make. The company's guiding principle is the Golden Rule – to treat others as you wish to be treated – and as such, Four Seasons strives to have a long-lasting, positive influence on the communities where we operate and on the people we employ and serve around the world. We believe that this goal is integral to our success as a company. This commitment is expressed consistently in our actions through three main areas of focus. By acting in a manner consistent with our corporate values, Four Seasons will continue to seek opportunities to enrich and contribute positively to the global community.

Building Communities

Four Seasons is committed to being a responsible and caring community partner by having a positive economic impact and supporting community goals, both within and outside the hotel. We engage in innovative training and mentoring programmes for young people, support those in need and celebrate the diverse cultures where Four Seasons operates.

Advancing Cancer Research

Four Seasons is committed to supporting both local efforts and broader campaigns whose goal is the eradication of cancer. Through the collective efforts of the company's hotels worldwide, Four Seasons annually raises significant funds and awareness for cancer research.

Supporting Sustainability

Four Seasons involves employees and guests in the common goal of preserving and protecting the planet. We engage in sustainable practices that conserve natural resources and reduce environmental impact. As importantly, sustainable tourism will enhance and protect the destinations where Four Seasons operates for generations to come.

Reprinted with permission from Four Seasons Hotels and Resorts (Ontario, Canada).

Common Personal/Organizational Values that Impact Employees and Other Groups
• Ethics (knowing the difference between right and wrong, then doing what is right)
• Social responsibility (doing the right thing for all groups and for the environment)
Ethics and Social Responsibility are Global Values because all other values can be subsumed under them.
• Honesty (equitable treatment)
• Respect/promoting self-respect
• Quality-of-life
• Diversity
• Sustainability
• Achieving one's potential
• High expectations of everyone
• Sense of accomplishment
• Sense of belonging/warm relationships with others
• Fun/enjoyment/excitement
• Security/stability

Values and Their Influence on Beliefs, Attitudes, and Behavior

The core of individuals' cognitive structure (a person's mind/brain/thought process) and hence their behavior is based on their values. The way values influence beliefs, attitude, and behavior will be explained in greater detail below, but briefly: values influence the development of beliefs; beliefs form the foundation of a person's attitude; and subsequently, the person's attitude influences their behavior (See **Figure 2.2: The Impact of Values on the Firm and Employees**).

<u>Beliefs</u> are what people *think* (and perhaps how they *feel*) about something—primarily specific cognitions/thoughts about the acceptance of something as true or false, important or not important, good/desirable or bad/not desirable. They are also the smallest element in the cognitive structure of the mind. For example, employees may have differing beliefs concerning the importance of customer service. One could believe it is important to do your best for the customer, another may feel employees should just follow company policies and do the basics, and a third may think that it is demeaning to serve people. Each of these beliefs would be accompanied by a number of additional beliefs. The employee who believes it is important to do her best for the customer may also believe that second best is not good enough, that all people deserve respect, that an employer who pays her well deserves her best, and that teamwork is important. The other two employees would also have additional beliefs related to their perception of customer service.

What has been described above is the cognitive aspect of beliefs or what people think about something. There is also an emotional component, termed *affect* that is associated with the belief (the "a" in affect is pronounced like the "a" in at). Where the cognitive aspect concerns what the person *thinks* about the stimuli, the affective component considers how the person *feels* about the stimuli. In research, cognitive measurements about a stimuli (e.g., I think this company cares about me.) can be combined in various ways with affective measurements about the stimuli (e.g., I strongly believe this company cares about me.) to obtain a person's overall belief toward the stimuli.

<u>Attitudes</u> are simply interrelated beliefs. That is, they are composed of two or more beliefs. In the above example, the employee who has several beliefs about the importance of excellent customer service will likely have the attitude that, "I will do my best to ensure customer satisfaction." If an employee had the following two beliefs: "It is important that I work with honest people" and "I believe that stealing hurts a business," may have the following attitude toward honesty, "We should not hire people who are dishonest because they can hurt a business." Conversely, if a person's *values* towards honesty were that stealing was okay, his *beliefs* may include, "the company can afford it, I need it more than the company, and I deserve better pay." This individual's *attitude* toward honesty might be, "I deserve whatever I can take." Additionally, attitudes, and the beliefs they are based on, are enduring (long lasting). That is, they provide psychological stability, allowing individuals to consistently respond to similar situations. Attitude is also a predisposition to behavior, that is, if individuals have a certain attitude, they are likely to act in a way that supports that attitude.

<u>Behavior</u> occurs when an individual is motivated to act on his or her attitude. Since an individual's values, beliefs, and attitudes form the basis for his or her behavior, the ability to understand these concepts allows managers to understand the basis of employee behavior. If an employee is not providing good service to people who are not well dressed, he or she may have the following beliefs, "People who dress poorly are probably not well educated," "People who dress poorly are lazy," "People who dress poorly don't have much money and can't afford to stay at our hotel," This employee's attitude may be, "I don't like people who are dressed poorly." By simply asking the employee *why* he or she acted that way, the manager can uncover this employee's beliefs and attitude and therefore understand why the employee is acting this way. The manager can also help the employee understand the basis for the behavior, which would ideally lead to an understanding that respect for all people is critical, and hopefully, a change in future behavior. This solution would likely be better and longer lasting than simply telling the employee to respect all people or else expect to be disciplined. It should also increase both the admiration of the manager as one who understands the complexity of situations and has enough respect for employees to sit down with them and pursue a reasonably full understanding of the situation.

The process of uncovering someone's beliefs is to ask simple questions, such as, "Why do you treat people who dress poorly with less respect than people who dress well?" or "Why did you do that?" Follow-up questions generally consist of asking for more reasons (beliefs) for the unacceptable behavior.

<u>Figure 2.2:   The Impact of Values on the Firm and Employees</u>

Values	Beliefs	Attitude	Behavior
•Honesty for the company	•Helps reputation •Improve morale and motivation •Right thing to do •Employees trust us •Community image	•Being honest is good/important	•Act honest
•Hard work (Being productive)	•What's in it for me •Others don't seem to work hard •For minimum wage? •I would work harder if I had better training	•Hard work is not worth it	•I'll do what I need to do to get by
•Mgt.'s lack of respect for employees	•Possible negative beliefs of mgt.?	•Possible attitude toward employees?	•Possible behavior toward employees?

Mission Statement and Values

The mission statement can be defined as a broad statement of characteristics (product and market), goals (profit and growth), and philosophies of a business (how it intends to treat its stakeholders) (Pearce & Robinson, 1991); or simply, its purpose and philosophies (Byars, 1984). It is also referred to as the company mission, vision, and brief excerpts, are referred to as the creed or credo. Most firms rely on a mission statement to express corporate values. The primary concern for Human Resources are the philosophies of the business, in particular, how the business intends to treat its stakeholders (Reich, 2000).

The mission statement is frequently thought of as being a nonsensical bundle of platitudes. For companies with little sense of direction, this is true. But, the mere putting down on paper of what general direction the company should take is essential, even if it does sound like every other company mission. "You've got to start somewhere!" A company that has not organized its thought process enough to know what it is, where it's going, and what it stands for will find it difficult to establish a secure future. The business purpose and business mission are rarely given adequate thought and are perhaps the most important single cause of business frustration and business failure (Drucker, 1974). Effective strategic leadership begins with an understanding of what the business should and should not be doing and a vision of where it needs to be headed (Thompson & Strickland, 1992). The following quote helps support the importance of the mission statements:

> Only a clear definition of the mission and purpose of the business makes possible clear and realistic business objectives. It is the foundation for priorities, strategies, plans, and work assignments. It is the starting point for the design of managerial jobs and, above all, for the design of managerial structures. Structure follows strategy. Strategy determines what the key activities are in a given business. And strategy requires knowing what our business is and what it should be (Drucker, 1974, 75).

Because today's mode of business can rapidly become obsolete, a set of principles, practices, and foundations is necessary to serve as a starting point for change. If management understands the firm's philosophies, then the firm will have a built-in mechanism to control the selection of new strategies. At most proactive and value-driven companies, the only sacred cow is their philosophy of doing business. Anything else can be challenged.

Peter Drucker (1974), perhaps management's most famous scholar, said that the central focus of discussions on mission statements should include "What is our business?" "What will it be (i.e., how will it change in the future)?" and "What should it be?" While the discussion of the three questions normally concerns the firm's products and markets, the first and third can also be used to derive the firm's appropriate philosophies. The questions then become "What are our current philosophies/values?" and "What should they be?" What the firm's philosophies/values currently are will probably be in writing, however, they should be defined by various stakeholder groups, such as customers, managers, and employees. Ideally, the only change in philosophies/values (what they should be) would be to make them stronger or to improve their implementation.

The following is the Mission Statement from Four Seasons Hotels and Resorts (**See Figure 2.3**).

Figure 2.3:   Four Seasons Hotels and Resorts Mission Statement

Many years ago, Four Seasons set out to create a corporate mission statement. Something that would guide the actions of everyone in the organisation. Our goals, beliefs and principles are the foundation of the work we do on behalf of our guests every day.

Who We Are

We have chosen to specialise within the hospitality industry by offering only experiences of exceptional quality. Our objective is to be recognised as the company that manages the finest hotels, resorts and residence clubs wherever we locate.

We create properties of enduring value using superior design and finishes, and support them with a deeply instilled ethic of personal service. Doing so allows Four Seasons to satisfy the needs and tastes of our discriminating customers, and to maintain our position as the world's premier luxury hospitality company.

What We Believe

Our greatest asset, and the key to our success, is our people.

We believe that each of us needs a sense of dignity, pride and satisfaction in what we do. Because satisfying our guests depends on the united efforts of many, we are most effective when we work together cooperatively, respecting each other's contribution and importance.

How We Succeed

We succeed when every decision is based on a clear understanding of and belief in what we do, and when we couple this conviction with sound financial planning. We expect to achieve a fair and reasonable profit to ensure the prosperity of the company and to offer long-term benefits to our hotel owners, our customers and our employees.

How We Behave

We demonstrate our beliefs most meaningfully in the way we treat each other and by the example we set for one another. In all our interactions with our guests, customers, business associates and colleagues, we seek to deal with others as we would have them deal with us.

Reprinted with permission from Four Seasons Hotels and Resorts (Ontario, Canada).

The Stakeholder Approach to Values

After the firm has determined its general philosophy toward stakeholders, it must specify how it will treat its various stakeholder groups. The stakeholder approach to values is the consideration of the legitimate interests of people and groups inside and outside the organization. There are two key stakeholder categories—internal stakeholders, which include employees, management, owners/stockholders/board of directors, and external stakeholders, which include customers, suppliers, local communities, and the general public, governments, and competitors. Each stakeholder group has certain desires. The challenge for management is that it is impossible to completely satisfy everyone's desires. For this course and HR, the key stakeholder groups are employees and managers. Their concerns will vary based on personal needs and personalities, but employees generally expect things, such as decent wages and benefits, appreciation for their efforts, the opportunity for growth, and a stable and secure job (see Morale and Motivation Factors later in this chapter for a more comprehensive list).

Social Responsibility and Values

Social responsibility is one of the key manifestations of value-oriented firms. It includes decisions and actions that take into account the interests of society as a whole, such as being considerate of the needs of employees, honoring diversity, charitable efforts, and environmentally friendly activities. Social responsibility has also been shown to be highly correlated with profit—firms do well by doing good (Kanji & Chopra, 2010).

Historical Business Philosophies Related to Social Responsibility

• **Profit Maximization**. This is the concept that management's primary duty is to return the highest possible profit to investors. It is government's job or individuals who want to help, to take care of the environment, the community in which it operates, and its people (Woods, 2002). Even today, there are some business people and economists that believe it is up to owners/stockholders of the business to determine what is done with their profits, not management. The people running the business should focus on what they do best--run the business as effectively and efficiently as possible. At first this appears to be a rational philosophy. However, if customers' and employees' image of the business is improved because of its socially responsible activities, then their argument is undermined.

• **Trustee Management**. Because of the many problems of society, many of which were caused by businesses (e.g., low wages, poor working conditions, long hours, environmental pollution, etc.), various governmental agencies began mandating change. In other words, since business did not take care of important aspects of the quality-of-life of society, the government needed to step in.

• **Socially Responsible Management**. Since government cannot take care of all needs of society, management must help by first doing no harm and second by seeking ways of bettering people's lives. In marketing terminology, this is referred to as the societal marketing concept.

Benefits of a Business's Social Responsibility Efforts

The following are among the benefits of a business's socially responsible efforts:

• The image of being a caring organization. All things being equal, most employees would rather work for socially responsible firms, especially when social responsibility is directed toward them (Reich, Xu, & McCleary, 2010). Customer loyalty is also improved.

• A strong society benefits the business. A vibrant community with equal job opportunities for all increases the likelihood of success of a business.

• It may be less expensive (monetarily and image-wise) to prevent a problem than to solve it later. Essentially, do it right the first time. Years ago, when someone had a badly upset stomach, the stomach flu was often blamed. In most instances it was not the flu, but spoiled food from restaurants or from home.

• Doing business in an ethical manner may minimize governmental intrusion and regulation. The leading cause of legal problems for hospitality firms is not treating employees with respect and consequently breaking various civil rights laws (e.g., discrimination based on age, race, color, religion, sex, national origin, pregnancy, etc.).

Social Responsibility Audit and Plan of Action

In a variety of courses, authors provide students with a means of auditing or reviewing a business concern and suggestions on putting together a plan of action to deal with it. The reality is that all of these audits and plans of action follow the same format—the functional plan (see Chapter One). For any business issue, you first review the firm's current performance (e.g., the internal analysis) and related activities of competitors, how customers view it, how it impacts potential applicants, and so forth (e.g., the environmental analysis). Subsequently you set objectives for the topic, in this case social responsibility; then you create strategies and tactics to achieve the objectives. Finally, you implement the strategies and design controls to monitor their implementation.

Strategies Supportive of Corporate Values/Ethics

The following activities are essential in helping firms create and support value-oriented philosophies and practices:

• There should be written and clear corporate values that encourage responsible behavior (and provide punishment for unethical behavior) (See the Four Seasons Hotel and Resorts Corporate Values earlier in this Chapter.)

• There should be frequent communication of corporate values (e.g., verbally, stressed in how work is done, written value statements posted in prominent places, etc.).

• Top management commitment to nurture corporate values. Management does things that exemplify various corporate values.

• If management is concerned about what to do, there should be a specific policy detailing a process or someone they should speak to.

• The firm should focus on the development of managerial awareness and competence through ethics training.

• A control system to monitor corporate ethical performance should be in place.

Questions for Resolving Ethical Dilemmas
What is the ethical concern?
Is it a legal obligation, fairness, respect, honesty, doing good, or attempting to avoid harm? Is it really an ethical issue? Am I afraid to do what I know is right?

• **Clear ethical issues.** Selling rockfish, when the menu says redfish—redfish can be three times the cost of redfish.

• **Single ethical principle problems.** An issue of fairness, honesty, commitment, or avoiding harm. Is it okay to pay similarly skilled and tenured employees different wages? Should we buy useful safety equipment for our kitchen that is not required by law? Should we allow a loyal, but subpar ten-year employee to continue working?

• **Complex ethical issues.** If we open a hotel in China, how will we treat nationals? The same treatment for everyone, different treatment from U.S. workers, or the same as we do in the United States? What about compensation and benefits? How much money should be set aside for social responsibility? Upon what criteria should donations be made? How should public relations be considered? Are bribes in one country simply a cultural phenomenon that should be respected? Decision-makers in many human endeavors rarely have the luxury of choosing between right and wrong, instead they may need to choose between the lesser of two wrongs.

Who else matters?
Who are the stakeholders who may be affected by my decisions? Can you use the Golden Rule in business?

Is it my problem?
Have I caused the problem or has someone else? How far should I go in resolving the issue?

Kew Gardens Principles (obligations)

1. Need—Is your participation needed?
2. Proximity—Are you close enough to the situation to help?
3. Capability—Do you have the ability to help?
4. Last resort—Are you the only one who can help?

What do others think?
Can I learn from those who disagree with my judgment? Does everyone feel comfortable in saying what is on his or her mind?

Am I being true to myself?
Do the actions support my personal Identity and character? What kind of person or company would do what I am contemplating? Could I share my decision "in good conscience" with my family, with colleagues, with public officials?

Friendship and the Employee-Supervisor Relationship
Central Features of Aristotelian Friendship (Brewer, 2005).
• A reciprocal wishing of the best for the friend.

• A mutual awareness of this reciprocal wishing.

• Resulting in equal exchanges of those things.

• True friendships are expected to last forever.

• True friendship is based on equality and equality is based on justice, or at least perceived justice.

Types of Friendship
There are three forms of friendship: virtue, pleasure, and utility friendships. The managerial dilemma is if any of these types of friendships should describe the relationship managers should have with their employees. Can a manager go to another restaurant with employees for a beer? Would such an event change the manager/employee relationship?

• **Virtue Friendships.**

• Share much in common.

• Are open about personal aspects of their lives.

• There are a limited number of virtue friends that you can have.

• Virtue friends encourage each other to live the good life and strive to help each other make this life possible.

• Our virtuous friends' character is important, since we share our lives with them.

• If people do not know what your interests are, their wishing you well is a somewhat empty wish. As admirable as their intent may be, they are not your virtuous friend.

• **Pleasure Friendships**.

Those who desire to be with each other for happiness.

• **Utility Friendships**.

• These friendships are based what the person can do for you.

• These friendships tend to cease when the relationship is no longer mutually beneficial.

• Though there is a basic understanding that the friendship will continue, it rarely does.

Philosophies from the Office of Trammel Crow

(Trammel Crow is one of the most successful real estate developers in the United States. One of his primary strategies for achieving this was to make his employees partners in the business. The following list came from a plaque in his office.)

Promise yourself to be so strong that nothing can disturb your peace of mind;

To talk health, happiness, and prosperity to every person you meet;

To treat every person you meet as the most important person in the world;

To look at the sunny side of everything and make your optimism come true;

To be just as enthusiastic about the success of others as you are about your own;

To forget the mistakes of the past and press on to the great achievements of the future;

To wear a cheerful countenance at all times and give so much time to the improvement of yourself that you have no time to criticize others;

To be too large for worry, too noble for anger, too strong for fear, and too happy to permit the presence of trouble.

Morale and Motivation

Once a firm's values are established, it can consider employee morale and motivation. Relative to employee productivity and the overall success of the business, there are few business concepts more important than morale and motivation. Think about this statement, "Your employees will allow you to succeed to the degree they want you to." Certainly it would be a stretch to say that employees have total control over the manager's success; however, if they are not satisfied with their work situation, their morale will be low and they will subsequently not be motivated to do their best. Of course, management could simply replace those with low morale, but this would likely be ignoring the more serious problem of why morale was low in the first place. Alternatively, if employee morale is high, they will be much more likely to support management in its goal to satisfy customers and help the business make a profit (Kale, 2007). There are entire books written on morale and motivation, in this chapter we will review the basic concepts. The following are general definitions of each term regarding employment:

• **Morale** concerns the attitudes and feelings (i.e., level of satisfaction) of employees toward their job and their managers.

• **Motivation** focuses on the level of energy employees are willing to commit to complete their tasks.

Even though the two terms can be defined differently, they are not mutually exclusive. Employees have different personalities and different needs. For example, for an individual employee, any one of the 24 Morale and Motivation Factors listed and explained later in this chapter may or may not influence morale and motivation. Benefits could be a morale factor for one employee, but not a motivator. For another employee, benefits may be a motivator, but not improve morale. Another important element in morale and motivation is that it is the combined or total impact of all existing influences on the employee that matters. The business could be doing a great job with everything except one item, and that one item ends up negating the great work done in 20 or so other areas. Most people have found themselves, at least in the short-term, upset with something at work that not only impacts everything they do, but makes them ignore or forget all the good things the firm does for them. One could say, "That which is least important, becomes most important." In other words, if management neglects one factor because it assumes that it is not important, it could end up hurting or even destroying the business.

The best way to describe the difference between morale and motivation is to consider morale as being those practices that allow management to motivate employees (i.e., management should focus first on morale, then on motivation). If employees are unhappy with morale factors that are important to them, it may be difficult to motivate them. When morale factors that are important to the employee have been satisfied, the employee will not necessarily be motivated, but will generally respond better to motivation techniques. This is evidenced by the fact that happy employees are not necessarily the most productive employees. The average employee will be motivated to uphold the standards of the business if he or she benefits from it in some way—appreciation, responsibility, achievement, and money being prime motivators.

Measurement of Morale and Motivation

Because of its direct link with productivity (both quality and quantity), turnover, customer satisfaction, and other critical areas, morale needs to be measured (Momeni, 2009). There are two primary means of measuring morale—conceptual and empirical.

• **Conceptual Measurement**. This is management's or others' opinion (concept) of the morale of employees. Logically and intuitively, managers know if morale is great, good, or poor. Two critical elements missing from the conceptual measurement are accuracy and the reason for the current level of morale. Each manager may have a different opinion. Also, because it is so highly related to managerial quality, there may be a great amount of bias in conceptually measuring morale. The reason for the current level of morale could be acquired from discussions, but because of the fear of saying what is on their minds, employees may not volunteer everything.

• **Empirical Measurement**. When random surveys of employees' perceptions of their morale are implemented, it is termed an empirical study or measurement. This could be measured by a single question—"Please describe your level of morale on the following 5-point scale: 1 = poor, 2 = fair, 3 = good, 4 = very good, 5 = excellent." This is the employees' overall attitude concerning morale. The problem with this result is that management has not exposed the specific areas that need to be addressed or changed. For example, if the result of the single-item survey was a score of 3.5, management can only assume that morale is average—not bad, not great. Exactly what to focus on is not known. Wages could be excellent, but a manager's inconsistent performance appraisals brought the score down. In other words, management does not have actionable data. A more effective option is to ask employees about the various factors that impact morale (e.g., quality of supervision, appreciation for their efforts, etc.), then incorporate the most common concerns into a multi-item survey. In essence, this will expose employees' beliefs that influence their attitude related to morale (morale is an attitude).

Although it could be measured in the same way as morale, because of the close relationship between the factors that measure and influence morale and motivation and the fact that motivation must generally be customized, it is not generally directly measured. In other words, if the firm is doing a good job with the various factors that influence morale and productivity is high (i.e., labor cost is low), then it will likely also be doing a good job with the factors that influence motivation. The key word here is *likely* as there may be some employees with good morale that are difficult to motivate. One key difference between assessing morale and motivation is that most employees do not need a customized morale package. Management simply does a good job with all the factors that influence morale and subsequently, employee morale should be good. The justification for this is that everyone is happy with more benefits, higher wages, better supervision, and so forth. Motivation requires a bit more personalized attention (Dunlap, 2010). For example, one employee may be motivated by responsibility, another by management's listening to them. Therefore, management must learn from each employee, which factor or factors motivate them, then utilize those for that particular employee.

Concepts Associated with Motivation

• **Manipulation versus ethical treatment/inducement**. Having employees do things for the good of management without considering their needs. Manipulation can actually be a good thing, *if* it is for the benefit of both the employee and management. To do this, management must find out what motivates employees, and then show them how working toward company goals can help them achieve their personal goals. Employee Stock Ownership Plans are an ethical way to get everyone working toward company goals. To be fair, that is, to not be viewed as manipulation, the amount of stock should be commensurate with the effort put forward by employees and the increased value of the firm.

• **Positive motivation versus negative motivation**. Providing positive and supportive reasons (i.e., positive motivation) for working hard, such as encouragement, challenges, incentives, and promotions can positively impact employee performance. Providing serious consequences for subpar performance (i.e., negative motivation) may occasionally have a positive impact on employee performance, but generally only in the short-term. Negative motivation is rarely successful, but is sometimes necessary. If the business is in trouble, a statement that the business will close unless sales and profits go up may be the only option. If management is attempting to keep from firing an employee and has tried almost everything, perhaps a little embarrassment away from customers, but in front of some other employees may help. This should not become a habit.

• **Self-Fulfilling Prophecy.** For thousands of years military leaders have knowingly utilized self-fulfilling prophecy (SFP), also known as the Pygmalion effect, to motivate soldiers to perform significantly beyond their potential. It is probably also true that most successful business leaders have utilized this concept in some manner to increase the motivation and performance of their subordinates. In business, the process of SFP occurs when managers develop expectations about the potential of an employee (Sutton & Woodman, 1989). These expectations are then communicated in some manner to the employee, who then begins to believe in the expectations and subsequently begins to perform up to (or down to) those expectations. To maximize the Pygmalion effect, managers should focus on the positive aspects of an employee's performance (as much as reasonably possible); provide tasks that enhance current strengths and build new strengths; and have a mentor available for coaching the employee to higher levels of performance.

• **Internal motivation versus external motivation**. Those who are internally motivated work hard because they know it will help them achieve their personal goals, help the business, or simply because they take pride in what they do. Those who require external motivation need to be spurred on by others or with some type of external incentive or threat before they will complete tasks or attempt to improve their performance. Perhaps the most important trait of a new manager and the most important judgment of them by their supervisor is whether or not they are internally motivated. The reason people are selected for management positions is because they willingly and even appreciatively take on responsibilities, learn everything they can about being a better manager—show up a little early and stay a little late and can be counted on to do whatever is necessary to make the business a success. Those who are not viewed as being internally motivated will unfortunately wonder why promotions have not come their way. While there are hourly employees who are internally motivated, most require some type of external motivation.

• **Management style**. Each manager has his or her own pattern of management, known as management style. There are two major styles, autocratic and democratic, with variations in between. Autocratic managers make most required decisions for the business and do not let emotions enter into decisions. Upholding company policies is their main focus and is carried out with a stern hand. The problem with the autocratic manager is that employees will quickly get tired of being ordered around and find employment elsewhere. Democratic managers solicit employee opinions for decisions (e.g., participative management) and, within reason, allow their emotions to impact decisions. Upholding company policies is still important, but the policies are enforced in a supportive manner. Employee empowerment is an important strategy for the democratic manager. This not only allows employees to help with decisions, but to personally address unique circumstances and problems as they arise. One study showed that firms that utilize empowerment experience greater sales growth than those that do not (Altinay, Altinay, & Gannon, 2008). Though the democratic style certainly has better long-term results than the autocratic style, some democratic managers are a bit too weak and place employee feelings before upholding company policies and therefore the success of the business. Regardless of whether the style is democratic or autocratic, the manager must be effective. The most productive managerial style tends to be somewhere between the autocratic and democratic styles, but closer to democratic approach. Generally, an effective manager is one who assertively guides the firm in the achievement of its objectives, steadfastly upholds the standards/policies of the business, and does so while having a good rapport with employees.

• **Money as a motivator**. Money is one of the most misunderstood of the motivators. Countless theories abound as to its effectiveness as a motivator, many of which contradict each other. The fact is that every individual reacts differently to increases in pay as a motivating tool based on their personal needs and psychological profile (i.e., how they perceive themselves or think others perceive them). Talking to employees to find out how they live and what they are trying to achieve for themselves and their families may help determine how money may motivate them. Usually there is a relationship between the need for money and the manager's power to use it as a motivator. Once the employee's need for money is met, additional money may not be a motivator. Since labor cost is the most volatile controllable expense in the hospitality industry, management should place reasonable limits on its use as a motivator. Primary options include using it for employees who deserve a pay increase and as a bonus/reward for achieving a goal. One reason why money is sometimes not considered a motivator in the hospitality industry is because since most firms pay about the same for someone with a certain level of experience for any specific position, there is little motivation to work harder or to switch firms for more money.

The relationship between money and morale (job satisfaction) is similar in some ways and different in others to the relationship between money and motivation. Like the money/motivation relationship, it varies based on the employees' psychological profile. If employees are not satisfied with their compensation (i.e., morale regarding their compensation is low), it will be difficult for management to motivate them. Employees' perception of the fairness of compensation will vary. For hospitality employees, typical concerns include: what employees doing the same job at the same business are earning; what employees doing the same job at other businesses are earning; what employees are making relative to how hard they perceive themselves to be working; the personal satisfaction they receive from the work; and the level of recognition from management, other employees, and customers.

• Fear of punishment as a motivator. Fear of punishment can be used as a motivator as long as the object of the employees' fear is a goal, not a person. If employees fear a person, they may develop a hatred for the person. If employees fear a goal of some sort, the worthy employee will be motivated to meet it. However, if the fear goes on for too long, employees will at some point become stressed, productivity will decline, and turnover will increase.

Morale and Motivation Factors
The following is a list of typical morale and motivation factors that impact employees (See **Figure 2.4: Typical Morale and Motivation Factors**).

1. Quality of Supervision. Management must be fair and consistent, make the employee's work as enjoyable as possible, always be in a good mood (except when disciplining employees), and show respect and appreciation for employees. Employees must feel that managers are not only making decisions in the best interest of the firm, but also in the best interest of the employees. When the latter occurs, morale, motivation and the desire to remain with the firm increase. Excellent managers not only let employees know when their performance is good, but also when it is not up to company standards. When the latter occurs, they help the employee learn the correct methods in a motivating and supportive manner.

2. Job Security. The longer the average tenure for all employees, the more secure each will feel about their chances of staying with the business. Tenured employees also increase everyone's enjoyment of working at the business because they are more professional and work better as a team. Common causes of high turnover are managers who terminate employees rather than properly training and counseling them, no enforcement of standards, inconsistent demands from management, no authority figure, and frequent unpleasant surprises.

Figure 2.4:   Typical Morale and Motivation Factors (Variables)

1. Quality of Supervision	13. Delegation
2. Job Security	14. Teamwork
3. Physical Working Conditions	15. Motivated Management
4. Wages	16. Interesting Work
5. Benefits	17. Adequate Staffing
6. Interpersonal Relationships	18. Effective Training
7. Personal Concern for Employees	19. Management's Communication and Listening Skills
8. Empowerment	20. Positive Corporate Culture/Minimization of Stress
9. Management Shows Appreciation	21. Company Goals/Shared Vision
10. Participative Management	22. Ethically Oriented Management
11. Personal Goals	23. Music
12. Incentives and Bonuses	24. Flexible Work Schedule

---

3. Physical Working Conditions. The business must be laid out efficiently and have the proper equipment and lighting available for required tasks. High standards of cleanliness and sanitation will not guarantee high morale, but low standards will generally assure low morale.

4. Wages. If employees are not reasonably satisfied with their compensation or the possibility of increases, they will probably not be happy with the job. If the business cannot afford to pay certain employees what they are worth, meet with the employee to decide what can be done in place of more money (e.g., better schedule for school, learning new skills, free meals, etc.) or whether continued employment is in the best interest of the employee. Ideally, wages should be commensurate with the employee's performance and what similarly skilled employees receive at other hospitality businesses with approximately the same volume.

5. Benefits. The hospitality industry has traditionally lagged behind most industries as far as benefits provided. Options, such as health insurance, paid vacations, bonuses, profit sharing, pension plans, and tuition reimbursement, will increase morale and keep employees on the job longer.

6. Interpersonal Relationships. When employees get along well as a group and work with people they have something in common with and with whom they consider friends, their morale will be higher. Most of our employees are young and young people generally value fun more than those who are older. An applicant's compatibility with present employees must be considered when making hiring decisions, but should not be a disqualifying factor. Compatibility based on differences protected by the Civil Rights Act is discriminatory and illegal.

7. Personal Concern for Employees. If employees know that management cares about them for more than the work they do, they will generally be motivated to do a better job. When the workday or shift begins, management should walk around the facility and greet each employee by name. About once a week have a short conversation with each employee to see how he or she is doing in both work and personal life.

8. Empowerment. When management lets employees know that it trusts them enough to make important decisions that impact their jobs, their morale, motivation, and performance will generally improve. The caveat is that management must place rational boundaries upon what an employee can and cannot do. Some luxury hotels give employees comp privileges of up to $5,000 (comp is short for complimentary—free). Whether it is a meal or $5,000, the concept is that when customers have a problem, they want it solved then, not later; not charging the customer for what was perceived as subpar service is often the best way to keep his or her business. Additionally, the true cost of the comp is generally between 35% for a restaurant (food cost) and as low as 15% to 20% for a hotel (the cost to clean the room and utilities).

9. Management Shows Appreciation. Lack of appreciation is one of the most common reasons employees quit their jobs. Do not compliment employee performance too often, or it will become meaningless. Use discretion when complimenting employees in front of others—it may make one employee feel good, but the others may feel neglected. In this case, try to compliment the entire group, then the outstanding employee. A sincere "Thank you" or "Good work today" at the end of the employee's shift promotes employee/management bonding and an attitude of trust.

10. Participative Management. Rarely will any individual manager know more about specific tasks in a business than the employees who perform the tasks on a daily basis. Therefore, when decisions need to be made, it best to ask those with the most knowledge. Soliciting ideas from employees gives them some control over their working life and it makes them feel that their opinions are valued. If employees are given credit for their input, their morale will be lifted and they will want to offer more ideas that will help the business. Participation is the key word here, as it is the manager who must decide what action must be taken and who has the final responsibility for the results.

11. Personal Goals. Help employees set personal goals while they are working for the business. When hiring employees, find out why they want to work for the business. If the employee is a student with career goals unrelated to the business, within reason be willing to help the employee work toward those goals. If an employee desires a career in the hospitality industry, set up a series of goals and accompanying training sessions to help the employee learn what is needed to advance. This means risking having employees leave because they are trained for a higher position than one's business can presently offer, but ultimately, a highly motivated employee who stays for one year is more valuable than an employee who just gets by for several years. The highly motivated employee will also have a positive influence on customer satisfaction and the morale of other employees. Employees who have no specific goals other than to make money can be encouraged to earn more by being the best they can in their position or possibly being trained for a better paying job where they work.

12. Incentives and Bonuses. Ideally, management should set goals with corresponding rewards for all employees. These goals should be beyond the normal standards of performance, such as service, cleanliness, and product quality. For example, sales goals for the best sales for a shift could be useful. Profit, food cost, beverage cost, and labor cost are additional possibilities. If goals are to be meaningful, the employees must have some degree of control over their attainment. Letting employees choose their own bonuses, within parameters, is a great motivator. While there are countless types of incentives and bonuses (See Chapter Three, Compensation, Benefits, and Incentives), some general thoughts include:

• Handout bonuses at a meeting (all-employee or shift meeting) to give the recipients recognition and to show other employees what happens when goals are achieved.

• Offer bonuses to individuals, to departments, or to the entire staff.

• Individual or department bonuses could include cash, trips, a day off with pay, or a free dinner for two.

• A bonus for the entire staff could be a party, a picnic, or a small cash bonus (but be careful, because in a large business, $100 or so per employee can quickly add up).

13. Delegation. Make use of the normal delegation of duties as a motivational tool. Tell employees that they are personally responsible for the completion of their assigned task, that it is important to the operation of the business, and that management is counting on them to perform it in a commendable manner. As an employee exhibits initiative, give them additional responsibilities. As responsibilities increase, so will confidence and morale because employees will realize that they are acquiring new abilities that will help them have a better future. When giving employees additional responsibilities, allow them to take risks. This means doing something they have not tried before. This is the only way a person can grow in ability. If employees have a problem, be there to help them figure out how to solve it. A good way to delegate responsibilities is by assigning trained employees temporary titles, such as kitchen shift leader or dining room shift leader. This title is good for that one shift only.

14. Teamwork. When employees willingly help others, employees feel more secure and confident that they can do their personal best and deliver the best service for the customer. While many employees naturally help others, some may need training, supervision, and encouragement.

15. Motivated Management. The manager should set the example for the employee. The average employee follows the manager's lead in personality, effort expended on work, and attitude toward the business.

16. Interesting Work. Many of the tasks in the hospitality industry can be boring and tedious. This leads to decreases in the employee's focus and motivation. Create ways to make mundane jobs more interesting and challenging. Add other tasks to the job or have the employee switch to another position or job after a few hours.

17. Adequate Staffing. Employees who are consistently faced with understaffed situations will feel that management is more concerned with making a dollar than taking care of employees or customers. They may also conclude that the business is either not doing well enough to hire more people, or that others simply do not want to work for the business. The management conundrum is that unless the business is always very busy, rarely can management consistently have the ideal number of employees. Therefore, management can make adjustments by being personally available when needed. For example, in many newer mid-scale hotels, the manager's office is right behind the front desk. That way, if a guest services agent needs help, the manager is a few seconds away. Restaurant managers should circulate throughout the restaurant to see if they are needed any place.

18. Effective Training. Since most training takes place during the employee's first few weeks or months on the job, proper attention communicates the company's concern for the employee. Well-trained employees are also more confident about themselves and their performance.

19. Management's Communication and Listening Skills. Some managers seem to think that employees can read their mind. If an employee needs to know something and they have not been told, tell them. This may be something that needs to be done (e.g., request from a customer or helping another employee) or perhaps they need to be shown the correct way of doing something. Managers must give each employee their undivided attention for at least the time necessary for them to say what is on their minds. Often, employees only need a few seconds to express themselves. The keys to being a good listener are focusing on what is most important to the person who is speaking, being aware that people communicate with their facial expressions and body language as well as with their voices, summarizing the important points that are being communicated, and remembering what has been said. To help them remember what employees and others tell them (and other things that need to be remembered), many managers carry a small note pad with them. Writing a brief note about what employees said also lets them know that what they have to say is important.

20. Positive Corporate Culture/Minimization of Stress. This is essentially the group personality of the business. When fellow employees have a positive outlook and do their best to get along, being at work is much more enjoyable. When most people go to work, their general happiness decreases. Employers who can help employees maintain their normal level of happiness or even improve upon it will find it easier to keep employees longer and to motivate them.

21. **Company Goals /Shared Vision**. If employees are working toward the same goals, teamwork becomes a natural component of the business. Management must frequently use the business's primary goal (for example, "customer satisfaction is our number one goal") in their discussions with employees so that all employees realize its importance and are motivated to work toward it. Management must show by its actions that they too support it as their main goal. When all employees work toward a common goal, teamwork naturally follows. One of the best motivators is to find ways of aligning the employee's personal goals with that of the firm (also discussed in Personal Goals above). For example, if an employee wants to become a chef, management can give them additional responsibilities in the kitchen. An employee who wants to become an accountant could help with bookkeeping. A marketing student could help with the business's marketing efforts and so forth.

22. **Ethically Oriented Management**. Honest, sincere managers will generally attract employees with similar traits. Employees without these traits who work for such managers will either find that acting ethical is an asset to their careers and accept it or leave because honesty conflicts with their values. Turnover in this case is good.

23. **Music**. Upbeat music that can satisfy both customers and employees can decrease stress, make work move at a rhythmic pace, and make the workday seem shorter. As long as the upbeat music is pleasant and melodic, it can also increase productivity (employees work faster) and increase table turns (customers eat, talk, and finish their overall dining experience faster). Fortunately, music, such as elevator music or hearing the same songs over and over again, that may be irritating to many, can generally be tuned out by employees.

24. **Flexible Work Schedule**. This refers to doing one's best at accommodating each employee's scheduling needs. Most restaurants have day and evening shifts. Hotels will have most employees working the day shift, however, some employees will work the evening shift (e.g., 4 p.m. to 12 a.m.) and some will work the night shift (e.g., 12 a.m. to 8 a.m.). Also, since there are many part-time employees, flexible scheduling is quite common and relatively easy to accommodate in the hospitality industry.

Classic Motivation Theories
Maslow's Hierarchy of Needs
Maslow's needs include: 1. Physiological (food, shelter, clothing), 2. Safety and security, 3. Social needs/love, 4. Esteem, 5. Self-actualization (i.e., achieving one's potential). The concept behind Maslow's work is that lower-order needs must be satisfied before the individual will be motivated to achieve higher-order needs. For example, improving the esteem of a low-paid employee who cannot feed his family may not be as effective of a motivator as an opportunity to earn money.

Herzberg's Two-Factor Theory
Though this has been one of the most popular motivation theories, it was found that Herzberg used a statistical technique (Critical Incident Technique) that was not appropriate for his study. The egregious result of this is that because Herzberg theorized that money was not an effective motivator, many managers and employees were not given raises. After his data was reanalyzed, it was found that money in fact could be a motivator (no surprise). It is generally recognized that the factors Herzberg studied could be both the basis for morale and motivation, depending on the personality and needs of the individual. To his credit, many of the factors that he learned of in his study have become widely used by other researchers.

Morale/Dissatisfiers. Herzberg considered these factors as dissatisfiers because dissatisfaction could result from their absence. In other words, only a low level of morale could be attained from a firm's efforts for the dissatisfiers. Examples include quality of supervision, job security, personal growth, physical working conditions, wages and benefits, and interpersonal relationships.

Motivators/Satisfiers. This category of factors could result in positive motivation, hence, labeled as satisfiers. Examples include concern for employees, listen, show appreciation, participative decision-making, responsibility, and challenging work. The above findings have been found to be invalid.

McClelland's Need for Achievement Theory
• According to the study, employees and managers have three needs: achievement, power, and affiliation. (In this instance, affiliation means, "wanting to be liked by others.")

• Most successful managers have a high need for achievement and power.

• People with high need for *affiliation* historically have ranked lowest on productivity.

• As society changes, might the above situation change (i.e., will affiliation become more important)?

Equity Theory
- Does the compensation I receive equal the effort expended?
- Is this compensation equal to others who perform similar tasks?

Expectancy
- Can I perform up to the firm's expectations?
- What are the results of meeting the firm's expectations?
- Are the rewards worth the effort?

Reinforcement Theory
- Stimulus (e.g., a customer places an order).
- Behavior (e.g., the server takes the order).
- Reinforcement/consequences. Positive or negative comments by the manager or supervisor, influences future behavior. As the manager/supervisor sees good behavior, it can be rewarded with a compliment. Behavior that does not follow policies should be called to the employee's attention so that it can be corrected/changed.

Case Study 2.1: Personal Problems of Hourly Employees

Margaret is a guest services agent (GSA) in a major downtown conference hotel where you are the manager. She has been working at the hotel for nine months. Because of intense competition for employees, wages are $2.00 per hour above the local average for the position. Margaret is a 24 year-old single mother with one child; she dropped out of school when she was 15 years old. Most of Margaret's work is acceptable, but she rarely seems to be happy. It appears that she feels life has little meaning and that extra effort at anything is just not worth it.

You are proud of your employees and their attitude toward doing whatever they can to help customers and other employees. Employees are mostly highly motivated and many customers comment on how gracious and helpful they are. Margaret's attitude is beginning to affect your ability to motivate the rest of the team, especially new employees who work during Margaret's shift. You've decided it's time to talk with Margaret.

Required: (Answer each question, explain your answer.)
1. Is this a morale problem, a motivation problem, or both? Explain your answer. Why could it make a difference?
2. Margaret has problems with her attitude, and this attitude directly influences her poor behavior. How would you go about finding out what Margaret's beliefs are? Since this is a case study and we cannot talk directly to her, what are the possible components of her belief system that subsequently influence her attitude and behavior? (See Values and Their Influence on Thinking and Behavior for a review of this concept.)
3. A. What are your strategies and tactics for getting Margaret to change her beliefs/attitude and take a more positive approach to life?
B. You are a hotel manager, not a psychologist. Do you feel you have a responsibility to help Margaret in her personal life? Do you feel you have a responsibility to learn why Margaret is behaving as she is, or should you just inform her of the company policies and let her know that they must be followed?
C. Margaret also has a commitment problem. How can you help Margaret develop a stronger commitment to your organization?
4. What would you do if your strategies did not work?
5. Which of the classic motivation theories (Maslow, Expectancy, etc.) would most apply to her situation (i.e., your solution)?

_____

_____

_____

_____

_____

_____

_____

_____

_____

Chapter Three: Compensation, Benefits, and Incentives

Strategy Review: Prepare a strategy review for this chapter (See back of Chapter One).

Case Study 3.1: Developing a Compensation Package

Chapter Objectives: After reading this chapter you should understand and be able to do the following:

1. List the main components of a compensation package.
2. Describe the perfect/best compensation package.
3. Explain compensation and payroll.
4. Describe communicating total compensation.
5. Explain fixed versus variable pay.
6. Discuss the impact of economic market factors on pay.
7. Explain gender disparity.
8. List and define government-mandated benefits.
9. Discuss voluntary benefits.
10. Define incentives (individual and group).
11. Explain the challenges for a good incentive program.

Compensation Package

A compensation package or total compensation is made up of three parts: *base compensation (base pay)*—wages and salary; *benefits*—indirect pay, such as insurance and retirement plans; and *incentives*—rewards for achieving a specified goal. Having an attractive compensation package is critical to the success of any business. It tells potential and current employees that the business truly values them. The main exception to this is when firms have such a poor reputation that they need to pay more to get employees to overlook the fact that job conditions are not very good. A good compensation package also helps keep employees happy, improves the image of the firm, and reduces employee turnover. As was discussed in Chapter Two, Values, Morale, and Motivation, pay is often not the number one motivator in the hospitality industry. The reason for this is that the pay for most firms for employees in the same position with similar experience will be in a very narrow range. Of course, what this means is that there is an opportunity for firms to focus on how they might improve their compensation packages to make it a motivator or a reason to work for them. The basic concept of a compensation package is simple—a paycheck plus some benefits and incentives. As managers begin determining starting pay, increases in pay for tenure and performance, which benefits to offer, and the astonishingly complex concepts of incentives, things get significantly more challenging.

The Perfect Compensation Package

The perfect compensation package does not exist. The best compensation packages generally combine the following:

• A livable wage (according to the living standards of the individual in any specific city).
• Fairness of the wage within the company.
• Fairness of the wage within the industry (i.e., what a worker with a certain level of experience receives from competing firms).
• A benefit package that is comparable to firms that are competing for employees with similar skills and firms within the same industry.
• Some type of incentives for outstanding effort and outstanding company performance.
• Without high morale, even the best compensation package may be of little value. Some of the key factors for keeping morale high include interesting and challenging work, good interpersonal relations with coworkers, offering a quality product, and recognition for employees' efforts (see Chapter Two, Values, Morale, and Motivation for more information on morale).

Compensation and Payroll

On the income statement (also referred to as the P&L or Profit and Loss Statement), compensation is generally referred to as labor cost and includes pay plus all benefits and incentives. Total labor cost, including pay, benefits and incentives for the average restaurant or hotel can vary based on the type of concept and unique factors, but it will generally be between 28% and 30% of sales. For hotels, this is often the largest controllable cost of doing business. For restaurants, labor cost is usually second to food cost, which averages around 32% of sales. Some expenses of the business, such as rent, are relatively difficulty to modify. Others, such as linens and utilities can be lowered, however, since their categories represent a very small percentage of sales, their impact on overall profit will not be significant. Of course, cumulatively, savings in many areas can have a great impact on profit. What this means is that even though management may want to pay employees well and provide them with good benefits and incentives, they are responsible for producing a profit and making sure that overall compensation is at an effective and efficient level. Effective, in this instance, refers to having enough employees available to provide excellent customer service. Efficient refers to the labor cost being proportionate to sales and as low as reasonably possible, while still maintaining both excellent customer service and employee morale.

Communicating Total Compensation

Unless a firm lets employees know what their total compensation is, they will often assume that it is simply the total pay shown in their paychecks. For example, an employee who has a salary of $36,000 per year and a 35% benefit package will have a total compensation of $48,600 (36,000 times .35 = 12,600; 36,000 + 12,600 = 48,600). Assuming the business is treating employees fairly and employees are happy with their jobs, an employee who realizes he/she is making $48,600, rather than $36,000 should have better morale. A 35% benefits package might include various types of insurance such as health, dental, life, unemployment, disability, and worker's compensation, plus vacation, sick leave, and the employer's contribution to Social Security, Medicare, and to the employee's retirement.

Base Compensation

There are many things to consider in determining base compensation, such as hourly wages versus salary, fixed versus variable pay, economic market factors (supply of those with appropriate skills versus demand for individuals with those skills), plus performance, experience, and seniority.

Hourly versus Salary

The first groups to consider are *hourly wages* versus *salary*. Employees working in non-managerial positions, such as front desk agents and cooks, are paid based on the number of hours they work. If they work over 40 hours in any one workweek (any seven consecutive days), per the Fair Labor Standards Act (FSLA), they are to be paid one-and-one-half times their normal pay (i.e., an employee earning $10 per hour would receive $15 for each hour over 40 for the week). For this reason, they are also referred to as nonexempt employees, that is, they are not exempt from time-and-a-half regulations of the FSLA. Managers are generally paid a set salary regardless of the number of hours they work and are therefore exempt from the time-and-a-half regulations of the FSLA. For example, if a manager works 50 hours during a week or 60, the pay is the same. Around 30 years ago, hospitality managers were working around 10 hours more per week than they currently are—about 60 then and 50 now. The reduction came about because it was found that managers were becoming fatigued, unable to function at their potential, and subsequently leaving establishments where 60-hour weeks were the norm. To take advantage of the exempt status of managers (i.e., no overtime pay), some employers in the past gave employees the title of supervisor and a low salary. This low salary not only allowed them to not pay time-and-a-half for overtime, but to not pay anything at all when the employee/supervisor worked over 40 hours in a week. The result was that some supervisors were earning less than minimum wage *and* working very long hours without overtime pay. The solution was that some states passed laws requiring that a supervisor on a salary spend the majority of their time supervising, rather than performing operational tasks and must be paid a specified minimum salary that is well above the minimum wage.

Fixed versus Variable Pay

There are two types of compensation, *fixed*—the same pay each pay period, and *variable*—pay varies based on some agreed-upon formula. While the vast majority of hospitality employees have a fixed pay rate, those involved in sales tend to have a compensation package with fixed and variable components. The variable portion will be based on the achievement of stated goals, for example, a percentage of the sales the employee made during a certain period of time. Variable pay could also be based on individual, group, or company-wide performance.

Economic Market Factors

Base compensation for hourly employees is also based on *economic market factors*. Simplistically, when the supply of employees with the skills demanded by most hospitality employers is very high—that is, supply is greater than demand, the price (pay, in this instance) goes down. For those with superior skills, such as a chef or skilled manager, where supply is much lower, the price (pay) rises. Relative to many other businesses, pay in the hospitality industry has been low. The primary reasons for this are: (1) most hospitality jobs do not require extensive experience, so they are often the first job for many young employees; (2) even though young people have many of the skills required for the hospitality industry (e.g., good attitude and pride in their work), they have the same rudimentary skills of many others who are seeking the same job; and (3) because of intense competition, the profit margins for the hospitality industry are relatively low, which makes it challenging to raise pay much beyond its present level. There are exceptions to the low-pay issue, such as when a hotel or restaurant has a substantial profit margin and decides to share the profit with employees through higher wages. When this happens, hospitality firms in competition with the better paying firm may need to improve their compensation to compete for the best employees.

Base compensation for salaried employees—mainly managers, and those with skills that can only be gained through education or experience (e.g., chef, sous chef, pastry chef, front desk supervisor, maintenance worker, etc.) has been steadily improving for many years and is generally competitive with most industries. In fact, there are a growing number of hotels and restaurants that are hiring new graduates from hospitality programs at salaries equal to that of graduates from engineering programs. Depending on their performance and internal motivation, some hospitality graduates will double, if not triple their starting pay within five years. The average graduate will triple their salary in about 10 years.

Performance, Experience, and Seniority

Perhaps the most commonly used criteria for setting employee and managerial pay are *performance, experience,* and *seniority*. Of these three criteria, performance is by far the most important, followed by experience. Seniority has some value, but is a distant third to performance and experience. The performance of an applicant must be based on management's perception of their potential ability—assuming that management has not seen them work. An existing employee's performance should be based on the results of their written performance appraisals and any other formal or informal assessments. The obvious justification for considering performance is that we pay people to perform certain tasks in such as way that meets the standards of firm and meets or exceeds customer expectations. Employees that can meet those expectations have one value, those who can exceed them have a greater value, and those who cannot meet them have little or no value to the firm. In virtually every position in every hospitality firm, there is a direct correlation between performance and pay. That is, employees whose performance is excellent have a higher wage or salary, those whose performance is average have an average wage, and so forth. When this does not occur, higher-performing employees can get frustrated and wonder why they are working so hard and receiving the same pay as others who do not perform as well. Subsequently, it is difficult for them to justify their hard work and their performance declines. Low-performing employees will feel they are being rewarded for their current level of performance and continue with their current efforts.

Experience is usually important. All things being equal, most managers would rather have a front desk agent with five years of experience than one with one year of experience. The more experienced agent has likely performed a greater variety of tasks and is therefore better able to handle unique and challenging situations. There are also situations where one employee has 10 years of experience doing the same thing and one has 10 years of experience at several key positions. Some people will say that the employee with 10 years of experience at the same position has one year of experience—10 times. In other words, what has been added to their ability over that period of time? The employee with 10 years of experience at different positions has a better overall understanding of how the business operates and can help in several different areas.

Seniority is related to experience in that it has a time component; however this refers to time at the particular business. A cook could have 15 years of experience at his/her profession, but only 4 months seniority at the current restaurant. Another cook at the same restaurant with no previous experience, but who has been there for one year will have more seniority than the cook with 15 years of experience. When determining pay levels, if seniority played a role, it would be to the advantage of the cook with less experience; if experience played a role, it would be to the advantage of the cook with 15 years at the trade. As previously discussed, performance and experience will in most cases carry a greater weight in the decision than seniority. The key to executing a pay policy concerning performance, experience, and seniority is that employees feel that they are being compensating fairly relative to these three criteria and to what others performing the same duties and tasks are being paid.

Gender Disparity

On average in the United States, women receive less compensation than men for doing the same job. This is obviously not a fair situation and is against the law (Equal Pay Act of 1963, see Chapter Four, Employment Laws).

Since enforcement of the law is not as aggressive as it should be and cases are sometimes difficult to prove, the problem persists. However bad the problem has been historically, it appears to be getting better in the hospitality industry. More and more firms have strong mission statements and value statements that specify equal treatment for all. Also, because of the competitive nature of the industry, firms that do not treat women equally will experience high turnover and poor reputations. Most pay disparity seems to be in the upper pay ranges (i.e., executives), where men occupy most of the positions. Sometimes the disparity is not caused by unequal treatment, but by the negotiation strategies of the person hired or promoted to the position.

Pay Secrecy

A common concern of managers is, "What happens if an employee tells another employee about his/her raise?" It is virtually impossible to keep employees from telling others what they make. In several ways, this is an advantage. First, it forces managers to be able to specifically explain to employees why they received a raise. Second, managers must be able to tell employees specifically why they are not receiving a raise or a small one. Some managers tell employees that, if they want a raise, they must tell the manager why they think they deserve it, rather than saying that a certain employee is making more and they think they should too. And third, employees who want to earn more money know what must be done to get it.

Benefits

Benefits are a form of indirect compensation, that is, generally not a direct payment to the employee, but a reward for being an employee of an organization. Examples include vacations, sick leave, life insurance, tuition reimbursement, and retirement plans. In the United States, there are also benefits that most firms must provide to employees, such as Social Security, Workers' Compensation Insurance, and Unemployment Insurance. In some countries, the government will take care of most benefit programs. In others, there are absolutely no benefits. The United States is between these two extremes. Mandated benefits in the United States help take care of only very basic requirements. Beyond this, employees need to either pay for their own health insurance, retirement, and so forth or work for a company that provides them as part of its benefit package. Historically, the cost of benefits for hospitality industry has been about 15% of payroll, however, because of intense competition, the percentage is going up.

Another advantage of benefits for employees is that they are generally not taxed as income. For example, an employee receives $5,000 in benefits that covers the cost of various types of insurance. If the employee had to purchase the insurance on his/her own, the purchase would be with after- or post-tax dollars, meaning that the employee would first pay taxes on the income, then purchase the insurance. If the employee's combined state and federal tax totaled 30%, the cost of the insurance in before tax dollars would be $6,500 ($5,000 ÷ .30 = $1,500; $5,000 + $1,500 = $6,500). Therefore, the employer's $5,000 benefit is actually worth $6,500 to the employee.

Government-Mandated Benefits

• **Social Security.** The Social Security Act of 1935 created a pension program to make sure that retired workers had at least a minimum level of income. Over the years other benefits have been added including disability payments (for workers that become disabled before they retire), survivor benefits (for spouses and dependents of workers who die before they retire), and Medicare (a federal health insurance plan for those who are 65 years of age and older). Through the Federal Insurance Contributions Act (FICA taxes), both the employer and employee are responsible for paying 50% of the tax. The employer pays 6.2% of the employee's wages/salary for Social Security and 1.45% of wages/salary for Medicare (i.e., not deducted from the employee's pay) and deducts identical amounts from the employee's pay. The employer is responsible for submitting the total of 15.3% pay to the federal government (6.2 + 6.2 + 1.45 + 1.45 = 15.3).

• **Unemployment Insurance.** Mandated by the Social Security Act of 1935, unemployment insurance is administered by each state as a payroll tax and provides a level of pay specified by the state when a worker loses their job. Employees who quit work are not eligible, as are employees who are fired for misconduct, or are receiving Workers' Compensation or Social Security, and who have turned down suitable jobs. The amount of the employer's unemployment insurance can go up or down based on the number of claims of employees. Before they can apply for benefits, employees must have worked for a certain minimum time and must be unemployed for a minimum time. They must also be available for work and be actively seeking employment.

• **Workers' Compensation Insurance.** When employees are injured at work, become sick, or die as a result of work, they may be eligible for Workers' Compensation. Medical expenses are covered and each state sets a minimum level of wages that will be paid until the employee can return to work. The employer is responsible for Workers' Compensation whether the employee was or was not following company policies. However, it is illegal if employees purposefully injuries themselves or fake an injury to receive benefits. The employer's cost for Workers' Compensation Insurance will vary according to their number of claims, their state, and their insurance carrier (i.e., the firm they purchase their Workers' Compensation insurance from). If firms can meet certain state requirements, such as purchase a bond large enough to cover potential claims, it can become self-insured for Workers' Compensation. Firms where workers have very few accidents can save a considerable amount of money by doing this. For example, if a firm experiences few claims, savings of $30,000 or more in a medium-sized hotel or full-service restaurant are possible.

• **Family and Medical Leave Act (FMLA).** Employees are allowed an unpaid leave of absence when they, their children, a spouse, or a parent have serious personal health problems (see Chapter Four, Employment Laws, for more information on this law).

• **Consolidated Omnibus Budget Reconciliation Act (COBRA)**. COBRA requires that employers allow employees to retain their health insurance after terminating employment. All costs related to the health insurance are paid for by the former employee and the firm can add up to a 2% fee for administering the benefit. The period of time that the benefit can continue varies from 18 to 36 months based on the qualifying event, such as whether there was a termination, reduced number of work hours, loss of dependent child status, divorce, and other events.

• **Uniformed Services Employment and Reemployment Rights Act of 1994 (USERRA).** USERRA protects those in the U.S. Armed Forces (e.g., Army, Navy, Air Force, Marines, National Guard, etc.) who need a leave of absence for military reasons (see Chapter Four, Employment Laws, for more information on this law).

• **Health Insurance.** The Healthcare Reform Bill of 2010 builds on the existing health care system, setting up health insurance exchanges where business with up to 100 employees and the self-employed will be able to obtain insurance at lower rates. Other provisions designed to lower rates include electronic medical records, insurance co-ops, greater enforcement of Medicare and Medicaid fraud, rewarding doctors for keeping patients healthy rather than for the quantity of their work, paperwork simplification, and medical malpractice reform. Beginning in 2010, businesses with less than 25 full-time employees that contribute at least 50% of their employees' health insurance premium will be eligible for tax credits of up to 35% of the employer contribution. A full tax credit will available for businesses with fewer than 10 employees who each earn less than $25,000 per year. In 2014, the tax credit for small businesses will rise from 35% to 50% (Small Business Majority, 2010).

Historically in the United States, employers were the primary providers of health insurance. Unfortunately, for hospitality employees, this was not the case for hospitality employers. In fact, until the 1980s very few hospitality firms offered their employees health insurance. The reasons for this situation were that: since most were not offering it, there was little competition or pressure to add it; the cost of the insurance relative to a hospitality employee's average pay was prohibitively high (e.g., often 30% to 40% of the employee's annual pay); hospitality employees are often part-time workers who as such do not qualify for health insurance and other voluntary benefits; many employees are dependants, and are therefore frequently covered by their parents; and being young, they do not have as great a need for medical care as those who are older. Currently, the vast majority of hospitality firms offer some type of health insurance benefit.

There are various types of health insurance, but most fall into two categories, Health Maintenance Organizations (HMOs) and Preferred Provider Organizations (PPOs). In an HMO, the employee selects a primary care physician from the physicians in the HMO's network. The employee will see the primary care physician for most needs and must consult them before seeing a specialist (e.g., dermatologist, physical therapist, etc.). The employee has no coverage for out-of-network physicians, except while traveling outside of the HMO's area. With a PPO, the employee can choose to see any primary care physician or specialist within the PPO's network. The employee can see a physician who is not in the network, but the reimbursement rate for the physician will drop from around 90% for in-network physicians to around 70% for out-of-network physicians. Given a choice most employees choose PPOs; however, they are generally more expensive than HMOs.

Costs for health care vary based on the services covered and the cost of those services. The average annual cost of a health insurance policy for a single employee in the United States is around $9,000; however, firms that promote healthy lifestyles saved an average of 12% on their health care costs (Towers-Perrin, 2009). There are many types of insurance plans where the rates can be substantially lower than $9,000, for example, around $3,000 to $4,000 per year. This is especially true of plans for younger employees that generally have fewer needs for medical care. Some "Cadillac" policies, those with few limits on services, can be in the $25,000 range. The average cost for a family is around $17,000 (Milliman Medical Index, 2009).

Voluntary Benefits

• Retirement Plans. To provide financial stability when people retire, most firms have some type of retirement benefit. For many years, the main type of retirement plan was a *defined benefit plan* or *pension*. Retired employees receive a monthly check for an amount that varies based on a particular formula selected by the firm. For example, it could be based on years with the firm, a specified percentage for each year, and the average of the employee's highest wage/salary over any three-year period (e.g., 15.6 years x 2 percent x $48,000 = $14,976 per year for retirement). Because of the high cost of providing pensions, fewer and fewer firms are offering them.

The other major category of retirement plans are referred to as *defined contribution plans*. These are growing in popularity because they cost less to administer and cost less to fund. The 401(k) plan is the most well known of these [401(k) is the section of the federal tax code where the law is located]. Here, the employer sets up accounts with an investment firm, such as Fidelity Investments or T. Rowe Price, then deposits a certain percentage of the employee's wages/salary into the account each month. Frequently, there is an agreement where the employer will match a certain level of employee contribution, for example, up to 5%. The employee can select the type of investment vehicle from mutual funds to money market funds and the level of risk they feel comfortable with. The employee does not pay taxes on the contributions when they are provided—they are tax-deferred. When the employee retires, the proceeds are taxed as income, however, since the retiree is generally in a lower tax bracket, the amount of tax is relatively low.

Simplified employee pensions (SEPs) were created for the self-employed and for employees who work for firms that do not have retirement plans. *Keogh plans* are a type of profit-sharing plan that allows the employer to modify the contribution amount based on the firm's profit.

• Paid Time Off. This is a general category of benefits that includes *vacations, sick leave,* and *holiday pay.* Vacations for hardworking employees are not only well deserved, but allow them to recharge themselves for when they return. Because of the high turnover rate in the hospitality industry, many employees do not stay the requisite one-year to earn their vacation. Therefore, the true cost is less than one would expect. Because of the potential for abuse, most hospitality firms do not offer sick leave for hourly employees. Holiday pay is also rarely offered in this industry, partially because most hospitality firms are open for business on holidays. Extra pay for working on holidays would certainly be appreciated by employees.

• Dental, Vision, and Life Insurance. These relatively low-cost forms of insurance help attract and keep the best employees. To reduce the employer's cost, the employee can be asked to pay part of the premium and the co-pay can be adjusted to make it reasonable for both the employee and the employer.

• Employee Meals. This is one of the most appreciated benefits an employer can offer. Most hospitality employees lead very busy lives, balancing school and work and often do not have enough time for a good meal. Also, being students, they are often short on money. Therefore, the employee meal satisfies their hunger and saves them a few dollars. The cost to the employer is minimal, for example, a bowl of soup and bread might cost a little over one dollar. The one dollar cost relative to the employee's daily pay is perhaps 2% or less. The benefit to the employer is a more motivated and appreciative employee who will provide better customer service.

• Employee Assistance Programs (EAPs). No matter how many employees a business has, some of them are going to have various types of personal problems. EAPs give employees a confidential place to turn to help identify the problem and find a solution. Typical problems addressed by an EAP include employees with alcohol or drug abuse problems, depression, eating disorders, and domestic violence. Another benefit of the EAP is that the employee knows that there is someone there to help in difficult times and that the employer cares enough about them to offer it.

• Employee Volunteer Programs (EVPs). As the cost of many benefit programs that have been popular with employees are rising, offering volunteer programs can be accomplished with little or no cost. Brenner (2010) offered nine reasons firms should offer EVPs: leadership opportunities, development of important skills (e.g., communication, organization, etc.), networking, corporate citizenship and support for corporate values, recruiting (i.e., more and more employees desire to work for socially responsible firms), improvements in retention, improvements in productivity, the health and wellness of people that volunteer is better than those that do not, and brand recognition.

• **Educational Support.** This could include help with tuition, conferences, and continuing education classes. Normally, a large percentage of hospitality employees are attending college. Helping them with tuition would certainly be something that would gain their loyalty. Of course, similar benefits must be offered to all employees. Generally, there is some type of completion agreement, such as needing to receive a C or better to be reimbursed and a minimum time on the job before the benefit can be provided.

• **Disability Benefits.** Disability Benefits from Workers' Compensation Insurance covers employees who are injured on the job and cannot work. It is however, only for about 26 weeks. Social Security covers individuals regardless of where they were injured; however, the benefit is small and does not go into effect for six months. Short-term disability benefits covers employees until Social Security begins. Long-term disability insurance also covers workers regardless of where they were injured, but the amount of the benefit is considerably larger than what is provided by Social Security. The range is generally between 50% and 67% of the worker's wage/salary (Gomez-Mejia, Balkin, & Cardy, 1998).

• **Perquisites (generally referred to as "Perks").** These are benefits that are closely associated with the employee's work, some of which have already been mentioned in benefits. Examples include a company car, gasoline, expense account with company credit card, business travel to nice places, personalized schedule, responsible for work completed (rather than being someplace from 8 a.m. to 5 p.m.), and so forth.

Incentives

Incentives, or pay-for-performance plans, are rewards provided to employees for achieving various organizational goals. There are two broad primary issues regarding incentives. First, the firm's overall performance (i.e., profit) depends upon its performance in specific areas (e.g., customer service, cleanliness, product quality, performance of the HR, Marketing, and Accounting departments, etc.). Overall performance and performance in specific areas subsequently depends to a large degree on the performance of employees. Second, to attract, retain, and motivate its employees, especially its best employees, a company needs to reward employees on the basis of their relative performance. The rewards could include cash, stock, stock options, time off with pay, a dinner for two, and merchandise, such as a shirt, hat, or jacket, and so forth—anything that motivates employees to achieve various company goals. Though the primary purpose of the incentive is to increase the likelihood that certain organizational goals will be achieved, other objectives include improving morale, reducing management and employee stress, reducing turnover, and making work fun.

When creating incentives, it must be understood that individual employees and work teams (or departments) differ in how they contribute and how much they contribute to the firm. Therefore, when creating an incentive, the reward should generally be tied to their key contributions. For example, restaurant servers contribute by making sure sales goals are achieved and that customers are provided with good service. Housekeepers contribute by making sure that rooms are clean and everything is neat and in its appropriate place. A Human Resources Department contributes by recruiting enough employees for the business, having great orientation programs, and by supporting other departments with information on employment laws, performance appraisals, and so forth.

Individual versus Group Incentives

The main advantage of individual incentives is that employees will generally work hard because they directly benefit from their own efforts. Some disadvantages include individual competition negatively affecting group performance (e.g., lower service quality, decreased morale from the stress of competition) and documentation and administration of rewards.

The main advantages of group incentives are that they promote teamwork, improve morale and motivation, and generally lead to improved customer satisfaction. Documentation of group incentives is easier than that of individual incentives because there are fewer calculations that need to be made and establishing the relationship between individual effort and specific results may be difficult. The main disadvantage of group incentives is that some employees will attempt to take advantage of the efforts of others. The term for this is *social loafing*, where as more people are added to a group, those inclined will seize upon the opportunity to do less, hoping their laziness will not be noticed. Another disadvantage is that the payout for achieving the goal must be carefully planned, otherwise it could be significantly larger than expected. Related to this is the fact that once you divide a sizable bonus by 100 or 200 employees, the individual bonus may not be large enough to please each employee. For example, $10,000 is a significant amount of money; however, if it is divided among 100 employees, it amounts to $100 per employee. Some may feel that this is not enough to justify their efforts. A final concern for group and individual incentives is that, once business slows down, incentives will also decline, which could make some employees unhappy. Employees who are using their annual incentive/bonus for a family vacation and receive $50 instead of $500 will likely not be pleased.

Some Additional Challenges for Incentive Programs

• The incentive must be something employees want (Dunlap, 2010). This means that employees should be involved in decisions on how they will be rewarded.

• Objectives must be explicit (understandable). Examples: sales (total company, specific department, or individual), service times, or a broad range of customer satisfaction scores (e.g., quality of service at front desk, room cleanliness based on number of customer complaints, food quality, etc.).

• Objectives must be fair and achievable. Employees will get frustrated if they always work hard and never achieve the specified goals to receive the incentive. Additionally, employees must be effectively trained to achieve the incentive.

• Measurement of performance must be reasonably objective and free of bias. When there is the perception that goal achievement is based more on management's opinion than on objective criteria, motivation to work toward the objective and morale will decline.

• Incentives should be paid/provided soon after the objective is achieved. Some incentives are based on daily performance. In this case, the incentive should ideally be paid out that day. For longer-term incentives, the reward should be in the first paycheck after the incentive is announced

• Once in place, the incentive program should not be changed or removed without serious consideration of the consequences. For this reason, considerable thought must go into their creation.

• If the incentive program influences employees to work beyond a comfortable pace, it can increase stress, job dissatisfaction, and reduced service quality.

Typical Incentives

• **Merit Pay.** Most firms have semiannual or annual performance reviews where, based on the employee's performance rating, a raise of some type will be given (e.g., a percentage of their current wage or a specific dollar amount). Merit pay is a long-term incentive because it is permanent and part of the new base pay. During recessionary times, firms have several choices, including, no merit pay increases, wage cuts, and whether or not to give cost-of-living increases.

• **Monetary versus Nonmonetary.** Whether money or merchandize or some other incentive will work best, depends on the needs and wants of each employee. Employees with financial responsibilities that can barely be met with their existing compensation will likely appreciate money more than various types of merchandise. However, even these employees will appreciate a non-monetary incentive that they cannot regularly afford for themselves or would have felt guilty purchasing with their limited funds (e.g., a nice dinner out for the family, a weekend at a resort, a day off with pay, etc.). Another option for these employees is a gift certificate for a grocery store or a gas card—sort of a combination monetary/non-monetary reward. Younger employees who live at home generally have few financial responsibilities, so a shirt or jacket with the company's logo may work best—giving them something to show their friends and validating their accomplishments. Cash incentives to these employees may simply go into their wallet with other cash they have and soon be forgotten.

While cash incentives are generally thought to be effective and desired, a recent finding shows that they can have a negative effect (Dewhurst, Guthridge, & Mohr 2010). For example, employees will work hard to achieve productivity and customer satisfaction goals when there is a monetary incentive. Unfortunately, once the incentive is gone, so is the motivation. Therefore, the act of attempting to do something positive for employees while at the same time improving business performance actually has the opposite effect. The authors suggest that praise from immediate supervisors, working closely with key managers, and opportunities for greater responsibilities can be more effective than monetary incentives. Of course, this assumes that employee pay is viewed as fair.

• **Cost-of-Living Raise.** Many firms offer annual cost-of-living raises that adjust the employee's pay for inflation. The Consumer Price Index, an index of various goods that the average person buys, is used as the measure of inflation. It is important to remember that while this represents an increase in the employee's actual wage, it only helps to retain the same purchasing power the employee had before the most recent inflation. Inflation in the United States is generally in the 2% to 3% range, sometimes reaching 5%. On rare occasions it has been in the teens or we have had deflation, where prices drop.

• **Bonuses**. These are generally individual or group pay-for-performance incentives. Bonuses differ from merit pay in that they are one-time payments to the employee and do not increase their base pay. Both individual and group bonuses function on the concept that what is rewarded is more likely to be repeated. Since some bonuses may small relative to an employee's pay, they should be presented with great appreciation. That is, not, 'Here's your fifty bucks.'

• **Profit Sharing**. This is a company-wide pay-for-performance plan where employees share in a certain percentage of the firm's profits. The focus of profit sharing is to create a positive overall corporate culture and commitment to the firm that will hopefully lead to increased profits. Since virtually everything that every employee does influences profits, each employee has a vested interest all aspects of the business from cost control to the firm's overall image. Profit-sharing is normally distributed in two ways, primarily as distributions to retirement plans and secondarily as checks for the employees' share of profits for a specified period.

Employee Stock Ownership Plans (ESOPS) are based on the performance of the firm's stock price. Employees are either given shares of stock or allowed to purchase shares at a reduced price based on a predetermined formula. The main difference between ESOPs and profit sharing is that the ESOP focuses on the long-term because the employee must hold the stock for some specified period of time. An additional benefit to the employee is that the shares are not taxable until they are sold. Employees who sell their stock when they retire will be taxed at a much lower rate. The main disadvantages are fluctuations in the stock price, especially when employees are close to retirement, and having a large percentage of their retirement savings in the stock of one firm.

• **Customer Service**. A relatively new type of incentive that is becoming more popular is one based on customer satisfaction. The amount of the incentive is tied to how the firm performs on a customer satisfaction survey. Each category in the survey, such as product quality, service quality, cleanliness, and so forth, are communicated to employees on a regular basis so everyone knows where they currently stand and where they need to improve. As time passes, it will be interesting to see if any hospitality firms adopt the practice used by many hospitals of openly posting customer satisfaction scores for everyone to see.

Case 3.1: Developing a Compensation Package

The Mount Joseph Resort located in Sedona, Arizona is having a hard time attracting and keeping its 100 hourly employees. The two major problems are that the cost of living in the city is about 30% higher than surrounding cities and that there are fewer potential hospitality employees in the area. Annual turnover (the percentage of employees who leave in one year) has been 200% (meaning the average employees stays for only 6 months). You have just taken over as General Manager of this resort. You examined the financial statements and realize that you can afford to pay anywhere up to double minimum wage for those with considerable experience and excellent potential (applicants) or actual performance (current employees). You also realize that more must be done to attract and keep employees, such as improving the benefits package and adding incentives.

Required:

1. You need to create a compensation package for front desk agents, housekeepers, and your maintenance staff. You need to be able to justify all of your decisions to the resort's owners and convince them that your decisions are logical, will improve employee retention, and will result in a better profit (i.e., why they should let you do this). It would be acceptable to show that profits may go down in the short-term, but will increase in the long-term.
2. Develop a base compensation schedule for each of the three above positions that will help attract new potential employees or help keep current ones. For each of the three groups there must be four different levels of base compensation: (a) no experience, but excellent potential; (b) up to one year experience (at the resort or with another hotel); (c) one to three years experience (at the resort or with another hotel); and (d) over three years of experience (at the resort or with another hotel). Each must factor in performance in some way.
3. Develop a benefits package that will not cost more than 30% of the employees' pay. You can use the highest category of pay for calculating benefits. Since you will not actually be pricing out various types of benefits, you can estimate what they might cost. In the case of health insurance, use $4,000 per employee, per year as the cost. You do not need to include coverage for the family.
4. Develop an incentive program for each group of employees that will not only motivate them, but do so in a way that covers its costs. For example, if the incentives cost the resort $10,000 per month, they must increase the resort's profit by $10,000 per month. Some relationships between what the employees do and profit may be easier to justify/explain than others. The incentives can be cash or anything else that can be reasonably justified.

_____

_____

_____

_____

_____

_____

_____

_____

Chapter Four: Employment Laws

Strategy Review: Prepare a strategy review for this chapter (See back of Chapter One).
Case Study 4.1: Chef Williams Is Pregnant
Case Study 4.2: Sexual Harassment Role–Play
Case Study 4.3: Dealing with Diversity
Chapter Objectives: After reading this chapter you should understand and be able to do the following:

1. Explain why discrimination has occurred in the United States and how it has impacted different racial, religious, ethnic, age, gender, and sexual preference groups.
2. Explain why the 1963 March on Washington was important and what it is most famous for.
3. Describe what types of jobs women and other minorities performed prior to enforced civil rights laws. Explain how and why their aspirations were limited.
4. Explain the main components of the Fair Labor Standards Act of 1938.
5. Describe the Equal Pay Act of 1963 and the basis for equal pay.
6. Describe the Civil Rights Act of 1964, EEO, EEOC, Title VII, and list the three principal roles of that organization.
7. Differentiate between disparate treatment and disparate impact.
8. Define retaliation as it relates to civil rights laws.
9. Explain what sexual harassment is and what a business should do to prevent it and deal with it.
10. Discuss circumstances when a business is liable for sexual harassment, when it is not liable.
11. Explain why there is a tendency to have more sexual harassment complaints in the hospitality industry than in other industries.
12. Differentiate between the two types of sexual harassment of quid pro quo and hostile work environment.
13. List the benefits of sexual harassment role-play.
14. Explain the reasonable person standard as it relates to sexual harassment.
15. List the major components of the following laws: Age Discrimination in Employment Act of 1967, Pregnancy Discrimination Act of 1978, Immigration Reform and Control Act of 1986, Employee Polygraph Act of 1988, Civil Rights Act of 1991, the Family and Medical Leave Act of 1993, the Uniformed Services Employment and Reemployment Rights Act of 1994, and the Genetic Information Nondiscrimination Act of 2008.
16. List three legitimate defenses that can be used by a business to defend itself against violations of the civil rights law—business necessity, bona fide occupational qualifications and seniority.
17. Define affirmative action and affirmative action plans and list which organizations are legally bound to uphold it.
18. Define diversity and be able to discuss the various aspects of diversity in the workplace, including reasons for encouraging it, stereotyping, factors that hinder diversity, and solutions to the diversity issue.
19. Explain the Americans with Disabilities Act and what makes an employee eligible under the ADA.

Discrimination
Historical Basis
Discrimination is excluding individuals from certain groups from the same opportunities enjoyed by other more powerful groups. The root cause of discrimination in the United States is that white people, white men in particular, felt they were superior to those who were different (e.g., women, racial and religious minorities, and those from other countries, of a different skin color, or who were perceived to be from a lower social class). This attitude led to the white majority's demeaning and taking advantage of those of minority status. This was first evident in interactions with Native Americans, next with African Americans, and subsequently with any immigrant with an accent, different skin color, or different religion (e.g., Irish, Italian, Jews, Asian, German, Mexican, etc.). Immigrants from England, for many reasons (e.g., same language, are most similar to us, and we were once part of the British Empire), were one of the few groups of people who generally did not experience moderate to severe discrimination. While there are many theories of why discrimination continues, two prevalent ones are the ability to create laws that limit the power of others and societal entrenchment/indoctrination of discriminatory habits. Since whites controlled the courts and legislature, they could either ignore existing discrimination laws or pass laws that codified discrimination (e.g., Jim Crow laws passed from 1870s to 1960s that included legislation, such as

the separate-but-equal doctrine that justified various types of discrimination and legalized voter discrimination). Even today, whites in the U.S. Congress and State governments make statements blaming minorities for a variety of societal problems. Because corporations and various other organizations through political action committees (PACS) provide lawmakers with campaign funds, these nongovernmental entities have the power to introduce legislation or to stop legislation they disagree with. For example, they have the ability to stop or limit the impact of health care legislation, banking regulation, pro-labor laws, and so forth that are good for employees, but may either increase business expenses or limit their ability to garner large profits. Social entrenchment or indoctrination of discriminatory habits occurs when people see others being discriminated against and accept it as the way things are, or are told that others are less honest, less smart, less able, and so forth. Soon the majority group, or segments within it, start to believe the insults or at least accepts it as "the way things are." Others attempt to carry discrimination a step further by verbally demeaning others, denying them equal treatment, or even resorting to physical violence against them. Hate crimes legislation, by which various crimes against individuals protected by civil rights laws carry increased penalties, has helped to protect minority groups.

In the United States there are three broad categories of discrimination—women, the disabled, and those with visible or cultural differences, such as color, country of origin, and religion. This categorization is an attempt to help provide an overview of the discriminated groups and to assist in understanding the obstacles each face. All discrimination is bad. The worst is discrimination against those with the fewest options to fight back, generally the young and old.

Women. Although African Americans and Native Americans were certainly the groups with the worst discrimination, women, young and old, have been the largest mistreated group. As late as the 1970s, a large number of women studying business in college were there to become administrative assistants (i.e., professional secretaries). Title IX of the Education Amendments of 1972 (now known as the Patsy T. Mink Equal Opportunity in Education Act) gave women parity in educational programs and activities in institutions receiving federal assistance (i.e., all public schools). Prior to this law the majority of school budgets for sports and many other activities went to activities for men. While Title IX helped, like civil rights laws, it did not automatically reverse society's attitudes.

Disabled. Historically, in the United States and most other countries, the disabled were rarely able to participate in routine societal activities (e.g., using a sidewalk, going to a business that had steps at its entrance, using a public restroom, etc.). Until a few decades ago, the most common sources of income for disabled adults were begging and government assistance. The term *handicapped* was derived from *cap-in-hand*, meaning beggar. After the Americans with Disabilities Act went into effect in 1991 (discussed later in this chapter), people, businesses, and communities became more accommodating of people with disabilities. Many disabled began finding jobs and leading fruitful lives. As virtually any employer of the disabled will tell you, they're dependable, do a great job, and their morale is higher than any other group of employees. Since the Americans with Disabilities Act (ADA) was passed, millions of disabled employees have found jobs.

General Differences. The third category consists of all other discriminated groups that have been penalized for simply looking different or coming from different cultures (e.g., race, color, religion, age, national origin, etc.). This group does not have disabilities or gender differences that can be used as an excuse for discrimination (e.g., they can't lift this or that), just 100% discrimination based on outward appearance.

Legal Reality

Moral employers will obey most employment laws even if they know nothing about them. That is, managers who treat people with respect and listen to their concerns will rarely have problems with employment laws. Of course, because the laws can be a bit complex and since everyone's morality can be different, managers need to know and understand employment laws.

Civil Right Marches and Riots

Though there were many peaceful marches, the most famous were the 1963 March on Washington for Jobs and Freedom and the three marches that took place between Selma and Montgomery, Alabama, in 1965. Civil rights, labor, and religious groups organized the March on Washington. Each of the groups had different reasons for supporting the march. Some wanted to support the President Kennedy's efforts at passing civil rights legislation, while others want to bring the issue of civil rights and economic issues to the nation's attention or call the Kennedy administration to task for not acting quickly enough on civil rights legislation. While the marchers were 80% African American, 20% were from other racial groups. There were many impassioned speeches at the event. The most famous was Martin Luther King's "I Have a Dream" speech (see a copy of his speech at mlkonline.net/dream/html). In it he spoke of America's failure to honor the words in the Constitution and Declaration of Independence and his hope that America would live out the true meaning of that creed—We hold these truths to be self-evident, that all men are created equal. Perhaps his most famous quote from that speech is when he spoke of his dream that his children would someday "live in a nation where they will not be judged by the color of their skin, but by the content of their character." That in essence is the foundation of Equal Opportunity Employment. Employment decisions must be based on a person's abilities and character, not their color or other characteristics unrelated to their ability.

The Selma marches were organized by Amelia Boynton, a Selma resident, vocal supporter of civil rights, and friend of Martin Luther King. King frequently used her home for meetings while in Selma. The main purpose of these marches was to promote voting rights legislation, in particular to remove literacy tests from voting requirements. Many of these tests were not just to make sure the voter could read. They allowed voter registration workers to ask questions of their choosing, such as "How many circuits courts are there in the state?" and "Name each of the judges in each court." The marches themselves were peaceful; however, state and local police attacked participants with clubs and tear gas. The first of the three, because of the brutality of the police, was known as Bloody Sunday. These particular marches helped influence the passing of the Voting Rights Act of 1965.

Prior to various laws being passed, the most notable of which was the Civil Rights Act of 1964, there were virtually no remedies for people who were discriminated against. The result was that beginning in the 1960s blacks in many U.S. cities rioted in the streets in order to bring attention to their plight. Though some criticized them for the violence, it does not take much to imagine the pain and suffering endured by blacks as they were turned away from good jobs, restaurants, hotels, and other routine activities enjoyed by white citizens. Imagine if your father was intelligent enough to be a doctor, but was a janitor, simply because of the color of his skin. The most famous riots were Harlem in 1964, Watts in 1965, and Detroit in 1967.

Jobs before Civil Rights Act

Prior to 1964, women, blacks, the disabled, and other minorities had limited choices for employment. The unfortunate reality is that many firms to this very day still discriminate against most anyone who is not a white male. Common jobs for women included teaching, nursing, and being secretaries. Blacks could be teachers in all black schools, laborers, maids, and janitors. Employment for the disabled was virtually nonexistent; the lucky got decent jobs, but were placed where customers could not see them. Many had to rely on the support of others (e.g., relatives, begging, and government assistance).

Legalized Discrimination

Is there such a thing as legal discrimination? Yes, businesses are able to select the most qualified individual for the job. An employer is never required to hire someone who is not qualified. The only time an employer is obligated to select a less-qualified applicant is when there has been significant cases of discrimination. Even in this case, the person hired must still be qualified for the position.

The Civil Rights Acts of 1866, 1875, 1957, and 1960

Though there were many civil rights laws passed, few had any impact because they were not defended in the courts. The ones listed here are just a sample. The 1866 law applied only to blacks for racial discrimination and allowed for both compensatory (e.g., back pay, and pain and suffering) and punitive damages (e.g., to penalize the firm for its actions). Unfortunately, for various reasons, it was rarely enforced, primarily due to the difficulty of getting a Southern jury to side with the black plaintiff. The 1875 law prohibited discrimination in public places such as theaters, trains, and hotels. It also prohibited discrimination in jury selection (U.S. Commission on Civil Rights, 2010). In 1883 the Supreme Court declared this law unconstitutional because they felt that the Fourteenth Amendment to the Constitution prohibited discrimination by the state, but not by individuals. While in place, the law was rarely enforced. The Civil Rights Act of 1957 was primarily a voting rights act. It gave more enforcement powers to the U.S. Attorney General and the Civil Rights Commission to investigate and report violations to Congress. The Commission on Civil Rights still exists today and laid much of the foundation for later civil rights laws. The Civil Rights Act of 1960 created penalties for anyone who attempted to keep someone from registering to vote or to actually vote.

The Fair Labor Standards Act (FLSA) of 1938

The FLSA includes minimum wage, overtime pay, recordkeeping requirements, and child labor protections for workers in the United States (U.S. Department of Labor, 2010). The FLSA has always included exemptions for certain executive, administrative, professional, and outside sales workers (e.g., managers are classified as exempt from FLSA laws).

Minimum Wage

The federal minimum wage provisions are contained in the Fair Labor Standards Act (FLSA). The current federal minimum wage is $7.25 per hour effective July 24, 2009. Many states also have minimum wage laws. When state laws specify a higher minimum wage; employers must comply with the state wage. The general rule for creation of state employment laws is that the standards in the state law must be at least as high as those in the federal law. The general rules for compliance with employment laws when there are both a state and federal version is that the firm should follow the version with the highest standard—usually the state's version.

Overtime Pay

Unless specifically exempted, employees covered by FSLA must receive overtime pay for hours worked in excess of 40 in a workweek at a rate not less than time and one-half their regular rates of pay. The Act does not require overtime or additional pay for work on Saturdays, Sundays, holidays, or regular days of rest. It is only the hours over 40 in a workweek that count. The Act applies on a workweek basis. An employee's workweek is a fixed and regularly recurring period of 168 hours—seven consecutive 24-hour periods. It need not coincide with the calendar week, but may begin on any day and at any hour of the day. Averaging of hours over two or more weeks is not permitted. Overtime pay earned in a particular workweek must be paid on the regular payday for the pay period in which the wages were earned. The pay upon which overtime is calculated is the employee's regular rate and does not include other remuneration such as bonuses or incentives. Where an employee in a single workweek works at two or more different types of work for which different straight-time rates have been established, the regular rate for that week is the weighted average of such rates.

Legally Required Employee Information (Recordkeeping Requirements)

According to the Fair Labor Standards Act, each covered employer must keep certain records for each nonexempt or hourly worker. No set form is required, only that the information be accurate. The following is a listing of the basic records that an employer must maintain (FLSA Recordkeeping Requirement, U.S. Department of Labor):

1. Employee's full name and social security number.
2. Address, including zip code.
3. Birth date, if younger than 19.
4. Sex and occupation.
5. Time and day of week when employee's workweek begins.
6. Hours worked each day.
7. Total hours worked each workweek.
8. Basis on which employee's wages are paid (e.g., "$9 per hour," "$440 a week," "piecework")
9. Regular hourly pay rate.
10. Total daily or weekly straight-time earnings.
11. Total overtime earnings for the workweek.
12. All additions to or deductions from the employee's wages.
13. Total wages paid each pay period.
14. Date of payment and the pay period covered by the payment.

Employers need to keep payroll records for at least three years. Records such as time cards on which wage computations are based should be retained for two years. These records must be open for inspection by the Department of Labor representatives and may be kept at the place of employment or in a central records office. Any type of timekeeping method may be used (e.g., time clock or having employees manually record their own time) as long as it is complete and accurate.

Employment of Children

There are special pay rates for students where they can be paid 85% of the mandated minimum wage and for workers under 20 years of age where they can be paid $4.25 per hour for the first 90 days of employment. Restaurants and hotels may pay these lower wages, but because of the intense competition for employees most need to pay at least the mandated minimum wage to attract workers.

• Hours Restrictions for Nonagricultural Employees.

Fourteen years old is the minimum age for nonagricultural employment covered by the FLSA. The basic rules for when and where a youth may work are:

• Youths 18 years or older may work for unlimited hours.
• Youths 16 or 17 years old may work for unlimited hours.
• Youths 14 and 15 years old cannot work:
    • More than 3 hours a day on school days, including Fridays;
    • More than 18 hours per week in school weeks;
    • More than 8 hours a day on nonschool days;
    • More than 40 hours per week when school is not in session.

Also, 14- and 15-year-olds may not work before 7:00 a.m., or after 7:00 p.m., except from June 1 through Labor Day, when their permissible hours are extended to 9:00 p.m. Under a special provision, youths 14 and 15 years old who are enrolled in an approved Work Experience and Career Exploration may be employed for up to 23 hours during school weeks and 3 hours on school days (including during school hours). On a case-by-case basis, they may be exempt from certain limitations on the use of hazardous equipment.

• Prohibited Occupations for Hospitality Industry Employees.

The child labor rules that apply to hospitality industry employment depend on the age of the young worker and the kind of job to be performed. The minimum age for hospitality employment covered by the FLSA is 14 years old. In addition to restrictions on hours the Secretary of Labor has found that certain jobs are too hazardous for anyone under 18 years of age to perform. There are additional restrictions on where and in what jobs 14- and 15-year-olds can work. These rules must be followed unless one of the FLSA's child labor exemptions apply.

• A youth **18 years or older** may perform any job, whether hazardous or not.
• A youth **16 or 17 years old** may perform any nonhazardous job. For the hospitality industry, they generally cannot (i.e., without an exemption) drive a motor vehicle or be an outside helper on a motor vehicle; work in meat-packing or processing (including the use of power-driven meat slicing machines); or use power-driven bakery machines (e.g., mixers, vertical mixers, powered dough dividers, etc.).
• A youth **14 and 15 years old** may **not** work in the manufacturing or mining industries, or in any hazardous job. In addition, a 14- or 15-year-old may **not** work in the following occupations: (a) communications or public utilities jobs; (b) construction or repair jobs; (c) driving a motor vehicle or helping a driver; (d) transporting of persons or property; (e) public messenger service; (f) manufacturing and mining occupations; (g) power-driven machinery or hoisting apparatus other than typical office machines; (h) workrooms where products are manufactured, mined or processed; and (i) warehousing and storage.
• A 14- or 15-year-old **may work** in retail stores, food service establishments, and gasoline service stations. However, a 14- or 15-year-old **may not** perform the following jobs in the retail and service industries: Baking; Cooking, except with gas or electric grilles that do not involve cooking over an open flame and with deep fat fryers that are equipped with and utilize devices that automatically lower and raise the baskets in and out of the hot grease or oil; Freezers or meat coolers work; Loading or unloading goods on or off trucks, railcars, or conveyors; Meat processing area work; Maintenance or repair of a building or its equipment; Operating, setting up, adjusting, cleaning, oiling, or repairing power-driven food slicers, grinders, choppers, or cutters and bakery mixers; Outside window washing, or work standing on a window sill, ladder, scaffold or similar equipment; and Warehouse work, except office and clerical work.
• The jobs a 14- or 15-year-old **may do** in the retail and service industries include:
• Bagging and in-store delivering of customer's orders;
• Cashiering, selling, modeling, art work, advertising, window trimming, or comparative shopping;
• Cleaning fruits and vegetables;
• Cleanup work and grounds maintenance—The young worker may use vacuums and floor waxers, but he or she cannot use power-driven mowers, cutters, and trimmers;
• Clean cooking equipment, including the filtering, transporting, and dispensing of oil and grease, but only when the surfaces of the equipment and liquids do not exceed 100° F;
• Errand and delivery work by foot, bicycle, or public transportation;
• Kitchen and other work in preparing and serving food and drinks, but not cooking or baking (see hazardous jobs);

- Office and clerical work;
- Pricing and tagging goods, assembling orders, packing, or shelving;
- Pumping gas, cleaning and polishing cars and trucks (but the young worker cannot repair cars, use garage lifting rack, or work in pits);
- Wrapping, weighing, pricing, stocking any goods as long as the young worker does not work where meat is being prepared and does not work in freezers or meat coolers.

The Equal Pay Act of 1963

The Equal Pay Act was a significant employment law; however, it has not been aggressively enforced. It was an amendment of the Fair Labor Standards Act of 1938.The Equal Pay Act requires that men and women be given equal pay for equal work in the same establishment (Mathis & Jackson 1997). The jobs need not be identical, but they must be substantially equal, performed under the same working conditions, in the same establishment. It is job content, not job titles, that determines whether jobs are substantially equal. Pay differentials are permitted when they are based on factors other than gender, such as seniority, merit, quantity, or quality of production. These are known as "affirmative defenses" and it is the employer's burden to prove that they apply. If a pay differential is discovered, it can only be corrected by raising the pay of the lower-paid employee (i.e., not lowering anyone's pay).

The Civil Rights Act of 1964

The Civil Rights Act of 1964 provided for protection from discrimination regardless of *race, color, religion, sex,* or *national origin,* in all areas of life. (U.S. Equal Employment Opportunity Commission, 2010—The vast majority of legal information in this chapter came from the EEOC and other U.S. government web sites.) The law was first proposed by President John F. Kennedy before his death in 1963. President Lyndon B. Johnson took up the cause and had it reintroduced. It was passed out of the U.S. House of Representatives by a vote of 290 to 130 on February 10, 1964 and in the U.S. Senate by a vote of 73 to 27 on June 19, 1964. It was signed by President Lyndon B. Johnson on July 2, 1964. The law that was passed was a weaker version of an earlier bill so it could get enough votes to pass. One congressman introduced the word, "sex" into the law, in an attempt to kill the bill. A congresswoman fought to keep it in the bill because it formed the basis for equal treatment of men and women. The law had 10 sections, referred to as titles [Title I. Voting rights, Title II. Relief against discrimination in places of public accommodation, Title III. Desegregation of public facilities, Title IV. Desegregation of public education, Title V. Created a commission on civil rights, Title VI. Nondiscrimination in federally assisted programs, **Title VII.** *Equal Employment Opportunity* (also created the Equal Opportunity Commission to help enforce EEO laws), Title VIII. Registration and voting statistics, Title IX. Federal intervention in civil rights cases, Title X. Community relations service (intervene in problems with cities and interstate commerce), Title XI. Miscellaneous (general provisions in support of the other titles of the Act)].

Title VII of the Civil Rights Act of 1964--Equal Employment Opportunity

Title VII of the Act was titled Equal Employment Opportunity and is by far the largest section of the Civil Rights Act. It also established the Equal Employment Opportunity Commission (EEOC) to enforce the Title VII/Equal Employment Opportunity (EEO) laws and regulations. These laws provide protection from discrimination in employment situations, making it unlawful to discriminate against any individual in regard to recruiting, hiring and promotion, transfer, work assignments, performance measurements, the work environment, job training, discipline and discharge, wages and benefits, or any other term, condition, or privilege of employment.

Job requirements must be uniformly and consistently applied to all persons, regardless of race, color, religion, sex, or national origin. Even if a job requirement or practice is applied consistently, if it is not important for job performance or business needs, the requirement may be found unlawful if it excludes persons of a certain racial group, color, religion, sex, or national origin significantly more than others. Examples of potentially unlawful practices include: (1) soliciting applications only from sources in which all or most potential workers are of the same race or color; (2) requiring applicants to have a certain educational background that is not important for job performance or business needs; and (3) testing applicants for knowledge, skills, or abilities that are not important for job performance or business needs.

<u>**Three Principle Roles of the Equal Employment Opportunity Commission**</u>. The EEOC is responsible for enforcement, legal interpretation, and compliance/monitoring of firms (Woods, 2002).

• <u>**Enforcement**</u>. The EEOC is the defender of EEO laws and the origination point for claims against employers (their web site is: www.eeoc.gov). Claims are generally referred to State EEO offices. Often the EEOC will not view the complaint as a violation of EEOC laws, but this does not mean that the claimant cannot still sue. For example, many employer acts are not illegal according to the EEOC, but are still illegal by other laws (e.g., someone is denied a promotion or pay raise because of a hostile work environment).

• <u>**Legal Interpretation**</u>. The EEO laws are known as *statutory laws* because they were developed by legislative statutes. What makes compliance so challenging is that there are thousands of different situations that can occur, each of which may need to be interpreted based on current laws, past interpretations, or similar court decisions (*case law*). For example, in a law suit, the investigator or lawyer would need to know things, such as if there were any related policies in place, who said what, who did what, what was the context in which the alleged incidents occurred, and had similar events occurred before without anyone complaining or without management doing anything. (Note: there are also *regulatory laws*, such as the health codes that restaurants must follow.)

• <u>**Compliance/Monitoring of Firms**</u>. Through the EEO-1 Report, the EEOC gathers compliance information from firms with 100 or more employees, 50 or more if the firm has government contracts of $50,000 or more. The EEO-1 Report has sections for male and female, different races (Hispanic or Latino, White, Black or African American, Native Hawaiian and other Pacific Islander, Asian, American Indian, and Two or More Races), and several sections for different categories of employees (e.g., professional, service workers, administrative support workers, etc.).

<u>**Discrimination Penalties**</u>

Unfortunately, the only recourse in the 1964 law was actual damages, in other words, only back pay—no punitive damages. Additionally, the employee needed to prove that he or she was discriminated against. No lawsuits were allowed under the 1964 law—a complaint would be filed at the EEOC. There were few complaints under the 1964 law because finding an attorney to present a case to the EEOC for back pay of perhaps $200 and to prove the client was discriminated against was difficult.

<u>**Collecting EEO or Affirmative Action Data**</u>

Employers may legitimately need information about their employees or applicant's race for affirmative action purposes (e.g., affirmative action plans). One way to obtain this information and guard against discriminatory selection is to use separate forms from the employee application. This lessens the chance of the information being used in the selection process.

<u>**Harassment/Hostile Work Environment**</u>

Title VII prohibits offensive conduct, such as racial or ethnic slurs, racial jokes, derogatory comments, or other verbal or physical conduct based on an individual's race/color. The conduct has to be unwelcome and offensive, and has to be severe or pervasive. Employers are required to take appropriate steps to prevent and correct unlawful harassment. An employer can reduce the chance that employees will engage in unlawful harassment by implementing an anti-harassment policy and having an effective procedure for reporting, investigating, and correcting harassing conduct. Likewise, employees are responsible for reporting harassment at an early stage to prevent its escalation.

<u>**Religious Discrimination**</u>

Employees cannot be forced to participate in a religious activity as a condition of employment. Employers must reasonably accommodate employees' sincerely held religious practices unless doing so would impose an undue hardship on the employer. A reasonable religious accommodation is any adjustment to the work environment that will allow the employee to practice his/her religion, such as flexible scheduling, voluntary substitutions or swaps, job reassignments and lateral transfers, reasonable modification of grooming requirements, and other workplace practices, policies, and/or procedures. An employer can show undue hardship if accommodating an employee's religious practices requires more than ordinary administrative costs, diminishes efficiency in other jobs, infringes on other employees' job rights or benefits, impairs workplace safety, causes coworkers to carry the accommodated employee's share of potentially hazardous or burdensome work, or if the proposed accommodation conflicts with another law or regulation (e.g., not wearing a hair restraint).

<u>**Language Laws**</u>

An employer may not base a decision on an employee's foreign accent unless the accent materially interferes with job performance. An English fluency requirement is only permissible if required for the effective performance of the position for which it is imposed. English-only rules must be adopted for nondiscriminatory reasons, such as when needed to promote the safe or efficient operation of the employer's business. An employer cannot prevent employees from talking in their native language as long as it does not interfere with work. For example, they can speak Spanish on their break, but could be required to speak English when working.

Retaliation

All laws enforced by the EEOC (and the Americans with Disabilities Act—ADA) make it illegal to fire, demote, harass, or otherwise "retaliate" against people (applicants or employees) because they filed a charge of discrimination, because they complained to their employer about discrimination on the job, or because they participated in an employment discrimination proceeding (such as an investigation or lawsuit). For example, it is illegal for an employer to refuse to promote an employee because she filed a charge of discrimination with the EEOC, even if EEOC later determined no discrimination occurred. An employee who complains about business practices unrelated to the EEO or ADA laws (e.g., financial mismanagement) is not protected by EEOC retaliation laws, but could be protected by other laws (e.g., harassment, hostile work environment, etc.).

Disparate Treatment versus Disparate Impact

The two basic types of discrimination are *disparate treatment* and *disparate impact*. Disparate treatment is essentially the intentional discrimination of individuals. This could be through prejudiced actions, different standards for various groups, and unequal treatment. Disparate impact (also referred to as *adverse impact*) is generally unintentional discrimination such as a test that applicants of a protected group have a disproportionately difficult time passing that does not directly relate to the job they are applying for. If it is determined that the actions of an employer were disparate treatment, civil penalties would generally be substantially greater.

Multinational Employers

U.S. firms that employ U.S. citizens outside the United States or its territories are required to abide by EEO laws. Non-U.S. firms that operate in the United States or its territories are required to abide by EEO laws.

Sexual Harassment

Sexual harassment is covered under the 1964 Civil Right Act under sex discrimination. The term itself has been credited to both faculty of Massachusetts Institute of Technology (MIT) and Cornell, both in 1975. The MIT usage was in a letter discussing the importance of protecting women from sexual harassment. At Cornell, they were attempting to make a poster for an event focused on sex discrimination and several terms came up, such as sexual coercion, sexual exploitation and others. When someone suggested the term *sexual harassment*, everyone agreed to it. Sexual harassment includes unwelcomed sexual advances, requests for sexual favors, and other verbal or physical conduct of a sexual nature when this conduct explicitly or implicitly affects an individual's employment, unreasonably interferes with an individual's work performance, or creates an intimidating, hostile, or offensive work environment (U.S. Equal Employment Opportunity Commission, 2010). Visual sexual harassment, though less common than verbal or physical actions, can occur when someone is constantly staring (e.g., elevator eyes) or shows pictures of a sexually explicit nature. Sexual harassment can occur in a variety of circumstances, including but not limited to the following (from EEOC law):

• The victim as well as the harasser may be a woman or a man. The victim does not have to be of the opposite sex.

• The harasser can be the victim's supervisor, an agent of the employer, a supervisor in another area, a coworker, or a nonemployee.

• The victim does not have to be the person harassed but could be anyone affected by the offensive conduct.

• Unlawful sexual harassment may occur without economic injury to or discharge of the victim.

• The harasser's conduct must be unwelcome.

Types of Sexual Harassment Under the Civil Rights Act

• **Quid Pro Quo Harassment** (Latin for, "this for that"). An employee must tolerate sexual harassment to keep a job, obtain one, or to keep or obtain a raise, benefit, or promotion. Essentially, this is an employment decision based on acceptance or rejection of sexual conduct.

• **Hostile Work Environment**. The harassment interferes with the employee's work performance or creates a hostile, offensive, or abusive work environment. The determination of whether the actions are hostile are based on whether the conduct was physical, verbal, or both; its frequency; and whether the perpetrator was a coworker or supervisor; and if others joined in the harassment.

Employer Actions to Limit Sexual Harassment

• The first step is to have a clear policy against sexual harassment (Woods, 2002).

• The policy must be communicated to everyone on a regular basis (during orientation and several times per year during employee meetings). Role play is one excellent means of communicating sexual harassment laws and their impact on others. It allows employees to better understand the details of each law and the unfortunate problems it causes its victims (See Case Study 4.2: Sexual Harassment Role-Play)

• There should be a simple means of filing a complaint and someone should be identified as the person employees can go to in order to discuss cases of harassment. Also, it should be a policy that, when an individual thinks they have been sexually harassed, he or she must notify a designated individual in the business (e.g., HR director, General Manager, corporate HR department, etc.).

• Each complaint should be thoroughly reviewed (i.e., do not take it lightly—"Oh, he's just friendly").

• Take action to correct past and current sexual harassment behaviors. In most cases, the firm's attorney should be consulted to determine the appropriate action.

Liability for Sexual Harassment

1. If the sexual harassment leads to a tangible employment action, such as loss of job, demotion, decrease in pay, or significantly different work assignments, the employer is liable.

2. When there is no tangible employment action, the employer is liable unless (a) it can prove that it has taken reasonable care to prevent and quickly correct sexually harassing behavior (e.g., having effective policies and complaint procedures that are widely communicated) and (b) the harassed employee failed to take advantage of the available complaint procedure.

Impact versus Intent

Intent is irrelevant in determining whether sexual harassment has occurred. It is the impact on the situation or individual that determines if sexual harassment has occurred. For example, a sexually explicit joke only has to offend one person for sexual harassment to occur. Intent versus impact applies to all forms of discrimination.

The "Reasonable Person" Standard

When the civil rights law regarding sexual harassment was first passed, there was confusion over what constituted *unwelcomed* advances or being made to feel *uncomfortable*. Sexual harassment complaints were being filed for someone simply saying, "You look nice today." The reasonable person standard was instituted to address this problem. It states that each case of sexual harassment will be judged offensive as interpreted by a "reasonable person." For example, in the "You look nice today." example, sexual harassment has not generally occurred. However, if the victim complains to management and either management does nothing or talks to the perpetrator and the activity continues, then sexual harassment may be a legitimate charge.

Major Employment Laws Following the Civil Rights Act of 1964

Of the laws included in this chapter, most are enforced by the EEOC (Dressler, 1997; Mathis & Jackson, 1997; U.S. Equal Employment Opportunity Commission, 2010; Woods, 2002), the exceptions being polygraph and USERRA (both by the Department of Labor) and immigration (Immigration and Customs Enforcement—ICE).

Age Discrimination in Employment Act (ADEA) of 1967

In relation to employment, people 40 years and older are a protected class, like race, religion, sex, and so forth. The 1967 law stated that the protected group was those between 40 and 65 years of age. In 1978 the upper limit was raised to 70 years of age. In 1986 the upper limit was removed making the protected class 40 years of age and above. This is the current age category. This group is protected when applying for a job and as an employee. Under the ADEA, it is unlawful to discriminate against a person because of his/her age with respect to any term, condition, or privilege of employment, including hiring, firing, promotion, layoff, compensation, benefits, job assignments, and training. It applies to employers with 20 or more employees. The ADEA generally makes it unlawful to include age preferences in job notices or advertisements. A job notice or advertisement may specify an age limit only in the rare circumstances where age is shown to be a "bona fide occupational qualification" (BFOQ).

The Older Workers Benefit Protection Act of 1990 (OWBPA) amended the ADEA to allow employers to reduce older workers' benefits in certain circumstances. Congress recognized that the cost of providing certain benefits to older workers is greater than the cost of providing those same benefits to younger workers, and that those greater costs could create a disincentive to hire older workers. Therefore, in limited circumstances, an employer may be permitted to reduce benefits based on age, as long as the money spent on benefits was the same as that spent on younger workers. In other words, a health insurance plan for a younger worker that costs the same as one for an older worker may provide significantly greater benefits; however, since it costs the same, the law may allow it.

Pregnancy Discrimination Act of 1978

Employers cannot refuse to hire a woman because she is pregnant, conditions related to the pregnancy, or because of prejudices of customers or other employees. They also cannot stipulate the beginning and ending of pregnancy leave; however, if women leave for a longer period than allowed in the Family and Medical Leave Act (FMLA), they may lose benefits or their job. If an employer provides any benefits to workers on leave, the employer must provide the same benefits for those on leave for pregnancy-related conditions. Additionally, it is up to the pregnant employee to determine if a situation at work is dangerous enough to harm their fetus. It is only the responsibility of the employer to make them aware of the danger. This keeps employers from developing reasons for asking pregnant women to leave, rather than leaving it up the employee.

Pregnant women can work as long as they are able to perform the essential functions of their job. If an employee is temporarily unable to perform her job due to pregnancy, the employer must treat her the same as any other temporarily disabled employee. For example, if the employer modifies tasks for temporarily disabled employees or allows them to perform alternative assignments or take disability leave or leave without pay, the employer also must allow an employee who is temporarily disabled due to pregnancy to do the same.

Any health insurance provided by an employer must cover expenses for pregnancy-related conditions on the same basis as costs for other medical conditions. Abortion coverage is not required, except when the life of the mother is endangered. The same level of health benefits must be offered for spouses of male employees as for spouses of female employees.

Immigration Reform and Control Act of 1986

The law makes it illegal to knowingly hire persons not authorized to work in the United States. It also makes it illegal to hire individuals without verifying or correctly documenting their identity and eligibility to work legally in the United States.

Verification begins with completion of the I-9 form and the employee's presentation of documents specified in the form. Employee eligibility can then be verified through a U.S. government-run Internet-based system called E-Verify. This allows an employer, using information reported on an employee's Form I-9, to determine the eligibility of that employee to work in the United States. For most employers, the use of E-Verify is voluntary and limited to determining the employment eligibility of new hires only. According to E-Verify administrators 96.9% of employees are either immediately confirmed as eligible for employment or are confirmed within 24 hours. There is no charge to employers to use E-Verify. The E-Verify system is operated as a joint initiative of the U.S. Department of Homeland Security and the Social Security Administration. The law is enforced by U.S. Immigration and Customs Enforcement (ICE).

When the law was first passed, Hispanic employment was said to have decreased because employers were concerned about verification. Another impact was the increased use of subcontractors who would take responsibility for verification. Since subcontractors need to charge a fee, this resulted in lower wages for employees. If employers are aware that any of the subcontractor's employees are illegal aliens, then the employer is liable.

Employee Polygraph Protection Act of 1988

Polygraphs are lawful only for the investigation of economic loss or injury. The requirements for giving a polygraph examination include: (1) the employee had access to the location of the incident being investigated; (2) reasonable suspicion that the employee was involved; (3) employer must provide a written statement to the employee with the following: (a) the incident being investigated; (b) the specific economic loss or injury; and (c) the employee had access to the property and can reasonably be under suspicion. The Employee Polygraph Protection Act (EPPA) is enforced by the Employment Standards Administration's Wage and Hour Division (WHD) within the U.S. Department of Labor (DOL). Violation of the law can result in a fine of up to $10,000.

Civil Rights Act of 1991

This law significantly strengthened the 1964 Civil Rights Act. The main changes include that it places the burden of proof on the employer, rather than the employee, and it allows for full compensatory damages, plus punitive damages. Damages for the employee can also be assessed by the EEOC in the following amounts (15 to 100 employees—up to $50,000; 101 to 200 employees—up to $100,000; 201 to 500 employees—up to $200,000; 500 or more employees—up to $300,000). The 1964 law required the employee or his/her attorney to prove that discrimination occurred and allowed only for recovery of back wages; that is, it did not allow for punitive damages or the recovery of other compensatory damages, such as back pay, pain and suffering, inconvenience, loss of enjoyment of life, or loss of a promotion because of discrimination. Therefore, when an employee was discriminated against, and the EEOC did not take the case, he/she had to find an attorney who was willing to sue with the hope of recovering perhaps a few hundred dollars. The alternative was for the attorney to take the case on a pro bono status (i.e., without compensation). Since the cost of an average lawsuit can start at $20,000 and more, it was very difficult to find an attorney who would represent a discriminated client in hopes of recovering a few hundred dollars. The size of the punitive damages is based on the size and value of the firm.

Family and Medical Leave Act of 1993

Requires employers with 50 or more employees to offer up to 12 weeks of unpaid leave for pregnancy, adoption, to care for an immediate family member (spouse, child, or parent) with a serious health condition, or when the employee has a serious medical condition. The employee must have worked for the company for a minimum of 12 months and 1,250 hours. The law does not cover the highest paid 10% of workers. If a husband and wife work for the same restaurant, it is lawful to limit their combined leave of absence to 12 weeks. The leave of absence must be in writing and approved by the manager.

Uniformed Services Employment and Reemployment Rights Act of 1994 (USERRA)

This law requires that upon their return, service members must be reemployed in the job that they would have attained had they not been absent for military service (the "escalator" principle), with the same seniority, status, and pay, as well as other rights and benefits determined by seniority. Special training must be made available to help the service member qualify for the position. Advanced written or verbal notice must be given to their employer unless for justifiable reasons it is not possible. The cumulative time that a service member can be absent is 5 years. Disabled veterans who are convalescing from military service or training have up to 2 years from the completion of their service to return to or reapply for their civilian job. Enforcement is through the Department of Labor.

Genetic Information Nondiscrimination Act of 2008

Now part of EEOC law, Title II of the law protects applicants and employees from discrimination based on genetic information in hiring, promotion, discharge, pay, fringe benefits, job training, classification, referral, and other aspects of employment. The Genetic Information Nondiscrimination Act (GINA) strictly limits employers' acquisition of genetic information and the disclosure of genetic information. Genetic information includes information about genetic tests of applicants, employees, or their family members and the existence of diseases or disorders in family members (family medical history).

Proving Discrimination and Defenses for Discrimination Charges

For an employee to institute an EEOC complaint, there must generally be some type of *prima facie* evidence (i.e., "on the face of it") that the employee has been denied his or her civil rights (Gomez-Mejia, Balkin, & Cardy, 1998). This is generally through the disparate treatment or impact covered earlier in Title VII of the Civil Rights Act. Once *prima facie* evidence has been presented by the plaintiff (through the appropriate means—EEOC complaint or law suit), it is up to the firm to prove that nothing wrong was done. A less common means of providing *prima facia* evidence of discrimination is the Four/Fifths Rule. This essentially states that relative to the group that makes up the majority, the firm must hire at least 4/5s or 80% of the qualified minorities (protected class) that apply. In other words, if 25% of white males are hired for a position, then at least 20% of the qualified minorities that apply must be hired (20% is 80% or 4/5s of 25%). Defenses for EEOC suits include the following:

Bona Fide Occupational Qualifications (BFOQ)

The firm needs to hire someone with specific characteristics for a particular job. For example, a country club could deny a job to a female applicant as a men's locker room attendant. If customers are requesting female masseuses, then the firm has the right to hire the requested gender. If the same request was for a particular race, the decision would likely be discriminatory. BFOQ is by far the most frequently used discrimination defense in the hospitality industry.

Business Necessity

This generally concerns requiring certain characteristics for the safe operation of the business. For example, a physically disabled person may not be able to function effectively or safely in a fast kitchen environment. Because air pressure can induce labor, a pregnant woman in her third trimester cannot work as a flight attendant.

Seniority

A policy specifying that seniority is used to determine promotion or other employment decisions is justified if it is applied in all situations without regard to minority status.

Affirmative Action

In 1965, President Johnson issued Executive Order 11246, which became known as affirmative action. Both Presidents Franklin D. Roosevelt and Dwight D. Eisenhower signed similar executive orders. A major difference was that Executive Order 11246 shifted affirmative action enforcement to the Department of Labor, which led to federal regulations. Where Equal Employment Opportunity are the laws included in Title VII of the Civil Rights Act that protect the current employment rights of individuals from certain groups, affirmative action is a set of guidelines designed to remedy past discrimination. No quotas are allowed. Covered employers must simply make a reasonable attempt to hire qualified people from minority groups and to as closely as possible have employees that mirror the community in which it operates. When determining availability of women and minorities, employers consider, among other factors, the presence of minorities and women having requisite skills in an area in which the employer can reasonably recruit. In other words, the applicants must be qualified.

It is required of federal and state agencies/organizations, other organizations that accept money from the federal government (e.g., most universities), and businesses with $10,000 in government contracts. When a business meets this threshold, every location of the business is required to be an affirmative action employer. If the entire business does $50,000 or more in total contractual business with the U.S. government, it must also prepare *affirmative action plans*. Affirmative action plans compare the demographic composition of the current workforce to the pool of qualified workers in the local labor force; establish dates by which specific underutilization problems will be corrected; and specify what actions will be taken to provide equal opportunities to members of a protected class. Examples of remedies include recruiting protected-class members, providing additional training, and removing barriers to employment (transportation, education/tutoring).

The Supreme Court has upheld affirmative action. Decisions can be made, in part, on non-job-related characteristics. However, to be permissible, the employment decision cannot be made solely on the basis of those characteristics. Before non-job-relevant characteristics can be considered, applicants must be essentially equally qualified on job-relevant characteristics. Affirmative action cannot be used in layoffs, even when it affects minority representation. At some point in the future, affirmative action will not be necessary. According to the Supreme Court, that point has not been reached. Whenever affirmative action is rescinded, EEO laws will still protect minority groups from discrimination.

In 1965, President Johnson gave the commencement speech at Howard University where he articulated the reasoning behind these new affirmative action measures. He said,

> But freedom is not enough. You do not wipe away the scars of centuries by saying: Now, you are free to go where you want, do as you desire, and choose the leaders you please. You do not take a man who for years has been hobbled by chains, liberate him, bring him to the starting line of a race, saying you are free to compete with all the others, and still justly believe you have been completely fair. Thus it is not enough to open the gates of opportunity. All our citizens must have the ability to walk through those gates. This is the next and more profound stage of the battle for civil rights. We seek not just freedom, but opportunity—not just legal equity but human ability—not just equality as a right and a theory, but equality as a fact and as a result.

Conflicting Philosophies/Strategies for Fair Employment

There are two rational and conflicting arguments related to affirmative action. One is that employment decisions should be made without regard to minority status (e.g., race, gender, religion, national origin, color, age, disability). Here, the decision is focused entirely on hiring the best person for the job. This philosophy, on its face, is logical. At the other end of the spectrum is the philosophy that the fairest employment policy is to make employment decisions at least partially based on minority status. Here, the decision includes the reality that people from minority groups have historically been denied equal employment. The question is at what point can we get rid of affirmative action? Can all U.S. employers be trusted to provide equal opportunities to applicants? Are there current applicants who have been discriminated against when applying for jobs and therefore deserve some level of extra consideration?

Diversity in the Workplace

Diversity can be defined as the characteristics of people that make them different from others (Gomez-Mejia, Balking, & Cardy, 1998). A critical element of a firm's values and commitment of upholding employment laws is its philosophy and strategy for honoring diversity in all areas of the business. While the vast majority of hospitality firms promote diversity in their employee ranks, they are less proactive for management positions. From the perspective of a minority employee (e.g., gender, race, religion, country of origin, color, age, pregnancy, disabled, etc.), how can they respect management and trust their statements on values, ethics, and honesty if management consists of mainly white men, while employees are mainly minorities?

Stereotyping

Stereotyping is forming judgments about one person based on your opinion of the group you associate them with. Another way of stating this is making the assumption that an individual will behave like most people from their group. The reality is that individual characteristics are more important than group membership.

Two Main Categories of Human Differences

• Variations that people have no control over (e.g., skin color, race, ethnicity, gender, age, etc.).
• Variations that people have some degree of control over (e.g., education, religion, marital status, values, beliefs, attitudes, behavior, etc.).

Different Views and Reasons for Encouraging Diversity

• Voluntary implementation of affirmative action and EEO laws.
• Maximization of cooperation, teamwork, and employee effort.
• Improves overall business performance.
• Creativity, problem solving, and flexibility are enhanced because people with different backgrounds have different views.
• Customers and potential employees, especially minority customers and potential employees, recognize and respect a firm's diversity efforts.
• Diverse firms have been found to have greater profits than those with less diverse employees (Staff, 2005).

Factors that Hinder Diversity and Maximization of Employees

• Male dominance in management positions and the "old boys" network.
• People tend to socialize with those who are most similar to them.
• Biological differences (pregnancy, physical ability of different people, and genders).

Solutions to the Diversity Issue

• Top management commitment to honoring and valuing diversity.
• Diversity training for everyone in the firm.
• Support groups geared toward empowering minorities.
• Accommodation of family needs.
• Direct support for minorities and others through mentoring, apprenticeships, and internships.
• Communication standards (not assuming that secretaries are women, substituting the term *secretary* with *administrative assistant*, not using "he" for managers and "she" for secretaries, and alphabetizing minority groups).
• Organized social activities.
• Diversity audits.
• Management responsibility and accountability.

Americans with Disabilities Act (ADA)

The first major disability law in the United States was the Vocational Rehabilitation Act of 1973. This law requires the federal government and employers with contracts with the federal government of $2,500 or more to institute affirmative action plans for hiring the disabled. The law was the forerunner of the Americans with Disabilities Act.

The Americans with Disabilities Act, passed in 1990 and enacted in 1991 for large employers (fully enacted for all employers by 1992), prohibits discrimination on the basis of disability in employment, state and local government, public accommodations, commercial facilities, transportation, and telecommunications. To be protected by the ADA, one must have a disability or have a relationship or association with an individual with a disability.

Disability as Defined by ADA

A. "A physical or mental impairment that substantially limits one or more major life activities." Examples: walking, speaking, breathing, performing manual tasks, sitting, lifting, seeing, hearing, learning, reading (e.g., dyslexia), and some psychological problems, such as depression or stress (if professionally diagnosed).

B. Record of such impairment

C. Regarded as having such impairment (Americans with Disabilities Act, 1992)

The ADA does not specifically name all of the impairments that are covered.

ADA Title I: Employment

Title I requires employers with 15 or more employees to provide qualified individuals with disabilities an equal opportunity to benefit from the full range of employment-related opportunities available to others. For example, it prohibits discrimination in recruitment, hiring, promotions, training, pay, social activities, and other privileges of employment. It restricts questions that can be asked about an applicant's disability before a job offer is made. Employers may not ask job applicants about the existence, nature, or severity of a disability. Applicants may be asked about their ability to perform specific/essential job functions. A job offer may also be conditioned on the results of a medical examination, but only if the examination is required for all entering employees in similar jobs. Medical examinations of employees must be job related (e.g., cannot include things like pregnancy or cancer testing) and must be consistent with the employer's business needs. It also requires that employers make reasonable accommodation to the known physical or mental limitations of otherwise qualified individuals with disabilities, unless it results in undue hardship. Religious entities with 15 or more employees are covered under Title I (A Guide to Disability Rights Laws, 2005, U.S. Department of Justice, Civil Rights Division, Disability Rights Section). Illegal drug use is not covered by the ADA.

Charges of employment discrimination on the basis of disability may be filed at any U.S. Equal Employment Opportunity Commission field office within 180 days of the date of discrimination, or 300 days if the charge is filed with a designated State EEOC office. Individuals may file a lawsuit in federal court only after they receive a "right-to-sue" letter from the EEOC. Field offices are located in 50 cities throughout the United States and are listed in most telephone directories under "U.S. Government."

Key Guideline for ADA Compliance

A qualified employee or applicant with a disability is an individual who can perform the essential functions of the job with or without reasonable accommodations.

Essential Functions:

• Major responsibilities (duties and tasks) in the job description.

• Things that every employee in that position must be able to do to be considered a good employee.

Reasonable Accommodations:

• Anything that does not cause undue hardship on the employer. Undue hardship is defined as an action requiring significant difficulty or expense when considered in light of factors such as an employer's size, financial resources, and the nature and structure of its operation. Additionally, an employer is not required to lower quality or productions standards to make accommodations.

• This is a subjective decision, based on the relative cost of the accommodation and the employer's resources. Reasonable accommodations may include, but are not limited to:

  • Making existing facilities used by employees readily accessible to and usable by persons with disabilities;

  • Jobs should be restructured to eliminate functions not essential to good performance;

  • Schedules must be reasonably modified for medical appointments or other needs;

  • Acquiring or modifying equipment or devices, adjusting or modifying training materials or policies;

  • If an employee becomes disabled, the employer should attempt to find another job suitable for the individual.

Case Study 4.1: Chef Williams Is Pregnant

The long-time chef of the Hill-Top Restaurant is 7 months pregnant and is beginning to find it difficult to get around the kitchen. Knowing the basic components of the Pregnancy Discrimination Act of 1978, the restaurant's manager is afraid to say anything for fear of breaking the law.

Required:

1. What are the basic rights of the Pregnancy Discrimination Act that protect Chef Williams?
2. Because the chef is slowing down a bit, does the manager have the right to (a) tell Chef Williams to take a few months off until she has the baby; (b) tell her to work at another position?
3. What would you do in this situation (consider the ability of the firm, the needs of Chef Williams, and the opinions and the feelings/emotions of other employees)?

_____

_____

_____

_____

_____

_____

_____

_____

_____

_____

_____

_____

_____

Case Study 4.2: Sexual Harassment Role–Play

Role-Play:

1. Your group is to prepare a short skit (anything up to 2 minutes) that shows an example of sexual harassment in the hospitality workplace. You can select from the following scenarios or you will be assigned one of them: manager to employee, customer to employee, employee to employee, female to male (use any of the previous employee/manager/customer categories for this or the remaining pairs), male to male, female to female, or any other possible combination.

2. It is best to have large groups so that if any students do not feel comfortable participating in the role-play, they can still participate in the discussion without worrying about having to participate in the role-play. Additionally, any student that does not feel comfortable with the topic, does not have to participate.

3. If your example includes touching, it cannot be in any erogenous area and no matter where it is, and it should not be excessive.

4. Before you prepare the skit, be sure you are familiar with the laws regarding sexual harassment.

5. You must review your skit/situation with the instructor before you act it out.

Presentation:

1. Explain your situation.

2. Present it.

3. How do you think the victim would feel in your role-play?

4. What do you think the perpetrator thinks about what was done?

5. What should the victim do?

6. What would you do as the manager?

_____

_____

_____

_____

_____

_____

_____

_____

_____

_____

_____

_____

Case Study 4.3: Dealing with Diversity

Nikki Nagurski has been the front desk manager of a 450-room hotel in San Francisco for the past three years. The current executive housekeeper has left and Nikki is interested in the position. One of the reasons she is interested in the new job is that it will require a greater use of her HR management skills.

In the new job Nikki would be responsible for a staff of 50 full-time employees and about 25 part-time workers. The number of part-time employees changes with occupancy rates, which vary by 20% throughout the year (from a high of 70% to a low of 50%). Additionally, the number of hours worked by full-time employees can, by necessity, also vary based on occupancy. About six months ago, new corporate policies were introduced that require housekeepers to be friendlier with guests, including engaging them in conversation.

One of Nikki's hesitations in accepting this position is that she has noticed that a great deal of conflict existed between the former executive housekeeper and the housekeeping staff. There have also been problems between the different ethnic/cultural groups of housekeepers (equally divided by African American, Asian, Hispanic, Native American, and White). You suspect that most of the problems are probably due to the diverse ethnic and cultural backgrounds of the employees.

Required:

1. Your group will consider Nikki's decisions as she reviews the pros and cons of taking the Housekeeper's position. In doing so, you must answer the following questions posed to Nikki from the executive committee.

   A. Do you feel that ethnic and cultural diversity plays a larger role in housekeeping than it does at the front desk? Justify your answer.

   B. Considering that, if you were not successful, this job could stifle your advancement opportunities in the company, do you want the executive housekeeper's position? Explain your answer.

   C. Assuming that you accept the position, what are your strategies and tactics for improving the work environment of the housekeepers?

2. The following is a philosophical question: Is there a viable solution to every problem? Explain your response.

_____

_____

_____

_____

_____

_____

_____

_____

Chapter Five: The Job Creation Process
Job Analysis, Job Design, Job Descriptions, and Job Specifications
Strategy Review: Because few firms publish information on their Job Creation efforts, there is no strategy review for this chapter.
Case Study 5.1: Management Problems at the Mount Aspen Resort
Case Study 5.2: Duties and Tasks—Be Specific
Case Study 5.3: Poor Service at the Abby Rose Hotel
Chapter Objectives: After reading this chapter you should understand and be able to do the following:
1. Explain how job creation components relate to each other.
2. Define job analysis and describe its two major components—duties and tasks.
3. Explain why the job analysis is one of the most important concepts in Human Resource Management (i.e., how it is used by employees and managers).
4. Identify how to tell if a job analysis is complete.
5. Differentiate the between the complexity of preparing qualitative and quantitative duties and tasks.
6. Create task lists for a qualitative duty.
7. List the advantages of increasing the specificity of job analysis components.
8. Identify who should have input into the creation of a job analysis.
9. Describe the methods of gathering job analysis information.
10. Explain the purpose of job design.
11. Describe the four types of job design.
12. Explain the primary components of a job description and how it is used.
13. Describe the two primary components of a job specification and give examples of what is typically included in each.
14. Create a job analysis, job design, job description, or job specification for any hospitality position.
15. Describe work-flow and the concepts of layout, work centers, work sections, and workflow analysis.

The Job Creation Process
There are two definitions for the Job Creation Process. One is from economics where new jobs are created so that workers who are either entering the job market or are seeking new jobs can find one. For example, when a hotel or restaurant opens new locations, jobs are created because it must hire employees for those new locations. The job creation process for Human Resources Management and for this book entails recording what each employee for each position will be responsible for. It also commonly includes the general characteristics expected of each employee. Running a business without the details of what each employee must do in writing, while not impossible, would be quite a challenge (Collins, 2007). There are four parts of the Job Creation Process: Job Analysis, Job Design, Job Description, and Job Specification. Each is briefly defined below and explained in more depth in the chapter.
• The *job analysis* records the duties and tasks, the specific details required to perform the job.
• The *job design* then analyzes the duties and tasks to make sure there are not too many or too few things to do, that the job is as interesting as reasonably possible, and if there are other positions at which people working this position could also be trained.
• The *job description* is typically a one-page abbreviation of the job analysis with additional job-related information.
• The *job specifications* are the general personal and behavioral characteristics people should have to perform the duties and tasks in the job analysis.
      Figure 5.1: Job Creation Process graphically presents a brief overview of the Job Creation Process and **Figure 5.2: Sample Relationships for the Job Creation Process**, provides an overview of how they function together.

Figure 5.1:   Job Creation Process

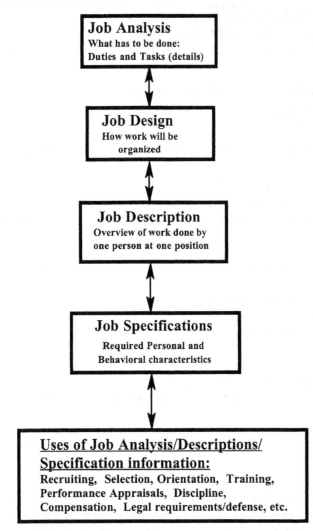

Job Analysis

The job analysis is a systematic process of collecting information used to make decisions about how jobs are performed—the standards or policies for each job (Gomez-Mejia, et al., 1998). The analysis must take into account that standards set must be somewhere between those that are minimally acceptable and the performance of exemplary employees. The higher the standards, the greater the challenge of virtually every aspect of management (e.g., recruiting, hiring, training, and supervising employees). In other words, if standards are set too high, then not only will employees have a hard time achieving them, but managers will become frustrated because it is too difficult to run the business according to the policies.

The key element in preparing a job analysis for any position is to identify the duties and tasks for the position.
• A **duty** is what must be done—a single requirement of a job. For example, make a bed, check in a guest, cook a steak, answer the front desk phone, and so forth.
• A **task** is how the duty will be accomplished—a basic element of work that is necessary to perform a duty. For example, if the duty is "Answer the front desk phone," the tasks could be: 1. Answer the phone within three rings. 2. Speak with a pleasant voice. 3. Use the following script: "Hello, Snowbowl Hotel. This is Jennifer, how can I help you?" The concept behind setting duties and tasks is that it increases the likelihood that each task will be performed as management desires. Duties and tasks ultimately become the firm's policies, also referred to as standards. **In Human Resources, there is no concept that is more important than the job analysis and duties and tasks**. This is how we

want things done, how we satisfy customers, how we determine who to hire, how we train, how we supervise and give performance appraisals, how we discipline employees, how we determine who should receive a raise, and more. Equipment utilized and standards associated with the position (e.g., close a cash drawer within $1.00 each shift) can be included.

Figure 5.2:   Sample Relationships for the Job Creation Process

Position: Guest Services Agent (GSA/front desk clerk)

Job Analysis

Duties

1. Recognize and assess needs of guests approaching the front desk
2. Check in
3. Check out
4. Answer phone, relays messages
5. Make reservations
6. Provide information

Tasks for duty #2, **Check in**

1. Have guest complete a registration card (if information is not on computer).
2. Determine, record, and approve form of payment.
3. Ask if there are any special needs during the guest's stay.
4. Determine type of room desired and whether nonsmoking or smoking is preferred.
5. Attempt to upsell higher priced room.
6. Assign guest room.
7. Provide room key, without mentioning room number.
8. Inform guest of hotel facilities (restaurants, specials such as a seafood buffet, exercise room, etc.).
9. Provide directions to room.
10. Offer assistance with baggage.

Job Design

Job Simplification: Let reservationist handle all reservations, add PBX operator.

Job Enlargement: Clean lobby area, restock brochures, business services.

Job Rotation: Restaurant hostperson, server, reservations, night auditor.

Job Enrichment: GSA can perform all tasks related to the front desk, help with marketing tasks (sales, telemarketing, etc.).

Job Description for Guest Services Agent

Job Identification Data: Reports to: Front Desk Manager. Pay range: $7.50 to $9.00.

Job Summary: Checks guests in and out and takes care of needs associated with making their stay comfortable and productive.

Responsibilities: (from the duties and tasks above)

1. Acknowledge guests by...
2. **Check in** guest by: making sure there is a registration card completed, recording form of payment, assessing special needs, type of room desired, attempting to upsell, assigning room, providing room keys, informing guest of hotel's facilities, providing directions, and offering assistance with baggage.
3. Check out guests by ...
4. Answer phone in a friendly manner with the following...
5. Make reservations if reservationist is not available. Inquire about dates...

Job Specifications for GSA

Pleasant and outgoing personality, likes working with others, caring attitude, ability to quickly assess situations and solve problems, ability to coordinate multiple tasks, honest, ethical, physically able to stand for long periods of time, able to work with minimal supervision, and able to work quickly.

There are a couple important quotes related to duties and tasks in the job analysis that help highlight their importance. "The quality of supervision is directly related to the specifics therein" (unknown author). Too often, employees are told to do something, but not provided the details/specifics of exactly what the manager wants done. When the specifics are known and understood (both duties and tasks), then there is a much better chance that the employee can perform up to the manager's expectations. Harry H. Pope said, "Policies must be in writing, communicated, and enforced" (Pope, 1972). The written policies are the duties and tasks. They are communicated through training, and enforced through supervision/informal performance appraisals (observing employees actions and correcting behavior that does not concur with the duties and tasks), and formal/written performance appraisals and discipline.

Once the job analysis is prepared, it is then analyzed to make sure it is effective and efficient. One way to measure this is to see if a new employee can follow the information in the analysis and complete the job up to management's standards with minimal requests for help. The reason for specifying a new employee is that there should be enough information so that someone without prior knowledge can perform the duties and tasks (at least at a rudimentary level). This should be done in a role-play situation without customers. When completed, the job analysis becomes the core of the *position manual*—the manual that is used to train employees for any specific position. Managers also use the job analysis for preparing performance appraisals and in disciplining employees. Since employees are trained according to the policies/standards in the Job Analysis (in the training manual), they should also be counseled on how well their performance measures up to the standards. Employees are given raises (compensation) based on how well they perform their duties and tasks. The job analysis is also used to help determine selection strategies (i.e., applicants must be able to perform the duties and tasks before managers can consider hiring them). **Figures 5.3 and 5.4 are Job Analyses for a Server and Restaurant Manager.**

Subsequently, the duties and tasks are reviewed to see if they are appropriate for the position, termed job design. Information from the job analysis is abbreviated and used to prepare the job description. The job analysis is also used to determine the general characteristics of employees that would be suited for the position. These characteristics are referred to as the job specifications.

Quantitative Duties and Tasks

These are duties and tasks that can be objectively measured. Consequently, they also allow for an objective determination of employee performance. Other terms for quantitative are numerical and objective standards. Quantitative standards are relatively easy for management to enforce. The employee either does it or does not. To set quantitative standards for any position, list the routine tasks for the position, then decide what the minimum quantitative standard should be. There are two basic factors involved in setting quantitative standards.

1. **Time**. The time it should it take to perform a certain activity. For example, clean a guest room up to the hotel's standards in 20 minutes.

2. **Quantity**. The measurable amount of work that can be completed during a certain period of time, such as 25 items at once for the broiler cook or no customer complaints for the day.

3. **Yes/No Quantitative Duties**. Related to quantity, a common standard is that the duty or task was either completed or not completed. In quantitative terms, completed one time. For example, the front desk is organized and ready for the day's business, when answering the phone use the following script, "Thank you for calling Ed's Inn," a confirmation number is given, the hotel's cancellation policy number is given, use the guest's name at least once during the check-in process, and so forth. Each of these is a quantitative standard because it was either done (yes) or not done (no). Each was either completed or not completed.

Examples of quantitative standards that could be a part of the duties and tasks for a broiler cook might include:

• Cutting steaks for Sunday to Thursday should be completed in two hours. (Obviously, allowances would need to be made when business is especially busy or slow.)

• Each steak should be within 1/4 ounce of its specified weight.

• There should be no more than 1/4 inch of fat on a sirloin steak. (Cutting each different type of steak would be a duty.) For example, Duty—Cut ribeyes (or filets and sirloins) into steaks. The tasks for each duty would include the specific steps involved in cutting the steaks: 1. Remove fat in excess of 1/4 inch. 2. The thickness of the cut steak should be even from one cut side to the other (i.e., not 1/2" at one end and 1" at the other end). 3. Each steak should weigh 10 ounces (plus or minus 1/4 ounce). 4. Each steak should be covered in plastic wrap and placed on a sheet tray. and 5. Steaks should be rotated so that the oldest is used first.

Other examples of quantified duties or tasks:
• Stocking the salad station should take 15 minutes (duty). How it is done would be the tasks.
• From the time an order is turned in to the kitchen until it is ready for pick-up should be 12 minutes or less (duty).
• Being able to start orders when called (task). The related duty could be prepare all orders in 10 minutes or less.
• Being able to restock and clean the station for the next shift in 30 minutes or less (duty).
• Wipe the seasoning shaker with a towel that has been soaked in sanitizing solution (task). The related duty would be sanitize all kitchen surfaces.

Qualitative Duties and Tasks

The goal of setting standards is to make sure that employee actions meet or exceed customer expectations and are consistently carried out. When standards are difficult to quantify, such as an employee's courtesy, respect, personality, interpersonal skills, working toward company goals, problem-solving ability, food quality, initiative, and so forth, management should attempt to set qualitative standards. Because of the many possible interpretations of these concepts, qualitative standards are much more challenging to create and assess than quantitative standards. It is, however, important to make an attempt. Otherwise, management leaves it up to the each employee to determine the meaning of "be respectful" or "take the initiative to do things." While the management of quantitative standards is relatively easy (the employee did or did not do it), maintaining qualitative standards is often what separates excellent from average managers. The key is to know when to say something about the performance (e.g., you could have been a little friendlier or here is how I would have solved that problem).

Qualitative standards are set by specifying/defining what is expected and through constant and consistent feedback. For example, for respect for guests, the requirement could include: Each employee should: (1) establish eye contact; (2) have a friendly and considerate expression on his or her face; and (3) in a pleasant manner, ask the guests, "How can I help you?" or whatever statement may be appropriate at the time. Yes, this requirement still contains subjective elements; however, it does establish guidelines that can be trained and supported. It is also much better to have a less than perfect policy than to not have a policy and allow employees or managers to set their own personal standards.

Implementation of these standards is accomplished through reasonably extensive training, usually role modeling (e.g., identifying someone who is excellent at a certain duty or task, and using them as a role model for others to follow), related videos and role play, repeating the duty or task with other employees until the trainee's performance is up to company standards. Since personal interpretation will often play a role in the performance of qualitative duties and tasks, having strongly held positive corporate values that are consistently communicated will increase the likelihood of effective performance. Maintaining these standards is accomplished through informal performance appraisals (i.e., observation and suggestions for improvement). Qualitative standards for food can include pictures and taste parameters. For example: Chicken Stock - 1. The flavor of the chicken should override all other flavors. No one should feel that the stock has a weak or watery flavor. 2. A blend of garlic, thyme, rosemary, onion, celery, and carrots should be the next flavors recognized. 3. It is okay to taste salt, but it should not be a predominant flavor.

Qualitative standards can be made more quantitative through the use of employee or customer surveys. For example, it is generally more objective to have the comments of 10 customers relative to an employee's personality, than from one manager. Whatever is attempted, they are still moderately subjective in nature.

Advantages of Increasing the Specificity of Duties and Tasks

• Employees begin to manage their own time because they know exactly what the minimum acceptable standards are for each major task. They know that, if they do not meet the standards, their performance level is not yet adequate; if they meet the standards, their performance level is adequate, but not exemplary; and if they exceed the standards, they can be proud of themselves because they know they are doing a good job.
• Employees who exceed the higher standards are happier with their work than those who do not, become good examples for other employees, and often become the restaurant's trainers.
• By creating reasonably high standards, management learns the most efficient, effective performance level for each major task.
• Managing productivity becomes easier because the manager quickly knows when employees are or are not meeting the firm's standards.
• The new standard becomes a goal that can make work more challenging and rewarding for all concerned.

• The key advantage of increasing the specificity of duties and tasks is that customer satisfaction is improved.
• the business will often attract a new group of customers.
• In support of the concept of increasing the specificity of duties and tasks, think about what separates the employee performance of mid-scale hotels from up-scale properties. It is the standards that they are trained for and that managers uphold.

An important question related to this topic is, "How do I improve what I'm now doing?" or "How do I effectively increase the specificity of my duties and tasks?" The answer is relatively simple; first determine what the standards should be. This should be something that existing and potential customers would desire, and that could be delivered at a reasonable cost. For example, customers expect higher standards for taking care of guests at the front desk. Next, work with current employees to determine how to meet those expectations, then exactly what those standards should be—the duties and tasks, and subsequently, write them down. If there are additional time and materials involved, they should be included to help estimate additional costs over what is currently being done.

Who Performs the Job Analysis?

The job analysis is generally performed by the HR department, job incumbent (i.e., the employee in the position), the department supervisor, the manager, or a combination of these. Because of their different bases of knowledge, a combination generally works best. For example, the dishwasher (employee) would have the most knowledge of the details of washing dishes. The restaurant's manager and servers would have good input on issues related to having enough dishes and their state of cleanliness. The HR department would know more about how to record the information and prepare the actual job analysis.

Methods of Gathering Job Analysis Information

There is not one best method for gathering job analysis information. Often a combination works best as each new method uncovers different information. Options include: *interviews* with those working at the position (i.e., the incumbent); *observation*—watching the incumbent and then recording what is done, *diaries*—have the job incumbent record each duty and task as it is completed, *questionnaires* that generally go beyond recording what is done and include questions about how to make things better; and *hands-on experience*—the HR department or whomever is responsible for gathering the information performing the job, then recording the duty and task information (Woods, 2002).

Figure 5.3:   Server Job Analysis (sample)

Title: Server   **Date prepared:** May 22, 20XX
Division: Operations   **Department:** Food & Beverage
Reports to: Food and Beverage Director   **Promotion to:** Dining Room Manager

GENERAL DUTIES (each could have specific tasks added to them)

1. Check that you have the following supplies before beginning your shift: three ballpoint pens, guest checks, a server bank if servers act as their own cashiers (amount decided by the management), and sugar substitute if it is not kept on the table.
2. Treat all customers equally and with respect, regardless of race, appearance, or socioeconomic level.
3. Speak plainly and clearly so that the customer can easily understand what you are saying.
4. Maintain reasonably correct posture when walking or standing.
5. Cooperate with fellow employees by helping them.
6. Complete all opening, running (during service time), and closing sidework.
7. Be able to explain the preparation of and briefly describe all items on the menu.
8. Stay informed about which items are not available or whether the kitchen is running low on an item.
9. If there is a special being served, know what it is and be able to describe it to the customer.
10. Provide proper seating, such as a high chair or booster seat for small children. If a child is loud, ask the parent whether the child would like something, such as crackers. If the noise is irritating other customers, tell the manager.
11. Never discuss tips during open hours or within hearing distance of any customers, suppliers, or guests of the restaurant.

ORDER-TAKING (Order taking is a Duty, the Tasks (8) follow.

1. If you cannot take an order immediately, acknowledge the party by saying, "I'm your server. I'll be right with you."
2. Write the date, table number, number of covers (number of customers ordering from the table), and your name on the guest check.

3. Use the "home base" method, also known as the "pivot point," when writing down orders. The home base seat for each table will be designated so that there are no misunderstandings.

4. Suggest to customers that they order items that will make the meal more pleasurable, such as appetizers or desserts that complement their entree. These additional sales increase your income and that of the restaurant.

5. When asked for a recommendation, recommend an item that you have tried and liked.

6. Write the order neatly, using proper abbreviations and all printed, capital letters.

7. Turn orders in to the kitchen (or bar) as soon as possible. Ideally, orders should not be held for more than two or three minutes. You may take orders from two or three tables at a time, as long as you turn the orders in to the kitchen immediately.

8. Before turning an order in to the kitchen, pre-check it (ring it up) in the restaurant's cash register or computer system. The kitchen is instructed not to prepare or serve any menu items unless the guest check is rung up.

SERVING FOOD AND BEVERAGES (a duty with 9 tasks)

1. Hot food is the server's number one priority. Make sure all food is served as soon as it is ready. (If a food runner system is used, where each server delivers any orders that are ready, each server should deliver his or her share.)

2. Check the order for problems such as spills, an unappetizing appearance, or improper portions before taking the order into the dining room. When necessary, politely ask the cook to correct the order. If the cook refuses, or if the problem persists, tell the manager.

3. Make sure you have everything you need to properly serve the order before delivering it.

4. Serve foods in the proper order: appetizer, soup, salad, entree, and then dessert.

5. Hold glasses by the stem or base, never by the top or rim. Serve all bar drinks, except wine, on a bar napkin.

6. Hold silverware by the handle. No water spots should be visible.

7. Set plates down quietly. Make sure when serving that you do not touch the food.

8. At tables, try to serve customers from their left side with your left hand and remove the plates from the customer's right side with your right hand. At booths, serve customers on the left with your right hand and those on the right with your left hand. All drinks are served on the customer's right side.

9. Most customers equate good service with quick service. But if a customer wants to eat leisurely, do not rush them.

SERVICE DURING THE MEAL (a duty with 13 tasks)

1. After delivering the food, ask customers whether there is anything else they might want.

2. Return to each table approximately two minutes after serving the customers or after they have sampled their food or drinks, to make sure that the customers are satisfied. Ask such questions as "How is everything?" or, if possible, be more specific, "Is the steak cooked to your liking?" If there is a problem, solve it immediately and inform the manager.

3. You must constantly be aware of what is happening in your station so you can take care of customer's needs in an organized manner. For example, normally every table will be at a different stage of service, some waiting to have their order taken, some waiting for food, some eating, and so forth. With this information you can make better, quicker decisions about what to do next.

4. It is important to anticipate the customer's special needs, such as more bread, tea, coffee, or water, before the customer requests it.

5. Make use of every trip made to and from the kitchen or food pick-up area and dining room. This is called consolidation. For example, on the way to the kitchen remove any empty dishes from tables and check whether any customers need something from the kitchen.

6. Remain polite at all times and give good service, even when you do not expect a large tip. You will make more money if you concentrate on proper service and forget about how big your tip will be at each table.

7. Try to be within sight of the customers most of the time.

8. Keep tables as clean as possible during the meal. Remove empty plates, silverware, glasses, and other items no longer needed.

9. Wait until most people at the table are finished with their meal or have pushed their plates aside before asking whether you may remove them. Do not remove one customer's empty plate while another is still eating. Do not continually ask the customers whether they are finished.

10. Empty ashtrays that have three or more cigarette butts in them. To remove an ashtray, cover it with its replacement before lifting it from the table to prevent ashes from flying out.

11. Do not sit down with customers when in uniform.

12. Do not spend too much time with any one customer or table; others may feel neglected.

13. Even the best servers will occasionally get extremely busy "in the weeds" and become frustrated and flustered. When this happens, relax, keep smiling, and maintain your composure so your customers will not feel that something is wrong. Take everything one step at a time, concentrating on things you can control. Ask other servers or management for help as needed.

DELIVERING THE CHECK (a duty with 8 tasks)

1. Make sure the customer does not wait too long for the check. At breakfast, the check is normally delivered with the meal. For lunch and dinner, deliver the check after everyone at the table has finished their meal, their plates have been removed, and they have turned down your offer of dessert. If they are having dessert, deliver the check after the customers have finished it.

2. Make sure the guest check is complete (all items rung up) and correctly totaled. Write the total on the back in one-inch-tall numbers and circle it to avoid any misunderstandings.

3. When presenting the guest check, say "I'll take care of this for you." Watch for customer's response to see if they want to pay out immediately. If so, wait for them to provide their payment.

4. If the customer does not pay out immediately, wait about two or three minutes after presenting the guest check, then walk to see if a credit card or cash is visible in the check folder. If not, smile, but do not appear impatient. This check-back should encourage the customers to pay promptly.

5. Since you are responsible for keeping your own bank, the following change is recommended: 1 $20; 2 $10s; 2 $5s; 5 $1s; 8 quarters; 4 dimes; 6 nickels; 10 pennies.

6. If the customer pays with cash, verify at the table that the amount is appropriate (<u>do not ask if the tip is included, this is rude</u>), go to wait station, calculate the appropriate change, return it to the customer.

7. If the customer pays with a credit card, pass it through the restaurant's scanner, verify authorization, retrieve voucher/receipt, and return this to the customer for signature.

8. At the end of your shift complete the server's checkout form.

SERVER'S BAR RESPONSIBILITIES (a duty with 5 tasks)

1. Know and observe the restaurant's alcohol service policy.

A. Before serving anyone a drink, observe whether they appear intoxicated. If so, take the order, but immediately contact the manager for a second opinion as to whether the customer can be served.

B. Each time a customer orders a drink, again assess their sobriety. Be extremely careful if a person is ordering their 3rd drink.

C. If a customer appears to be intoxicated, see the manager. The manager will assess the situation, and if appropriate, politely tell the customer that we can no longer serve alcohol to them, and offer them some complimentary coffee.

D. At this point, the restaurant is responsible for making sure that the customer has a safe ride home. If there is not a designated driver accompanying the intoxicated customer, a taxi can be called at the restaurant's expense.

2. If a customer appears to be under 25 years of age, politely tell them, "If someone appears to be under 25, I need to ask to see their driver's license." A driver's license is the only acceptable proof of age. Other forms of identification may be acceptable, but only by the manager. If a customer becomes difficult, tell him or her, "I'm sorry, but it is company policy to ask for identification." Check for the following on the license:

A. Date of birth. Does it appear to have been altered?

B. Is there anything else on the license that appears to have been altered?

C. Does the photograph match the person presenting it?

D. Has the license expired?

If there is an obvious problem with the license, return it to the customer an say, "I'm sorry, but I can't accept this license." If it is questionable, tell the customer you will be right back with it, then ask the manager for approval.

3. Know abbreviations and prices for all beverages.

4. After taking a table's beverage order (any beverage order), place a napkin to the right of one of the customers silverware/place settings. This will let the host know that you have visited the table. Place all beverages, except wine, on a beverage napkin.

5. To place an order at the bar:

A. Pre-check the order in the computer terminal.

B. Call "order" to the bartender. The bartender will reply with "call" if the drink can be made immediately, or, if there will be a wait, the bartender will reply with the number of orders that are before it by saying, "four back" or whatever the number is.

C. When the "call" response if given, call the order in the following sequence: (1) frozen or ice cream drinks,

(2) mixed drinks, (3) beer and wine. After making a drink, the bartender must draw a red line through each drink noted on each guest check.

      D. If the order cannot be prepared immediately, leave the order at the bar and return in a few minutes.

Manager's Daily Duty List

This is an adaptation of the job analysis where duties are divided into the time in which they will be accomplished (**See Figure 5.4**). It also shows students the reality of the many responsibilities of a restaurant manager. A Manager's Daily Duty List for a hotel General Manager could as extensive and would depend on the number of departments and department manager. This list would accomplish the following objectives:

• It focuses owners and supervisors on what the restaurant needs and expects from management.

• It assists managers in keeping track of what they are responsible for and the primary activities of the restaurant's employees.

• It helps managers to use their time effectively. If a manager cannot complete all duties and related tasks on the list within the appropriate time frame, he or she can delegate less critical tasks to other employees. If most managers are unable to complete all duties and related tasks on the list, the list can be reduced by permanently assigning certain duties or tasks to other employees or by reducing the amount of work required of managers.

• It is an excellent training tool for new managers. A manager-in-training should refer to the list frequently each day until he or she becomes familiar with it.

      There should be a list for each shift, such as the day shift or night shift. The following is a management duty list for an average full-service restaurant. A list could be developed for a hotel or any business.

Figure 5.4:   Manager's Daily Duty List for Full-Service Restaurant

DAY SHIFT

7:30 a.m.
• Examine exterior of restaurant for possible intruders.
• Enter restaurant through the front door (ideally). Turn off alarm.
• Turn on air conditioner or heater.
• Read manager's log book.
• Make urgent telephone calls (for example, equipment problems and product shortages).
• Tour restaurant and make notes on the previous night's closing.

8:00 a.m.
• Kitchen manager (the kitchen shift leader or chef) and one cook arrive.
• Kitchen manager completes prep list and accepts deliveries. Turn on dining room lights.
• Dishwasher arrives and starts cleaning dining room and restrooms.
• Fill out employee roster and get guest checks ready.

8:30 a.m.
• Complete daily sales report if not completed during previous night's shift.
• Prepare change order, if change funds need to be replenished. Armored car service picks up deposit and leaves necessary change.
• Complete the daily labor cost sheet for the previous day.
• Third and fourth cooks arrive.
• Count reserve bank.
• Prepare register bank for the bar.
• Complete the par stock order list for all items, except for produce and meats, on Monday and Thursday. (All orders are placed one day in advance.)
• Complete the par stock order list for produce every day except Saturday.
• Complete the par stock order list for meat, poultry, and seafood on Sunday, Tuesday, and Thursday, or as needed.

9:00 a.m.
• Monitor food preparation.
• Monitor progress of dining room and restroom cleaning.

- Conduct a two- to five-minute shift meeting each Monday and
Thursday with all cooks on duty.
10:00 a.m.
- Monitor food preparation.
- Check the dining room for cleanliness.
- Check restrooms for cleanliness and supplies.
- Busser arrives, picks up trash around exterior of building, cleans front doors, and does other work assigned.
10:30 a.m.
- Make sure the cooking line is properly set up or that setup is under way.
- Bartender arrives, receives bar register bank, and gets bar ready for lunch.
- Servers arrive and begin sidework.
10:45 a.m. Quickly tour exterior of building.
- Check server sidework.
- Check the complete cooking line for food quality and proper setup.
- Taste all items that require cooking or seasoning.
- Host arrives and completes a seating floor plan for the day shift, and opening sidework.
- Turn on cash register.
- Inspect tabletops, chairs, and booth seats for cleanliness.
- Inspect table condiments to be sure that containers are full and clean.
- Make sure the bartender is ready to open.
- Issue register banks to the bartender and cashier.
10:50 a.m.
- Conduct a two- to three-minute meeting each Monday and Thursday with all servers, bussers, cashiers, and hosts on duty. These meetings can be held every day, if needed.
- Food coordinator arrives and checks supplies in the pickup area.
- Turn on music and set volume.
- Turn on dining room lights to proper level.
11:00 a.m.
- Turn on "open" sign.
- Turn on all exterior signs on cloudy or overcast days. Unlock front doors.
- Accept only important telephone calls between 11 a.m. and 1:30 p.m.
- Arrange to have messages taken for all other calls.
- Do not accept deliveries between 11 a.m. and 2 p.m. unless a particular delivery is expected.
- Monitor servers for courtesy and speed of service.
- Monitor the performance of bussers, making sure that all dirty tables are cleared and cleaned as quickly as possible.
- Monitor the kitchen area for food quality, food appearance, proper portions, and speed in preparation.
- Refill customer's water and tea; ask them how everything is or something similar.
1:30 a.m.
- Start closing server stations.
- Servers should concentrate on sidework.
- Continue to monitor all aspects of customer service and food quality.
- Start accepting server checkout sheets, referred to as server checkouts.
- Late servers (those who are last to leave on the day shift) examine the sidework of the early servers and sign their time cards denoting approval.
- Sign all employee time cards when they leave and examine their work unless it was checked by another employee, such as a dining room manager, the last server on the shift, or kitchen manager.
- Write the number of hours each employee worked on the employee roster as employees leave.
- Examine the cooks' prep work; sign their time cards as they clock out.
- Ensure that the kitchen manager completes a produce par stock list.
- Place a produce order.
- Tell host to leave when business is slow enough for servers to watch incoming customers. Let servers know that they are responsible for watching for new customers.

3:00 p.m.
• Work on non-service tasks such as paperwork, telephone calls, and ordering.
• Dishwasher cleans all dirty items, dishwashing and potwashing areas, and other assigned duties before leaving.
• Manager or kitchen manager examines dishwasher's work and signs time card denoting approval.
• Busser picks up trash around the exterior of the restaurant, cleans restrooms, and completes other assigned work before leaving.
• Examine busser's work and sign time card denoting approval.
4:00 p.m.
• Confirm that servers, cooks, busser, and bartenders have completed all assigned duties and special projects.
4:30 p.m.
• Meet with the night manager to discuss the day's business, potential night business, product quality, service, cleanliness, personnel, and any other pertinent topics.
• Finish accepting server checkouts.
• Complete bartender checkouts (cash register checkout sheet).
• Complete any day shift paperwork, get the deposit ready, and separate and total credit card (charge) vouchers.
• Record pertinent information in the manager's log book.
5:00 p.m.   End of shift.

NIGHT SHIFT
4:00 p.m.
• Night manager arrives.
• Inspect the exterior of the building before entering.
• Read manager's log book.
• Inspect the interior of the restaurant for cleanliness and make sure that all sidework and food prep is complete or is being readied for the night shift.
• Dishwasher arrives, completes the work that remains from the day shift, and prepares for the night shift.
• Bartender arrives, receives register bank, and makes sure that the bar is set up (examines all garnishes, mixes, alcoholic beverages, and miscellaneous supplies), and completes setup, as needed.
• First two night cooks arrive, begin checking the kitchen line, and complete necessary prep work.
• Meet with day manager to discuss pertinent topics.
4:30 p.m.
• First (early) night shift servers arrive and check the previous shift's sidework (early server on night shift examines entire sidework of day shift and signs late server on day shift's time card, denoting approval).
• Pickup area should be ready for the night's business.
• Host arrives and completes a seating floor plan for the night shift.
• Make sure the cooking line is properly set up or that setup is under way.
• Check the complete cooking line for food quality and proper setup.
• Taste all items that require cooking or seasoning.
5:00 p.m.
• Busser and last two cooks arrive.
• Check their respective stations.
• Conduct a one- to two-minute meeting with all cooks on duty on Monday and Thursday.
5:30 p.m.
• Next group of servers arrives.
• Set lights to proper level.
• Check music volume.
• Make sure that the dining room temperature is comfortable.
6:00 p.m.
• Last group of servers arrives.
• Conduct a two- to three-minute meeting on Monday and Thursdays with all servers, bussers, cashiers, and hosts.
• Monitor servers for courtesy and speed of service.
• Monitor the performance of bussers.
• Make sure that all dirty tables are cleared and cleaned as quickly as possible.
• Monitor kitchen area for food quality, food appearance, proper portions, and speed in preparation.

6:30p.m.
- Refill customers' water and tea; ask them how everything is or something similar.
- Second host and busser arrive on Friday and Saturday night.

7:00 p.m. to 8:30 p.m.
- Dim lights slowly as the sun goes down.
- Continue to monitor kitchen, dining room, dishroom, and other areas, as needed.
- Check bar for potential problem drinkers.

9:30 p.m.
- Start closing server stations.

10:30 p.m.
- Servers begin closing sidework.
- Start accepting server checkouts.
- Late servers sign the time cards of early servers, denoting that their sidework is completed.
- If night business is slow, let a cook who came in at 4 p.m. clock out.
- Sign all employee time cards when they leave and examine their work unless it was checked by another employee, such as a dining room manager, the last server on the shift, or kitchen manager.
- Make sure late-night customers are properly taken care of.
- Walk through the restaurant 30 minutes before closing time to check for customers who may have had too much to drink.
- Try to get all the food orders to the kitchen by closing time.
- Give a last call for food orders for late customers five minutes before closing time.

11:00 p.m.
- Close the kitchen at 11:00 p.m. Sunday through Thursday, midnight on Friday and Saturday.
- Close the bar at 11:30 p.m. Sunday through Thursday, 12:30 a.m. on Friday and Saturday.
- Give the last call for the bar 15 minutes before closing.
- Exit doors should not be locked from the inside when there are customers in the restaurant.
- Finish accepting server checkouts.
- Bartender completes cash register checkout sheet.
- Inspect all closing sidework with the last server to leave.
- All exterior doors must be locked (from the outside) and remain locked after the last customer has left.
- The manager or a designated employee should let employees out. Depending on safety concerns, management or employees should walk female employees to their vehicle.
- When the restaurant is closed, tour the restaurant to look in all places where a thief could hide.
- Inspect the closing cleanup of the cooks, bartenders, bussers, and dishwashers before they clock out.
- Sunday through Thursday at 11:30 p.m. and at 12:30 a.m. on Friday and Saturday, ask all servers to present any remaining guest checks for payment.
- After all checks have been paid, take a Z tape or total sales reading on the main cash register.
- Complete night shift paperwork, get the deposit ready, and separate and total the entire day's credit card (charge) vouchers.
- Prepare and mail American Express vouchers.
- Place all monies in the safe and lock it. Spin the dial to be sure it is locked.
- Check all areas of the restaurant to be sure that everyone is out.
- Make sure all equipment, except the refrigerators, freezers, and ice machine have been turned off (review kitchen closing checklist).
- Turn off the lights and music.
- Adjust the thermostat to the proper temperature.
- Set the alarm system.
- Do not leave the restaurant at night with a cash bag.
- As you are leaving, inspect the premises for anything unusual.
- End of shift.

Job Design

The job design focuses on determining how the work will be organized, that is, which tasks and duties should be performed for each job (De Cenzo & Robbins, 1996). Rare would be a situation where the job analysis was prepared and everything was perfect. The job design process is the same as what was used to create the job analysis, different people that have applicable knowledge of the duties and tasks or how to organize them help review the job analysis to determine what changes should be made.

Four Types of Job Design

1. Job Simplification. If there are too many duties and/or tasks for the position, then some can be assigned to other positions (e.g., fewer duties and tasks).

2. Job Enlargement. If there are too few duties and/or tasks for the position, then either additional work can be assigned or the position's hours can be reduced.

3. Job Enrichment. Attempting to make the job more interesting and productive by modifying work requirements and giving employees autonomy and responsibility for all duties and tasks in a certain area (kitchen, front desk, etc.). Many of the duties and tasks in the hospitality industry are highly repetitive. Finding ways to make these jobs more interesting is not always easy, but they must be found. Two common solutions are to set high goals that are rewarded on a daily basis (e.g., all orders from the kitchen went out within 10 minutes of receiving the order) and having the employee work at something else to break up their routine (e.g., a server could work as a bartender, the front desk agent could help with marketing).

4. Job Rotation. This is a generally considered as a separate component of job design, but it is actually a type of job enrichment. For job rotation, a requirement could be added to job description that the employee must be trained and be able to perform at different positions (job descriptions). The alternative positions for rotation are general those that require similar employee characteristics. For example, a housekeeper could be trained in the laundry room, for general cleanup around the hotel, and for other routine maintenance duties.

Job Description

The main function of the job description is to summarize all major duties of the position so that applicants (and potential applicants) will know what is expected of them. To a lesser extent it is used by management for preparing questions to ask or criteria for making hiring decisions, however the job analysis and job specifications are much more important for that purpose (Chapter Seven, Selective Hiring explains this in more detail). The specific manner in which the duties are performed (i.e., tasks) can be included, but for sake of brevity, are usually not. Rarely will a job description for an hourly position be more than one page in length. Firms without job descriptions or ones that are poorly written will rarely be operated in an effective or efficient manner. **Figures 5.5, 5.6, and 5.7 are Job Descriptions for a Hotel General Manager, Server, and Busser.**

Job Description Components

• **Job Identification Data.** Job title, department, supervisor's title, subordinates' title(s), pay range, next position for promotion, etc.

• **Job Summary.** This includes between one and a few sentences that describe the major responsibilities and objectives of the position and perhaps its relationship/interactions with other positions.

• **Job Duties/Responsibilities.** Most firms will simply transfer the duties from the job analysis to the job description. Others will include what are termed responsibilities. This is a sentence that includes the duty and its primary tasks. It is somewhat redundant from the job analysis, but the main reason for preparing responsibilities is to have a reasonably detailed description of what someone will be required to do (i.e., a bit more than the duty alone), without including the every single task involved.

• **Job Specifications.** These are the desired personal and behavioral characteristics of the applicant (covered later in this chapter). Even though it is a separate part of the job creation process, it is becoming common to include the job specification for the position in the job description. It is used as part of the interview process when management attempts to determine if an applicant has the appropriate general characteristics to perform the duties and tasks of the position they are applying for.

Job Descriptions Uses

• **Recruitment, Selection, and Orientation.** Employees will know from the job description what will be required of them. For example, potential applicants can see the job description online, prequalify themselves, and perhaps feel confident that the job should be a good fit for their skills. It also limits surprises; such as finding out they will need to perform tasks that are normally not associated with the job. When posting the job description on a firm's web site, a heading similar to the following can be used: If you have experience with the following duties, you may be qualified to apply for the position (the job description would follow). Management can use it as a tool to help choose the applicant who is most compatible with the requirements of the position.

• **Training, Performance Appraisals, and Operations Management.** Management can use job descriptions as an overview to help trainees understand what they should be learning. Since the job description is usually one page, as opposed to the multiple past job analysis, it is easier to post as a reminder for employees of what they are responsible for. Management and employees can then refer to the job descriptions whenever employee responsibilities are in question.

• **Legal.** As a requirement of the job, each employee should sign an orientation sheet stating that he or she has read, understands, and accepts the duties listed in the job description. It can also be used to show that the firm made its best attempt at hiring the most qualified applicant.

Figure 5.5:   Hotel General Manager Job Description (sample)

Title: General Manager   **Date prepared:** May 22, 20XX
Reports to: Regional Manager   **Promotion to:** Regional Manager
Pay Rate: According to Qualifications
Summary:

     The General Manager is responsible for the profitable operation of the hotel, guest satisfaction, and employee satisfaction, retention, and productivity.

Duties:

1. Monitors employee performance and corrects deviations from policies.
2. Trains and/or monitors training of new and existing employees for compliance with applicable company policies. Must be knowledgeable about the duties and tasks of each position in the hotel.
3. Regularly meets with other managers in the hotel to make sure everything is going according to current plans/policies. When things are not going according to current plans/policies, makes necessary corrections or seeks ways of improving how things are done.
4. Sets budgets for each department and monitors implementation of the budget. Performs inventories as appropriate.
5. For hotels without a sales/marketing manager. Performs duties of sales and/or marketing manager, including public relations in the city (e.g., works with Convention and Visitor's Bureau, Chamber of Commerce, United Way, etc.), sales calls (in person and via phone), and marketing research (e.g., room rate and occupancy comparisons, business and personal services, and amenities).
6. Establishes competitive room rates.
7. Works with corporate headquarters on hotel promotions.
8. Maintains the building, equipment, furniture, and fixtures with internal maintenance personnel or outside services.
9. Performs daily, weekly, and monthly sales and expenses reports. Makes sure the hotel's accountants have the appropriate information to prepare and file necessary tax forms.
10. Inspects at least five rooms per day and reports findings to executive housekeeper.
11. Except when assigned to someone else, the General Manager must be available 24 hours per day for emergencies.
12. Banks deposits must be made on a daily basis according to company policies.

Job Specification:

• Be able to lift 30 pounds
• Excellent communication skills
• Pleasant personality
• Professional demeanor/manners
• Customer service orientation
• Team leader
• Ability or address customer concerns or complaints in a friendly and satisfactory manner
• Helps other employees as needed
• Well groomed and good personal hygiene

Figure 5.6:   Server Job Description (sample)

Title: Server   **Date prepared:** May 22, 20XX
Division: Operations   **Department:** Food & Beverage
Reports to: Food and Beverage Director   **Promotion to:** Dining Room Manager
Pay Rate: Full minimum wage
Summary:
        The server is responsible for managing the customer's dining experience and ensuring that their expectations are met or exceeded.
Duties:
General
• Maintain a positive attitude while at work.
• Be ready for the shift at the appropriate time.
• Treat all customers equally and with respect, regardless of race, appearance, or socioeconomic level.
• Speak plainly and clearly so that the customer can easily understand what you are saying.
• Teamwork.
• Complete all sidework.
• Never discuss tips during open hours.
Order-taking - Take the order in the proper manner and submit it to the kitchen. Understand preparation methods and ingredients for all menu items.
Serving food and beverages - Serve in a professional manner according to the restaurant's policies.
Service during the meal - Make sure customers' meals please them and check back several times during the meal in case they need anything.
Delivering the check - Deliver the check after the customer has declined dessert or has finished dessert.
Server's bar responsibilities - Serve alcoholic beverages according to the restaurant's policies. Make sure that: no one under 21 years of age is served alcohol; no one is allowed to become drunk at our restaurant; and if someone appears impaired, management is immediately contacted—before the customer leaves the building.
Server's Job Specifications (Over the years, it has become common practice to include the job specifications with the job description):
• Be able to lift 30 pounds
• Pleasant personality
• Professional demeanor/manners
• Customer service orientation
• Understands the details of good customer service for restaurants
• Ability to multitask
• Team player
• Ability or address customer concerns or complaints in a friendly and satisfactory manner
• Unselfish and willing to help other employees as needed (teamwork)
• Well groomed and good personal hygiene

Figure 5.7:   Bus Person Job Description (sample)

Title: Bus Person   **Date prepared:** May 22, 20XX
Division: Operations   **Department:** Dining Room
Reports to: Manager on Duty   **Promotion to:** Other positions as qualified
Pay Rate: Minimum wage or higher based on skills
Summary:
        The bus person is responsible for making sure that tables are cleaned and sanitized in a professional and quiet manner, as soon as possible after customers leave.
Duties:
1. Helps create a hospitable atmosphere for our guests.
2. Continuously monitors the dining room to see when guests leave.
3. Cleans and sanitizes tables and brushes off food and visible debris from seating.
4. Promptly and properly resets tables with appropriate silverware and napkins.

5. Cleans floors in dining room and lobby areas.

6. Always has appropriate equipment and solutions ready.

7. Keeps your uniform clean and follows the appearance and dress code.

8. Assists host persons, servers, and dishwashers as needed.

9. Works quickly, efficiently, and quietly.

10. Follows appropriate sanitation and safety rules.

11. Keeps work areas neat and clean so that if customers see it, they will be impressed.

12. Checks, cleans, and stocks restrooms every 15 minutes (male to check men's restroom, female to check women's restroom). Between 1 p.m. and 5 p.m., restrooms can be checked as time allows, but at least each 30 minutes.

13. Completes assigned sidework.

14. When appropriate, thanks guests for coming in and/or says goodbye.

Bus Person's Job Specifications:

• Be able to lift 40 pounds

• Pleasant personality and outgoing

• Professional demeanor/manners

• Customer service orientation

• Anticipates needs of customers, servers, and host persons (i.e., knows what to do next)

• Reliable

• Team player

• Unselfish and willing to help other employees as needed (teamwork)

• Well groomed and good personal hygiene

Job Specifications

The job specification lists the personal qualifications or characteristics normally required to perform the job effectively. It is used in the interview process as an aid in accessing the potential success of an applicant. To create the job specifications, managers review each of the tasks in the applicable job analysis, then determine what general skills an employee should possess to accomplish it in an effective manner. For example, a cook should have a high level of manual dexterity; a server should have an outgoing personality; and so forth. **Figures 5.9 and 5.10 are Job Specifications for a manager and for an entry-level hourly employee** (e.g., busser, dishwasher, housekeeper, grounds maintenance, host person, counter help in quick-service restaurant, etc.). Each is by necessity general, but comprehensive enough to be modified for any hospitality firm's use.

Figure 5.8: Typical Job Specification Categories shows the two job specifications categories, personal characteristics and behavioral characteristics, along with examples of each.

Figure 5.8:   Typical Job Specification Categories

Personal Characteristics

1. Education

2. Experience

3. Legal right to work in United States

4. Physical ability/stamina

5. Age (minimum age in the state to deal with alcoholic beverages)

Behavioral Characteristics

6. Positive attitude/enthusiasm/conscientiousness

7. Ethics/honesty

8. Neat appearance/hygiene

9. Written communication skills

10. Oral communication skills

11. Respect for others

12. Responsible/reliable/conscientious

13. Personality/interpersonal skills/friendliness

14. Love of service/passion for service

15. Intelligence

16. Productivity

17. Manual dexterity

18. Willingness to learn

19. Internal/self-motivation/pride in personal performance

20. Potential for accepting external motivation

21. Willingness to work toward company goals

22. Teamwork/cooperation	23. Creativity
24. Math reasoning	25. Decision-making/problem-solving skills
26. Analytical ability	27. Ability to follow directions
28. Memory	29. Loyalty to the firm
30. Composure under pressure	31. Accomplishment of goals
32. Ability to delegate (for managers)	33. Ability to motivate (for managers)

Figure 5.9:   Sample Job Specification for Management
(with explanations and justifications)

• **Age**. Ability is more critical than a minimum age. There is no upper age. Under normal circumstances, the minimum age for a manager should be 18 years. If you serve alcohol, the age requirement should be the minimum serving age for your area.

• **Education**. A college degree is preferred, though with excellent work experience, a high school diploma can be considered.

• **Job knowledge/experience**. The prospective manager should either have managerial experience or be willing to complete an in-house training program, which includes a reasonable amount of time spent working at designated positions.

• **Physical requirements**. Be able to stand and work for long periods without noticeable fatigue.

• **Mental requirements**. Have average or better than average intelligence and the ability to quickly respond to questions and to solve business-related problems. Applicants must be able to complete the necessary paperwork and withstand stressful situations, accepting them as the challenge of the job.

• **Planning and goal achievement**. Be able to accurately assess situations inside and outside the business and develop objectives, strategies, and tactics that help the firm maximize those situations.

• **Communication skills**. Be able to write and talk so that others will understand exactly what is being communicated.

• **Interpersonal skills**. Be able to comfortably converse in an intelligent and respectful manner with people of all socioeconomic levels and ethnic backgrounds.

• **Delegation**. Employees should know what they are responsible for, how to perform each duty, and when they are supposed to perform it. Managers should be able to focus on the overall operation of the unit, rather than doing work that employees should be doing.

• **Maximization of employee effort**. The encouragement of new ideas and risk-taking, teamwork, the use of tactful discipline, and knowing the appropriate balance between encouragement and pressure.

• **Time management**. Have a time management system and be able to set priorities.

• **General character/attitude**. Have a pleasant personality, display enthusiasm toward work, and demonstrate a willingness to cooperate.

• **Neat appearance**. Managers must be well groomed.

• **Goals**. The prospective manager must understand the goals of the business and be enthusiastic about supporting them. The primary goals are customer satisfaction, employee satisfaction, being recognized as a competitive player in our market, and achieving a reasonable long-term profit.

Figure 5.10:   Sample Job Specifications for Hourly Employees
(with explanations and justifications)

• **Age**. Hiring children 13 years of age or under is not permissible by the U.S. Department of Labor. (There are some exceptions for children who work for parents or guardians.) Hiring 14- and 15-year-olds is permissible by federal law, although legal limitations may interfere with the normal operation of the business. Fourteen- and fifteen-year-olds can only be employed in certain occupations, under conditions that do not interfere with their schooling, health, or well-being. They may not be employed

      a. during school hours, except as provided for in work experience
          and career exploration programs;

      b. before 7 a.m. or after 7 p.m., except from June 1 through Labor Day, when they may be employed up to
          9 p.m.;

      c. more than three hours a day on school days;

d. more than 18 hours a week when school is in session;

e. more than eight hours a day on nonschool days; and

f. more than 40 hours a week when school is not in session.

Under most circumstances, 16 years of age should be the minimum age requirement. The major limitation for 16- and 17-year-olds is that they cannot serve alcohol or use a commercial mixer or other potentially dangerous mechanical equipment. Additional or updated information about child labor laws may be obtained from the Wage and Hour Division of the U.S. Department of Labor.

• **Education.** It is best not to require any specific level of education for hourly employees. Applicants' educational level may or may not be related to their ability.

• **Job knowledge.** No previous experience is necessary for most positions. Experienced employees may be required for new hotel or restaurants or when certain skills cannot be developed within a short training period. Previous experience may be a plus when a decision must be made between two applicants who are equal in all other areas. The employee with no previous experience is occasionally easier to train because he or she has no old work habits to deal with from previous jobs.

• **Physical requirements.** The prospective employee should be able to work for long periods without noticeable fatigue.

• **Mental requirements.** The prospective employee should have average intelligence and attention span, and the ability to quickly respond to questions and requests.

• **General character/attitude.** The prospective employee should have a pleasant personality, have a good attitude toward work, and be willing to cooperate. These characteristics are most important for employees who have contact with customers.

• **Personal appearance.** All employees must be well groomed.

Work-Flow

Ideally, everything in the business was laid out in an effective manner when the building was built. However, since things change over time, furniture and equipment needs to be moved or new pieces must be sought to accommodate the changes. The four basic concepts in work design are *layout, work centers, work sections,* and *workflow analysis.* The redesign of business processes to increase efficiency (lower costs relative to sales, increase speed) and effectiveness (quality of goods and services) is generally referred to as *business process re-engineering.* While an architect or a professional designer will usually head a design team, it should rely heavily on input from those with extensive operational experience. Countless restaurants and some hotels are designed in such a way to make operating the business quite difficult. One restaurant was designed so that the dining room was over 100 feet from the kitchen, requiring a 200-foot walk by the server each time a customer needed something from the kitchen. The result was fatigued servers, slow service, high employee turnover, and only servers that could not get a job at better restaurant would work there.

Layout

This is the logical placement of all major activities in a way that allows employees to work at maximum efficiency. Traditionally, the theory has been that the layout should be based on the development of the *work centers* and *work stations.*

Work Centers

The *work center* is the smallest group of closely related tasks that are normally performed by one person. The primary goal of a work center is to reduce the time and number of steps an employee must take to complete his or her normally assigned duties and tasks. The ideal length is about four feet, but can be up to six feet if more work area, equipment, or supplies are required. All equipment needed in a work center should be within reach and there should generally be minimal space between related work centers.

Work Sections

Work sections are a group of related work centers where one type of production or activity occurs. Examples include the front desk area, human resources office, kitchen, wait-stations, the bartender's work area, and dining room.

Workflow Analysis

This is the examination of how work moves through the organization. The basic concept is to make sure the work flows smoothly, in the smallest reasonable space and time possible, and does not interfere with the work of other employees in the same or different work sections.

The following are typical standards for efficient workflow:

• **Sequence.** The work should proceed in sequence, with as little backtracking or wasted movement as possible.

• **Shortest Distance**. People, goods and services, and information should move the shortest possible distance and as quickly as possible to reduce labor cost, employee fatigue, and time.

• **Shortest Time**. Customer service times should be the shortest time attainable, compatible with the concept.

• **Maximize Floor Space**. Floor space should be used efficiently and economically.

The following is a very brief sample of a workflow analysis for a server:

• Customer places order with server;

• Order is forwarded to the kitchen;

• Order is received in the kitchen and cooks begin preparing the food;

• The cooks plate the food;

• The food order is assembled for the server and the server is notified;

• The server places the food order on a tray and takes it to the customers that ordered it;

• The server places the food ordered in front of the customer that ordered it;

• The server monitors the meal for the customers to make sure they are having a good experience;

• The server removes empty plates and clears any other unnecessary items from the table;

• When the customers are finished with their meals, the server offers dessert; if declined, the bill is delivered and the customers are thanked for dining at the restaurant;

• The server waits for the customer to leave before picking up the bill.

Case Study 5.1: Management Problems at the Mount Aspen Resort

Because of the many problems of past GMs at the Resort, you have been asked to spend some time there to straighten things out. One of the areas that appear to have been neglected is the preparation of adequate job descriptions, especially for the GM's position.

The Resort has 350 rooms and is located on the side of a mountain just outside Aspen, Colorado. The hotel has meeting facilities, spa, tennis courts, racquetball, a golf course, and an indoor swimming pool. The corporate rate is $385 per night, suites are $575. The Resort is positioned in the luxury market (Ritz Carlton, Four Seasons, etc.).

Required:

1. Prepare a new job description for the GM's position for the Resort. It should be comprehensive enough to assure that the GM knows what his or her duties are. That is, if they take care of the duties included, the Resort will be operated successfully. You do not need to include tasks with the duties.

2. The job description must include the job specifications for the GM.

3. If requested by your instructor, include tasks for the duties that you listed.

_____

_____

_____

_____

_____

_____

_____

_____

_____

_____

_____

_____

Case Study 5.2: Duties and Tasks—Be Specific

Select any position in the hospitality industry (or one will be assigned to you by your instructor). Select two duties for that position, and then create a detailed task list for each duty. Read over your tasks. Is every reasonable thing a person would do (the tasks) to complete the associated duty on your list? Remember, if either something is not included or the manner in which management wants it done is not specified, it will likely not get done. Present the duties and tasks to the rest of the class and the instructor for their opinions.

Case Study 5.3: Poor Service at the Abby Rose Hotel

The Abby Rose Hotel, a large resort hotel with spa, tennis, golf, swimming pool, hiking, and five restaurants has been receiving complaints from its guests about the general lack of knowledge and service orientation on the part of employees. More specifically, when guests ask for help with something that is not generally part of an employee's regular job description, the employees are not particularly knowledgeable or helpful (e.g., 1. Needs from other departments, e.g., how housekeeping, maintenance and bell staff work with the front desk; 2. Dealing with anything that is not currently in the employee's job description—"It's not my job!" and 3. Directions to local attractions, restaurants, shopping, business districts, etc., etc.). Several frequent guests have said that they would not come back to the hotel. The General Manager has discussed this problem at employee meetings, telling employees how important it is and that those who do not treat guests properly will be disciplined. Most employees are very concerned about doing a good job, but there has been no training in this area and the job descriptions for each position only mention the fact that a service orientation toward guests is important. There is no job analysis or effective training manual for any position.

Required: (Your instructor may give you or your group one or more of the following assignments and specify the problem to solve and the position.)

1. Prepare one duty and its related tasks that employees can follow to solve the problem of not being helpful with duties/tasks that are not part of their job description and one duty and its related tasks for the problem of lack of knowledge in the case study. The tasks will be evaluated based on their potential for solving the problem and their thoroughness. Your instructor may assign two or more duties for this requirement.

Positions: 1. Guest service agents, 2. Bellperson, 3. Housekeepers, 4. Maintenance workers, 5. Room service server.

2. One of the GMs has said that service orientation is an attitude and it was not necessary to write it down in any specific manner. What do you think of this?

3. Select what you feel is the most important duty for your position, then prepare the tasks for that duty.

Chapter Six: Recruitment

Strategy Review: Prepare a strategy review for this chapter (See back of Chapter One).
Case Study 6.1: Recruitment Planning
Case Study 6.2: Recruitment Efforts for Potential Employers
Case Study 6.3: Creating a Schedule for the Front Desk
Chapter Objectives: After reading this chapter you should understand and be able to do the following:

1. List the challenges that face hospitality firms in recruiting employees.
2. Explain the term, applicant pool, and its importance for human resource managers.
3. Describe the criteria for recruits.
4. Define turnover costs.
5. Discuss the importance of turnover to your career and the success of hospitality firms.
6. List the typical causes of turnover.
7. Describe how to calculate the turnover percentage.
8. Explain the importance of the situational analysis to recruitment.
9. List sources of recruits.
10. List the best source(s) of recruits.
11. Know where to place recruitment ads.
12. List the pros and cons of recruiting from internal and external sources.
13. Discuss traits of a good recruiter.
14. Create an employee schedule (to know how many employees must be recruited).

Recruitment

Recruiting is the process of attracting and screening of qualified applicants for employment. Because the hospitality industry has such a high turnover rate—the rate at which employees leave any particular business, managers must constantly be aware of sources for applicants. They must also have an *applicant pool*—a pool of hirable applicants on file that can fill positions as they arise. Excellent firms have large pools of highly qualified applicants. Lesser firms rarely have qualified people that want to work for them, so unfortunately they need to settle for less qualified applicants—the best of the worst. The level of effort for recruitment is directly tied to the level of turnover for the business. With minimal turnover, the business has minimal needs for recruitment. The vast majority of recruitment for hourly employees of hospitality firms is done in-house, that is by managers of the restaurant or by the Human Resource department in the hotel. Recruitment for entry-level management positions is mostly done in-house or through internal promotions, while recruitment for experienced managers may be done in0-house, through internal promotions or through various types of agencies or organizations that specialize in recruiting. The most common are general employment agencies that recruit for most types of businesses. There are also niche agencies that focus specifically on restaurants or hotels or the overall hospitality industry. Headhunters, specialists that focus on finding highly qualified managers, often within a particular industry, may work for any type of employment agency. The goal is to find a source, such as other employees, a university, high school, trade or culinary school, and other potential sources that supply the firm with employees to replace those that are lost and to provide for expansion.

The *criteria for recruits*—the basis for qualifying applicants for any specific position were developed in the job creation process. The firm needs to hire employees that can perform the duties and tasks in the job analysis and have the general characteristics listed in the job specifications for the position (See Chapter Seven: Selective Hiring for this process). For purposes of recruiting, the general rule is that they should ideally meet the requirements in the job specifications and ideally have some experience at the position for which they are applying, or be able to demonstrate the ability to perform critical duties and tasks for the position.

Turnover

Turnover is the number one issue related to recruitment for the hospitality industry, and one of the most important overall issues of concern for hospitality managers. A key objective of management is to do whatever is reasonably necessary to keep turnover at a reasonable minimum (Kuo & Ho, 2010). This is generally accomplished through quality recruitment and hiring processes and by making sure that morale is high. Low turnover is correlated with high satisfaction for employees, customers, and managers. Experienced employees—those with longer tenure, have fewer work-related problems and are better prepared to deal with the difficult situations that come up in the industry. Experienced employees who are happy, productive and experienced will generally provide quality service to customers, certainly better than disgruntled employees that are thinking about leaving or are ready to leave (Kintoghiorghes & Frangou, 2009). Managers of businesses with low turnover can focus on ways of improving the business, rather than dealing with problems caused by new employees that have not been fully trained. It is human nature to see the grass as being greener on the other side of the fence, so management must do what it can to minimize employees' desires to give other firms a try.

Costs of High Turnover

The costs of high turnover are considerable. The most critical is that customer satisfaction suffers when quality experienced employees leave and are replaced with inexperienced employees. Imagine the difference between managing a business where the average employee has been there for five years and everything runs to perfection versus a business where the average tenure is nine months and the manager is continually focused on finding and training replacements and dealing with customer complaints. The following is a brief list of typical turnover costs: recruitment costs, recruitment time, interviews, background checks, orientations, paperwork (insurance forms, payroll, etc.), training, uniforms, low morale and productivity of departing employees, mistakes and waste, increased supervision, disruption of teamwork (e.g., the negative impact of the departing employee on other employees), loss of competitive information (e.g., a manager goes to work for a competitor and takes all the knowledge that was learned over several years, and customer complaints (from both the departing employee and the newly hired, but not fully trained replacement) (Somaya & Williamson, 2008).

Calculating Turnover Percentage

To calculate the turnover percentage, divide 12 (months) by the average tenure of employees in months, then multiply by 100. For example, 12 divided by 6 = 2; 2 times 100 = 200%. The average turnover for hourly employees in the hospitality industry for both hotels and restaurants is about 100%, meaning the average time hospitality employees spend at a job is 12 months (12/12 months = 1; 1 times 100 = 100%). A common and viable objective for progressive hospitality firms is to lower their turnover percentage to 50% (12/24 = .5; .5 times 100 = 50%). The average tenure for hospitality managers is 48 months, so the turnover percentage is 25% (12/48 = .25; .25 times 100 - 25%). The turnover percentage can also similarly be calculated for departments, positions, and voluntary (left on their own) versus involuntary terminations (fired).

Causes of High Turnover

The following are some of the most common causes of high turnover.

• **Pay**. Hourly pay in most segments of the hospitality industry is relatively low. However, they are entry-level jobs that serve as many individuals' first job. This allows them to get valuable experience that will form the basis for their work habits and future success. While pay at hospitality segments with minimal service (e.g., quick-service restaurants and budget hotels) is generally low, pay at segments with greater levels of service is usually higher. Servers at some fine-dining restaurants in larger cities can make in the $100,000 range per year. Pay for managers for the different segments mirrors the stratification for employees—less service, lower pay, more service, higher pay. The difference is that managerial pay in the hospitality industry has increased significantly with the proliferation of competition. Graduates from university hospitality programs routinely start between $32,000 and $45,000 per year and even in recessionary time, the number seems to be going up. As they get more experience and prove themselves, they can double to triple their pay in about five years. The average pay for casual dining restaurant general managers (GM) is around $90,000, while full-service hotel general managers can make up to $150,000 per year and more. The average time to become a restaurant GM is five to six years. For full-service hotels, the time is eight to ten years, however, those with excellent skills can do so in less time. Employees who move up to corporate headquarters can make significantly more, depending on the size and type of business and their position.

• **Reputation as Temporary Job—Lack of Career Path**. Because many of the jobs in the hospitality industry are entry-level positions, there is no way to get around the fact that most hourly jobs in the industry *are* temporary jobs. Most of our employees have other priorities such as high school, college, just doing something that is fun while they finding out what they want to do in life. The argument against our industry as a place for temporary employment is two-fold. First, if someone wants to stay with a particular business or the industry in general, there are no limits to their potential success. Countless success stories have been written about a kids that started at a restaurant as a dishwasher and who ended up being President or a front desk agent with a hotel chain who worked her way to a Vice President of Operations post. The second challenge to the temporary reputation is that any individual hospitality business can decrease its turnover percentage by taking better care of its employees. A busser does not leave one restaurant to become the manager at another. He or she leaves to take a busser's position at another restaurant because of lack of appreciation or respect, better schedules, more fun, and so forth. If morale is high, turnover is low.

• **Lack of Respect**. Some years back, very few hospitality managers had college degrees, were well trained, or had a decent salary. All of this has changed. Both the National Restaurant Association and the American Hotel and Lodging Association have worked hard to improve the image of our industry—and they, along with the many restaurants and hotels have succeeded.

• **Unrealistic Job Previews/Information**. Every job has both good and bad points. When the recruiter or manager only informs the applicant about positive aspects of the job, the applicant may develop an unrealistic opinion of the position they are interviewing for. The name for this is an *unrealistic job preview* or the converse, *realistic job preview (RJP)*. When this occurs, the new employees will often quit after the shock of finding out how different reality is from their expectations. It also makes the job of management more difficult, because new employees may feel the manager is to blame. If the recruiter was honest in their presentation of what working at the firm is like, new employees would be more likely to stay because they know what to expect. For many management positions, there may be a formal job preview where the potential new managers are introduced to various unit and corporate managers with the firm, given tours of the business, provided information about the culture and history of the firm and either dine at the firm's restaurant(s) or stay at their hotels (i.e., experience the firm's products and services).

• **Schedules**. Hospitality schedules generally work out nicely for most hourly employees. They go to school during the day and need someplace to work in the evening and on weekends. If they are full-time, they can work virtually anytime they want. For managers, first the bad news—hospitality managers often work when others are not working, such as nights, weekends and holidays. However, things are changing. Successful businesses are either hiring an extra manager to allow for more time off for each manager, or are having experienced employees handle a slow shift to give managers a bit more freedom with their scheduling. Several decades ago many hospitality managers worked about 65 hours per week. Because of the concern for managers' quality-of-life and effectiveness on the job, most hospitality firms today rarely have managers work over 50 hours per week.

• **Quality of Supervision and Overall Working Environment**. This is an area that has probably experience the most change. Thirty years ago and before, it was not very common to find college graduates beginning their careers in the hospitality industry, especially in restaurants. Today, there are over 200 university and over 400 community college hospitality programs graduating many thousands of well-educated and capable future managers each year. This fact has significantly increased the professionalism with which hospitality firms are operated. Related to this is the fact that competition has increased to the point that the weaker organizations, those that are not run professionally, will at some point fail. Along with this increased professionalism has come a significantly better working environment—everything from the physical facilities to treatment of employees, pay and benefits. Today, many hourly employees enjoy benefits, such as stock options and health insurance that few managers received in the past. Employees that are asked to do excellent work without excellent supervision, training and equipment will quickly begin thinking about other places to work.

• **Training**. Employees that are not properly trained do not perform well. Employees that do not perform well are disciplined and subsequently, get very upset if they are being disciplined because of a shortcoming of the manager or the business. In one study, multi-unit managers said that their greatest desires were for more training in human resources management, employee development, and leadership skills (Murphy, Dipietro, Rivera, & Muller, 2009).

Recruitment Planning Decisions
Situational Analysis

The situational analysis (i.e., internal and environmental analyses) should be reviewed for factors that impact potential employees' decisions to apply for various positions with the company. Managers will have varying degrees of control over factors that impact the firm's ability to recruit the best employees, so they should focus on areas that will produce the best results (see **Figure 6.1: Recruitment and Control Over Situational Factors**). For the internal analysis, manager should ask questions such as:

• How does your staff describe you?

• What do they like/dislike about working for you?

• Do they have opportunities to better themselves (personally and professionally)?

• What do you offer by way of perks, benefits, good locations, and work/life balance?

• How flexible are you? Have you considered part-time, custom schedules, job sharing, and other new ways of working?

• How can you be more welcoming to underrepresented groups, such as older workers, those with a disability, women, minorities, etc.?

Employer-of-Choice. The overall goal for firms regarding employees is be known as the *Employer-of-Choice*—being the first employer quality applicants think of when looking for work. The advantage these firms have include: (1) the best applicant apply at these businesses; (2) very low turnover relative to similar firms; (3) minimal hiring needs because of the low turnover; (4) there is very little need to advertise for positions that need to be filled (5) higher employee satisfaction/morale; (6) higher customer satisfaction, sales, and profit; (7) when employees need to leave they give advanced notice; and (8) current quality employees recommend quality applicants.

For the environmental analysis, the most important factors to consider are: expectations of potential applicants, potential applicants' overall image of the business, and the availability and quality of applicants in the area (see Human Resources Planning Guidelines). Other important environmental factors to consider are the competition and the economy. Management should know as much as possible about each primary competitor's HR activities, such as their pay and pay range for each position, employee morale, training programs, reputation as good place to work, and so forth. Where the marketing department is competing for customers with other businesses, HR is competing for employees with other businesses, especially other similar hospitality firms. When the economy is good, most people that want jobs have them, so it may be difficult to hire employees. Good employees may need to be attracted from competing firms by offering better pay. When the economy is bad, there are plenty of employees looking for work. The problem is that they may only stay until the economy is good again, when they can go back to what they were doing before the downturn.

Figure 6.1:   Recruitment and Control over Situational Factors

Situational factors that management *generally does not* have control over:
• Physical working environment: layout of business, heating, air-conditioning, etc.
• Benefits: insurance, bonuses, pensions, etc.
• Pay: outside of a designated range. (Part of a manager's pay may be based on controlling labor cost—having the lowest reasonable wage.)
• Local employment characteristics: (a) Number of employees available; (b) Competition; (c) Seasonality; (d) Quality of applicants
• Actions of managers higher in the chain of command
• Past reputation for being a good or bad place to work

Situational factors that management *generally does* have control over:
• Hiring/selection decisions
• Quality of supervision
• Job security
• Physical working conditions (cleanliness, maintaining equipment, purchasing necessary low-cost equipment)
• Incentives that are relatively low in cost, such as free meals or other services of the firm, a day off with pay, etc.
• Interpersonal working conditions
• Training, personal growth, and development
• Having a personal concern for employees
• Listening to employees concerns (job and non-job related)
• Showing appreciation
• Participative decision-making
• Delegation
• Empowerment

Sources of Recruits

The sources given here are by no means all-inclusive. Ingenuity is necessary and an acknowledgment that the business is competing with other hospitality firms for both customers and employees. Another key overall focus should be on recruiting for diversity. Looking for employees from all demographic groups not only increases the potential number of recruitable employees, is the right thing to do from an ethical perspective, and for the firm's growth and advantage over competitors (Staff, 2005).

Walk-ins

Usually most of the applicants, especially for new businesses, will come from walk-ins. Review their applications thoroughly and try to have at least an initial talk with them when they pick up or turn in the application. This is because there is no prior knowledge of their abilities or character and many walk-ins are *job hoppers* (employees who do not stay very long at any one job). On the positive side, these applicants have taken the initiative to come in and apply.

Employee Referrals

Historically, this is the best source for new employees and certainly one of the least expensive. The employee has probably told the applicant, a friend, that the hotel or restaurant is a good place to work and there may be a feeling of responsibility on the part of the new employee toward their friend to do a good job. The higher the morale and the better the working conditions, the more likely excellent employees will recommend the business to excellent applicants. Recruiting bonuses can be offered to employees who bring in applicants who are hired and perform exemplary for a minimum of three or more months.

Managers should be careful not hire too many friends for the same shift because they may encourage a lackadaisical attitude toward work, encourage horseplay, and other activities that decrease production. On the other hand, young employees like to work with their friends and have fun. If management can simply make sure all employees uphold the standards of the business in an atmosphere where the two can successfully coexist, both the employees and the business should benefit.

Internal or External Promotions/Recruitment

As management and supervisory jobs come open that require more than basic skills, the first source to fill them should be from inside the firm. If no one inside the firm is capable, then outside recruitment efforts can be commenced. Historically, it is better to hire someone from within for two main reasons. First, the current employee knows more about the business than someone from outside the business and second, hiring from within raises morale. Employees realize that loyalty toward the business is rewarded. For this reason, it is generally better to have an existing employee take on a management position that is slightly less skilled than a potential applicant. If management feels the skill difference is too great, then the outside applicant should probably be hired (**see Figure 6.2: Advantages and Disadvantages of Promoting or Recruiting Internally or Externally**).

Figure 6.2:   Advantages and Disadvantages of Promoting/Recruiting Internally or Externally

Pros and Cons of Internal Recruiting

Advantages
- Improves morale of promoted employee
- Can improve morale of staff (those who see it as an opportunity for themselves)
- Costs less than hiring from outside
- Lowers training time and cost

Disadvantages
- May lower morale of employee not promoted
- Managing former peers may be challenging
- Fewer new ideas
- May be viewed as political—promote friends

Pros and Cons of External Recruiting

Advantages
- New ideas
- Forces HR to examine competitors' employees
- Already trained/experienced
- May show others that you're expanding

Disadvantages
- May show others you have a high turnover
- Morale suffers if current employee is passed over
- It may take time for the new employee/manager to understand and adopt the firm's culture

Recruitment Ads

Ads must be legal according to EEOC laws. That is, nondiscriminatory (e.g., non-gender or age specific, not racially biased, etc.). They should also be placed in media that is cost effective (see options below).

• **Newspapers**. Though newspaper circulation is down, it is still an important consideration for recruitment in most cities. Running ads in newspapers can be very expensive. This is especially true for small businesses that are considering advertising in major newspapers in large cities. For example, if the city has a population of over 1 million and is spread out over 300 or so square miles, the small business with most employees living within four miles will be spending the majority of its recruitment dollar on potential employees who live too far away to consider applying. Employees who need work badly may take a job that is too far from where they live, then quit after a few weeks because they get tired of the commute or they found a job closer to home. Ideally, other sources should be exhausted first. But if newspapers must be used, include the following information in the ad: the name of the business, the address, the positions available, time to apply, and who to ask for. A telephone number may tie up the business's phone lines. Hospitality firms with hiring problems may need to keep a small ad running continuously. Smaller neighborhood newspapers can provide a less expensive alternative. They are also generally more effective, because potential candidates will come from the local area.

• **Magazines**. Industry magazines and trade journals, such as those focused on the hotel or restaurant industry, generally have advertisement sections in the back where firms advertise for management positions (Raub & Streit, 2006). This is often a good source for management jobs because these firms have the money to insert the ad and have put much thought into the production and placement costs of the ad.

• **Internet**. Initially, the Internet was primarily used to attract and hire managerial candidates. Today, as computer use increases, it is also being used for hourly employees. Virtually every business has a web site, so simply adding an employment section where potential employees can complete an application, is relatively simple. Another advantage of recruiting from the firm's web site is that current employees can see new openings and opportunities as they arise (Millar, 2010). Privately run web sites, such as Careerbuilder, Hospitality Online and Hcareers are becoming popular with both hospitality firms for recruiting and with potential employees that are looking for jobs.

Schools

Many excellent employees have been hired through high school work-study programs. When the student employee is given a grade, he or she has a greater incentive to do a good job. Call a few local high schools and ask for the counselor in charge of the work-study program. The counselor will request information about the job openings and the business. Many local junior colleges, four-year colleges, and universities have employment offices geared toward finding part-time work for students.

Internships

Most large hospitality firms have internship programs where college students work in various positions with a firm and get introduced to life in management with the firm. If the intern is later hired, he or she may start work as a manager, since the management training program may have already been completed.

State and Federal Employment Agencies

Governmental sources can occasionally be helpful. Screen all employees to make sure they are not drifters or have any type of problem that could interfere with job performance.

Private Employment Agencies

In hospitality these agencies are generally used for managerial positions only. The downside is their cost, normally between 10% and 20% or more of the new employee's or manager's first year salary. The upside is that these employment counselors may have excellent contacts. Some of these agencies will use aggressive tactics, such as directly calling managers of businesses to see if they are interested in a new opportunity. The term for recruiters that utilize this tactic is *headhunter*. A new segment of private employment agencies are those that specialize in temporary positions in the hospitality industry (e.g., if the business is short one cook, the agency will send out a cook). The problem with this concept is that the business may be better off with fewer knowledgeable employees, than with an extra employee who does not know what to do.

State Vocational and Rehabilitation Agencies

These agencies will supply information on disabled people who are able to fill certain positions in a business. Additional screening may be necessary to ensure that these employees can function in the available positions. The benefit to hiring the disabled is that they are often very loyal to employers, have a positive attitude toward their work, and generally perform their duties and tasks well above company standards. Also, there may be state or federal sponsorship in the form of tax credits or direct payments during a training period.

The Elderly

There are generally retired or older people in every neighborhood that can qualify for certain positions. Their maturity and experience can be a positive influence on younger employees. These employees should be properly trained and treated like all other employees. Consider including "senior citizens welcomed to apply," when advertising for employees. Though employment ads cannot show preference for most groups, specifying disadvantaged groups is generally not a problem.

Homemakers

Many hospitality businesses need employees for part-time work (e.g., during lunch). Neighborhood homemakers, women and men, may be a viable source for these positions. An ad could read "Homemakers—Spare cash for your spare time."

Help Wanted Signs

Use these signs only as a *last resort* as they communicate to customers that the business is having problems hiring and retaining employees, and that product or service quality may be less than ideal. Relative to its impact on the business's image, help wanted signs are similar to the "Under New Management" signs that used to be quite common 40 or so years ago. On the positive side, potential applicants in the area will see these signs. New businesses can successfully use a *now interviewing* sign without hurting their image.

Competitive Surveillance Recruiting

In relation to recruiting, this is finding employees at their current business. When shopping, staying in hotels or eating in other restaurants, keep an eye out for people who would make good employees for one's firm. If they are dissatisfied with their present employer for a legitimate reason, or are being underutilized, it may be a good opportunity for them. Use caution and good judgment when talking to a prospective employee at his or her place of work. A simple compliment and letting the employee know that you are the manager/owner of a certain business is usually enough. Leaving a business card that could end up in the hands of the manager-on-duty may prove embarrassing and unethical.

Selecting Recruiters

Large chain hotels and restaurants will generally have one or more full-time recruiters, while smaller chains and individual properties will have various employees, some in HR, some not, help out with recruiting efforts. Since the recruiter may be the only person potential applicants have contact with from the firm, their ability to project a positive image of themselves and the firm is critical. Honesty is critical. Too often recruiters will make the job seem better than it really is, discussing only the great things about it, leaving out the part about cleaning toilets and grease traps.

      The typical characteristics of a good recruiter include: ability to make potential applicants feel comfortable, enthusiasm for the firm and the industry, loyalty toward the firm, good communication skills, knowledge of the various positions, patience with applicants who do not know how everything is done (reasonable expectations of those being interviewed), honest/ethical, and the ability to make preliminary judgments of an applicant's potential. Recruiters without these characteristics will find it difficult to represent the firm effectively and perhaps tarnish its image with potential employees.

Evaluation of Recruiting Methods (Control)

Like any form of control for business, management should continue what works, discontinue or modify what does not, and always search for new methods. Professionally run businesses that are geared toward satisfying both customers and employees will generally have lower turnover and therefore, less need for recruitment. While everything a business does must be monitored, doing things right minimizes the amount of time spent on controlling outcomes.

Creating an Employee Schedule

An important step in recruitment is the calculation of the number of employees required for any specific level of sales. This process is used for businesses preparing to open and for existing businesses. The goal of effective scheduling is to have the lowest number of employee labor hours that still allow the business to serve customers without compromising its standards. Basically, the goal is to strike a balance between keeping labor costs as low as possible and keeping the business functioning properly. Use caution when reducing labor hours or lowering labor cost. A 15% labor cost means nothing if service and product quality are low and customer counts are dropping. Experience with the business is the only true guide management has in figuring out its most efficient schedule.

The first step in developing an effective schedule is to decide on the appropriate (i.e., lowest optimum) number of employees, labor hours, and labor dollars possible for any given level of sales. Since hourly employees are paid 1.5 times their regular rate for overtime (i.e., more than 40 hours per week), limit scheduled and actual hours worked to no more than 40 hours per employee per week. During the first few weeks after opening a new business, it is excusable to be slightly overstaffed because the business must make a positive first impression on customers and there is no way to know exactly how employees will perform or what the sales volume will be. Scheduling too many employees after the first few weeks is wasting money. A form such as **Figure 6.3: Joseph's Bistro Monthly Projected Labor Cost** can be used to establish pre-opening estimates of the number and types of employees needed, the projected hours for each position, and projected labor costs (weekly and monthly). The form can also be used for existing businesses to establish ideal schedules relative to sales.

Steps in Creating an Effective and Efficient Employee Schedule

1. What positions must be filled? This depends on the type of business, requirements of customers, and sales volume. For example in a high volume restaurant, bussers are generally needed. In lower volume restaurants, servers may be able to buss their own tables. A busy or large hotel will need designated employees for the laundry. In a smaller hotel, housekeepers can do the laundry.

2. What the reasonable production capacity is for each position in the business. Someone with a reasonable level of experience in each position must be able to analyze the specific duties for each position and determine the production capacity for the position. If there is more than one employee, then the production capacity for each of the employee in the work section may vary and must be determined. Knowledge of the different levels of production ability for each employee must be factored in, when determining what a standard should be.

Some firms add standardized times and production quantities to duties and tasks or job descriptions (e.g., ability to work broiler station on $8,000 night – 350 items). This assists recruiters in determining whether an applicant has the potential to meet the standards of the position. It also helps the applicant decide whether they are capable of meeting the firm's standards.

3. How many employees will be required? Management must match the number of employees necessary for various levels of sales to the potential required production volume. Essentially, this is matching demand/sales volume (customers) with supply (employees). For example, three cooks may be able to handle 200 to 300 meals, while four cooks are required for more than 300 meals.

4. Forecasting demand. This is a part subjective part objective analysis and comparison of:

      a. sales for the last scheduling period;

      b. last year's sales for the planning period; and

      c. unique factors (reservations, significant events, weather, competitive dynamics, etc.) .

Sample Process for Creating Schedule

Kitchen Example:

- HR headquarters, 1,000 restaurants
- 5 positions on cooking line for lunch
- 65 items to prep for customers
- How can management decide how many prep cooks are needed and how many hours they will be needed?

1. Find out how long it takes the average skilled employee to prep each of the 65 items.

Where could you get this info? <u>Job Analysis</u>, ex. Cut salad lettuce.

Time each of the tasks: cut salad lettuce, including each of the tasks—make ice bath, get lettuce, open box, remove heads, remove outer leaves, remove core, etc.

2. Group items by similar foods, skills, and equipment.

3. Divide prep duties among the five positions based on each employees' assigned position, skill level, and information from preceding item (#2).

4. Sum the times for each item on a position prep list (e.g., 15 minutes, 20 min., 25 min. = 60 min.).

5. Make adjustments to position prep lists. Times can be evened out or some cooks can be given more or fewer hours.

6. Make adjustments to cooks' schedules.

      Some, in at 8 a.m., others at 9 or 9:30 a.m.

      If there is extra time, management could choose to reduce employee hours or add other items.

- If 4 hours per day was saved, how many hours were saved for the year?

      One restaurant: 4 x $10 x 360 days = $14,400

For the chain of 1,000 restaurants: $14,400 x 1,000 restaurants = $14,400,000
Examples of possible production capacity for the cooking line (based on experience with business):
    5 cooks for 300 or more customers
    4 cooks for 220 or more customers
    3 cooks minimum (regardless of volume)

Figure: 6.3 **Joseph's Bistro** Monthly Projected Labor Cost										
Shift & Position	Rate of Pay	Mon.	Tues.	Wed.	Thur.	Fri.	Sat.	Sun.	Total	$$/Wk.	$$/Month
Day Shift:											
Cook #1	$10.00	7	7	7	7	7	7	7	49	$490	$2,122
Cook #2	$8.50	4	4	4	4	4	4	4	28	$238	$1,031
Cook #3	$8.50	7	7	7	7	7	7	7	49	$417	$1,803
Cook #4	$8.50	4	4	4	4	4	4	4	28	$238	$1,031
Server #1	$7.50	4	4	4	4	4	4	4	28	$210	$909
Server #2	$7.50	4	4	4	4	4	4	4	28	$210	$909
Server #3	$7.50	4	4	4	4	4	4	4	28	$210	$909
Server #4	$7.50	4	4	4	4	4	4	4	28	$210	$909
Manager	$125.00	8	8	8	8	8	8	8	56	$875	$3,789
Day Shift Labor Cost										$3,098	$13,412
Night shift:											
Cook #1	$8.00	5	5	5	6	6	6	5	38	$304	$1,316
Cook #2	$8.50	4	4	4	4	4	4	4	28	$238	$1,031
Cook #3	$8.50	7	7	7	7	7	7	7	49	$417	$1,803
Server #1	$7.50	4	4	4	4	4	4	4	28	$210	$909
Server #2	$7.50	4	4	4	4	4	4	4	28	$210	$909
Server #3	$7.50	4	4	4	4	4	4	4	28	$210	$909
Server #4	$7.50	4	4	4	4	4	4	4	28	$210	$909
Manager	$125.00	8	8	8	8	8	8	8	56	$875	$3,789
Night shift Labor cost										$2,674	$11,576
Day and Night shift Labor Cost (Subtotal)										$5,771	$24,988
Related Labor Costs (Taxes, insurance, etc.) 15% of labor cost subtotal										$866	$3,748
Total Weekly Projected Labor Cost										$6,637	
Total Monthly Projected Labor Cost		(Monthly total equals 4.33 times weekly total)									$28,737
Employee and Management Labor Detail											
Employee Labor Cost											$17,411
Employee Related Labor Cost											$2,612
Total Employee Labor Cost											$20,023
Management Labor Cost											$7,578
Management Related Labor Cost											$1,137
Total Management Labor Cost											$8,714
Total Employee and Management Labor Cost											$28,737

The Process of Developing a Schedule Consists of Staffing for Shifts and Schedules
Review the following problem and solution:

- One guest services agent (GSA—front desk) can handle 25 transactions in an hour (the productivity standard for one GSA).
- Monday day shift averages 50 transactions per hour.
- From 7 a.m. to 11 a.m., transactions per hour average 60.
- From 11 a.m. to 3 p.m., transactions rarely average less than 35 per hour.

1. How many employees for the Monday day shift?

- 7 to 11 a.m.—Three employees are needed for four hours (60 divided by 25 equals 2.4, so, unless the manager or someone else can help for brief periods of time, three employees are needed for this four-hour period).
- 11 a.m. to 3 p.m.—Two employees are needed for four hours (35 divided by 25 equals 1.4, so two employees are needed for this four-hour period; again, unless someone else can help for a brief periods of time).

2. How many hours will each employee work?

Two employees are needed to work 8 hours (7 a.m. to 3 p.m.) and one employee to work four hours (7 a.m. to 11 a.m.).

The same process would be used to develop the schedule for the week. In the case of hotels, especially budget and midscale hotels, it is becoming common to place the manager's office directly behind the front desk. This way, if extra help is needed, the manager will generally be close by. It also helps when customer issues arise.

Solve the following problem:

Preparing a schedule for Monday through Friday for three (day shift, evening shift, night shift), eight-hour shifts each day (5 days times 3 shifts each = 15 shifts).

- One GSA can handle 25 transactions in an hour.
- Monday to Friday day shifts have 65 transactions per hour (7 a.m. to 3 p.m.)
- Three evening shifts have 50 transactions per hour (3 p.m. to 11 p.m.).
- Two evening shifts have 23 transactions per hour.
- Five night shifts have less than 25 transactions per hour (11 p.m. to 7 a.m.)

Staffing for the above front desk needs:

1. How many full-time GSAs do you need?
2. How many part-time GSAs do you need?
3. How many shifts must the part-time employee cover?

Solution:

- Five shifts (M–F day) requires 3 GSAs (65 transactions ÷ 25 or the number of transactions per hour for each GSA = 2.6, rounded to 3; 5 shifts times 3 GSAs for each shift = 15 employees needed)
- Three evening shifts require 2 GSAs (50 ÷ 25 = 2; 3 times 2 = 6)
- Two evening shifts require 1 GSA (23 ÷ 25 = .92; 1 times 2 = 2)
- Five night shifts require 1 GSA (5 times 1 = 5)
- Total 8 hour shifts to cover = 15 + 6 + 2 + 5 = 28
- Total full-time employees (FTEs) = 5 (28 ÷ 5 = 5 with 3 shifts left over)
- Total part-time employees (PTEs) = 1 for three 8-hour shifts

Case Study 6.1: Recruitment Planning

Required:

1. Develop a brief SWOT analysis for Taco Bell or any hospitality firm you have a reasonable knowledge of or are assigned by your instructor. This SWOT will be prepared based on a hypothetical situational analysis. In other words, just assume that you have the internal and environmental analyses prepared and you are recording the SWOT factors from it. The focus should be on the firm's ability to recruit hourly employees. See the HR planning project guidelines for information on preparing a situational analysis and a SWOT analysis.

    A. The strengths and weaknesses (i.e., from the internal analysis) must include information for the 10 areas of Human Resources covered in the course, plus Operations (i.e., information about your local Taco Bell for each HR area) (See ideas in the Internal Analysis in the HR Functional Plan Guidelines in the Appendix for help). For example, what is the quality of their efforts (Strength or Weakness) at Selective Hiring, Morale and so forth?

    B. The opportunities and threats from environmental analysis must include operating environmental factors of Human Resources, Customers, and Competitors (again, See the Environmental Analysis in the HR Functional Plan Guidelines for help).

2. With the objective being to help improve the Taco Bell's ability to recruit employees, based on the information you accumulated, what strategies would you recommend to:

    A. correct any weaknesses;

    B. take advantage of opportunities; and

    C. defend against threats.

_____

_____

_____

_____

_____

_____

_____

_____

_____

_____

_____

_____

Case Study 6.2: Recruitment Efforts for Potential Employers

Required:

Through any means, such as the firm's web site or a phone number, contact a company you might consider working for. It does not have to be the exact firm that you desire to work for. Tell them you are working on a project for your Hospitality Human Resources class. Ask them for information on their recruitment process (i.e., requirements such as job descriptions and job specifications, recruitment brochures, web sites, recruiter's names and phone numbers, when and where they personally recruit, the best way to get a job with them, etc.).

_____

_____

_____

_____

_____

Case Study 6.3: Creating a Schedule for the Front Desk

Productivity Standards:

• One person can check in or check out 25 people in one hour;

• Minimum requirement: You need one GSA/auditor at the front desk at all times (3 shifts per day for 7 days).

• Shifts are 8 hours long (7 a.m. to 3 p.m.; 3 p.m. to 11 p.m.; 11 p.m. to 7 a.m.)

Guest Forecast:

• Monday through Friday, between 7 a.m. and 7 p.m. there are 30 to 35 transactions per hour.

• Remainder of shifts: maximum of 15 transactions per hour.

Required:

   1. How many full- and part-time GSAs do you need for a week's schedule (7 days) and how many hours will each work? (Hint: One means of solving this problem is to prepare a schedule for one week with the three time periods.)

   2. If your objective was to have as many full-time employees as possible, how many full- and part-time employees would you need and how many hours would there be for the part-time employee(s)?

_____

_____

_____

_____

_____

Chapter Seven: Selective Hiring

Strategy Review: Prepare a strategy review for this chapter (See back of Chapter One).

Case Study 7.1: Managers' Favorite Interviewing Tactics

Case Study 7.2: Assessing Job Description Criteria

Case Study 7.3: Assessing Job Specification Criteria

Case Study 7.4: Interviewing Hourly Employees

Case Study 7.5: Good Question/Bad Question

Chapter Objectives: After reading this chapter you should understand and be able to do the following:

1. Discuss what you as a manager are looking for in a good employee.
2. Describe the challenges of hiring employees with skills that match those in a firm's job analysis/descriptions and job specifications (ideal versus reality).
3. Define the Warm Body Syndrome.
4. Explain Multiple Hurdle and Compensatory hiring strategies.
5. List the purposes of the application.
6. Know the legal retention time for applications.
7. Describe the filing system for processing new applications.
8. Understand the reason for Pre-employment Waivers.
9. Discuss things to look for when examining an application.
10. Discuss the topics reviewed in a Background Check.
11. Explain the purpose of Prequalifying Questions.
12. Explain the primary objective of an employment interview.
13. Describe the process for developing interview questions.
14. Describe common assessment problems with interviews.
15. Know the purpose of structured interviews.
16. Discuss questions that generally cannot be asked of applicants during an interview.
17. Explain why behavioral and situational questions are important for job interviews.
18. Understand the purpose of a multitasking interview question and be able to create one.
19. Discuss why or why not you would use employment tests and provide examples of different types.
20. Discuss the importance of the probationary period.

Selective Hiring

The process of selective hiring involves the interviewing and hiring of applicants based on their compatibility with company philosophies, goals, and policies. It is also critical that the overall hiring process is legal. Management must be as selective as possible about the applicants it hires. Remember, each employee is a direct representative of the business and its management. Managers should be proud of everyone working for them and confident in their ability to perform at their positions in an acceptable manner. Choosing employees is essentially the same as choosing your friends. You have basic requirements, such as someone that can make you laugh, enjoys some of the same things you do and you definitely want someone you can trust. The difference is that for friends, personal compatibility is most important (compatibility with your characteristics), for employees, work compatibility is most important (compatibility with the characteristics and needs of the firm).

Many HR managers consider attitude (i.e., conscientiousness and personality) and intelligence (i.e., general mental ability) to be the key desired characteristics of hospitality employees. The predominate thinking in the hospitality industry is to first consider attitude—an easy argument to make, then intelligence along with other desired characteristics. Several recent studies have found that general mental ability or intelligence is more important than personality, even for servers (Tews, Michel, & Lyons, 2010). One potential problem with these studies was that personality was measured by a self-assessment, rather than by an unbiased third party (Schmidt, Shaffer, & Oh, 2008). Another study found that both personality/attitude and intelligence were important, but at different times in the career of the employee (Tracey, Sturman, & Tews, 2007). Intelligence was found to be more important for new employees, while conscientiousness or attitude was more important for more experienced employees. Even allowing for potential validity problems with the measurement of personality, these findings make intuitive sense. A new job requires quick learning, intelligence, while once the job duties and tasks are understood, an employee's attitude or conscientiousness could play a larger role.

In spite of this research, hiring is more complex than looking for intelligent employees with a good attitude. A broader view is to find employees who are intelligent and goal oriented (i.e., regardless of age, have achieved significant goals in their life) and whom managers feel can measure up to the Five Responsibilities of Employees (See Chapter Eight, Orientation, The Employee Handbook): (1) dependable, (2) personable (good attitude) and customer-service-oriented, (3) willingly work with and help others (teamwork), (4) performance oriented (i.e., are productive, customer-oriented, and exhibit pride and enthusiasm in their work), and (5) who have high standards of personal grooming and personal hygiene. If there are future expansion needs for the business, some of the employees hired should have long-range potential to supply the current and successive locations with qualified managers and supervisory personnel. Management applicants should also be intelligent and goal oriented, exhibit the Five Responsibilities of Employees, plus be consensus builders, outgoing, open to new ideas, conscientious about their work, and emotionally stable (Oh & Berry, 2009).

The benefits of an organized selective hiring policy include: a applicant pool (i.e., larger base of recruits) from which to hire; more knowledge about the prospective employee, which will make for better hiring decisions; fewer poor hiring decisions made due to incorrect first impressions; and prospective employees know that management is very concerned about who they hire.

Ideal versus Reality

The business may have the ideal job description and other policies, but management may not be able to hire the ideal employee for the job. The two biggest hiring challenges in the hospitality industry were discussed in Chapter Six—Most applicants have other priorities and work for a firm for less than one year (e.g., being students and others trying to find their life's calling) and entry-level pay is relatively low. The situation would be likely be different if entry-level hospitality jobs had a starting pay of $30,000 per year, but that would only happen if we could raise our prices by about 35 percent—not a likely occurrence. Because of this predicament, managers have a few options. One is to hire only employees who meet all their requirements. There are plenty of bright applicants looking for work. For example, many of the students working in our industry will someday be Presidents of corporations, lawyers, doctors, and perhaps hotel or restaurant managers. As managers do this, they must understand that while these individuals will generally do a great job and work very hard, they will stay with the business for a short time before they leave for college or go home from college for the summer break. When managers cannot hold out for the ideal employee who will stay with the firm for at least a few years, they must sometimes make adjustments in their expectations (i.e., lower them a little) and increase efforts at training, supervision, and making the job a little more exciting. While this may seem to be a bit of a defeatist attitude, it is a rational response to the reality of hiring young people and offering a relatively low starting wage. One of the key attributes of a good manager is the ability to have the business function at a high level when some employees may not be best suited for their job.

Warm Body Syndrome

Some managers will hire almost anyone who walks through the door. While many managers will blame this on the unavailability of good employees, the most common cause is being known as a bad place to work. This reputation is usually gained through poor operational standards, such as low product or service quality, cleanliness and state-of-repair problems, poor training, and management indifference. What employee with great potential would want to work at such a place, or stay after finding out how bad it is? Businesses with reputations for excellence will often become known as *Employers-of-Choice*, and will attract the best applicants, minimizing the likelihood of the warm body syndrome (also known as the warm body theory).

Validity, Reliability, and Efficiency in Relation to Selection

Validity is the test of whether the selection process yields quality employees (effectiveness). Reliability is the test of whether the process is consistent over time (effective each time the company needs to select an employee). Efficient refers to whether the process is cost-effective and not overly burdensome or time-consuming. A firm could have an invalid selection process, but it may produce consistent/reliable results. Alternatively, a firm could have a valid process that may not be reliable in all situations or over the long term. The objective is to have a valid method of selecting employees that is reliable and efficient.

Selection Strategies
Multiple Hurdles Strategy
This strategy supports the concept that each employee hired must meet all requirements for the position—mainly job specifications and be able to perform each task in the job analysis (Linder & Zoller, 2010). This strategy is mostly used by firms with superior levels of service and reputation, such as fine-dining restaurants and luxury hotels. These firms can hold out for the best-qualified employees because their pay is generally higher and hiring less skilled employees could hurt their reputation. When customers are paying $400 or more per night for a hotel room or $100 per person for dinner, anything less than excellence is unacceptable to both the customer and company.
Compensatory Strategy
The compensatory strategy states that since few employees will be able to meet all requirements in the job specification and be fully qualified to perform all tasks in the job analysis, applicants with some weaknesses can be hired. The two primary justifications are that their weaknesses can be overcome and sometimes, this is simply the best that can be done. The fact is that it is very difficult for any firm to find the perfect employee, because few are strong in every job requirement. This is not the same as the Warm Body Syndrome where some firms' reputations are so poor that they can only hire unqualified employees or anyone and hope for the best.

The Application
Like most everything in business today, lawsuits have forced management to carefully analyze what is included in the application. For this reason, it is best not to go to a local office supply store to purchase a pad of applications. Since laws change virtually daily with the settlement of each related case, what was acceptable yesterday might not be acceptable today. The hiring process is so important that even small firms that feel they cannot afford an attorney or HR expert to review their hiring process should simply find the funds someplace. Often, the cost can be between $500 and $1,000 for a review of the needs of the business and providing required forms. At the minimum, the employment application must not have anything that is potentially discriminatory per EEOC laws. **Figure 7.1, Employment Application**, is a generic application that is included to help familiarize students with the various sections. The primary purposes of the application are to:
• have a written record of the person applying for work;
• allow the firm to abide by various federal and state laws; and
• to make sure there is enough information to make a hiring decision (including background checks).
Retention Times
The retention time for applications according to the Equal Employment Opportunity Commission (EEOC) is one year for applicants who are not hired; who are hired, then quit (voluntary termination); and for employees who are terminated (involuntary termination). One option for storage is to keep applications on file for a one year period (for example, those received during one year, January 1 through December 31 are discarded after December 31 of the following year. Even though the retention times for the various categories are the same, it is best to keep them in separate files (e.g., not hired, hired and quit, hired and terminated) to make searches easier. To help defend against lawsuits, most firms hold on to applications for longer periods of time, especially those for terminated employees. Keeping applications for terminated employees for 10 years is not uncommon.
Filing System for Processing New Applications
 Applications should be alphabetized and put into four separate folders corresponding to the four categories listed below. These folders should be easily accessible to answer applicant's questions about whether they are being considered for a position.
• **Potentially hirable**. No interview or background check completed.
• **Hirable**. Interview and background check completed, but no openings for the position applied for. If desired, the folders for potentially hirable and hirable employees could be subdivided into categories for each position in the business. When employees have great potential but there are no openings, management may consider hiring them anyway. The justifications for this are: if turnover is high or even average, there may not be an opening today, but there may one be very soon; perhaps the quality applicant can work at a position different than the one applied for; and there may be a current marginal employee that management would like to limit work time for or replace.
• **Not hirable**. For whatever rational and legal reason, if management feels the applicant should not be hired, it is generally best to not hire them.

• **Call for orientation**. If the applicant is hirable and there is a position available, the application should be kept on the manager's desk until the applicant is contacted and asked to come in for a second interview and/or orientation.

Pre-employment Waivers

Most firms have employees sign waivers giving them permission to do a background check. The waiver increases the chances of obtaining information from past employers, schools attended, credit checks, personal references, and so forth. It makes it easier to acquire information since signing it, the applicant waives the right to sue previous employers for releasing information (See the example at the end of Figure 7.1).

Reviewing the Application

• Check the position the applicant is applying for and his or her telephone number.

• Check that the application is complete. Management must make sure that each appropriate blank on the application is complete. This is done to make sure the firm has all reasonable information possible that the applicant is not trying to hide something, and to limit discrimination suits for having some applicants fill in all information, but not others. An incomplete application may also be an indication of work habits and lack of attention to detail. If the applicant does

---

Figure 7.1: Employment Application

Position applied for _____ Date _____

Name _____ Social Security # _____

Address _____ Telephone # _____

City _____ State _____ Zip _____

Date able to start _____ Pay expected _____

Are you available for full-time work? Yes (   ) No (   )

If not, what hours can you work? _____

High school attended _____ Did you graduate? Yes (   ) No (   )

College attended _____ Level attained (e.g., Junior) _____

Major/minor _____ Did you graduate? Yes (   ) No (   )

Other education or training _____

Career Goals _____

Hobbies, interests _____

Employment experience

(Start with most recent job; include month and year for Dates of employment)

  1. Name of company _____ Dates of employment _____ to _____

     Name of supervisor _____ Telephone # _____

     Job title _____ Reason for leaving _____

  2. Name of company _____ Dates of employment _____ to _____

     Name of supervisor _____ Telephone # _____

     Job title _____ Reason for leaving _____

  3. Name of company _____ Dates of employment _____ to _____

     Name of supervisor _____ Telephone # _____

     Job title _____ Reason for leaving _____

Applicant's Signature _____

With your signature you are verifying that, to the best of your knowledge, the above information is true; that you are giving our firm the right to perform a background check including contacting anyone or any organization that may help us determine your qualifications; and that you hold harmless anyone that provides such information.

Disclaimer: This is a generic application that may or may not comply with applicable laws in your areaand it may need to be customized for your needs.

not have anything to place in a section (e.g., only two jobs and there is room for four) ask them to place N/A (non-applicable) in the space.

• Review general information: date able to start; pay expected; full- or part-time employment sought; and if the applicant would be involved in the process of serving or handling alcohol, if the applicant is old enough to do so (i.e., is the applicant meet the state's age requirement for serving or handling alcohol). Do not ask the applicant's age without a specific and legal reason.

• Check the applicant's educational background. As mentioned in the position specification section, the employee's level of education may or may not have anything to do with ability.

• Look for special training, hospitality-related or not, that indicates the applicant has a desire to better him or herself.

• Adding a question on the applicant's goals is a good way to learn about them. People who have realistic goals and have a history of working toward them often make excellent employees.

• See how long the applicant worked for his or her last employer and how long he or she normally stays on a job. Is there a history of job-hopping? In the hospitality business, job-hopping is working in several businesses for about nine months or less for each. A short stay at a job may not be the fault of the employee, a short stay at many firms generally is. If there are questions about the potential of an employee, attempt to verify his or her reason for leaving by calling the past employer. Are there telephone numbers for references?

Calling Job References

It is important to call several of the applicant's past employers listed on the application. Often an applicant will make a good impression, but have a poor job history. Many very bad employees have been hired because the manager did not take the time to check references. Past employers will often have only good things to say about everyone, or it may be their company's policy to give out only a limited amount of information. It is sometimes possible to tell by the sound of an employer's voice what would be said if the manager was allowed to give out more information. To increase the likelihood of obtaining helpful information, managers should get to know other managers in the area (i.e., networking).

• **Reference Questions to Ask**. If the employer is willing to answer a few questions, ask as many of the following as time allows. Even companies that refuse to freely discuss the employee's performance will generally say whether they would rehire the person. (a) Dates of employment?; (b) Position held?; (c) Would you rehire?; (d) What was the employee's salary (salary history)?; (e) What was the person's reason for leaving?; f) Was the employee able to work without supervision?; (g) How did the person get along with others?; (h) Was the employee a team player—helped others?; and (i) Was the employee reliable?

• **Blacklist Laws**. Many states have what are referred to as Blacklist Laws. These generally specify that a business can provide information about employees' work-related actions as long as it is provided *without malice* or *intent to mislead*. That is, without malice toward the employee (e.g., trying to make sure the employee will not be hired because of a personality conflict, or telling the employee, "I'll make sure you can't get a job in this town."). Intent to mislead would be saying something good about the employee that is wholly or partially untrue. For example, a current employee who has a bad attitude and poor performance is looking for another job. When the competitor calls for a reference, they are told that the employee is an excellent worker. The key is that for whatever information the business provides, that management has written proof to support it. This way if a past employee's attorney considers a lawsuit for your saying something negative about their client (or a business claiming it was given misleading information), the attorney will reconsider when proof of what was said is seen.

A common reason that businesses do not give out references is that since few others do it, being known as one who does may keep managers or the HR department busy with calls. Alternatively, if management will take the time to learn their state's laws in this area and communicate it to other hospitality managers, perhaps there can be a mutual sharing of information that makes getting reference information easier to obtain.

• **Public Relations**. If employers provide any information at all, thank them for their time and offer assistance in the future. If the applicant is still in high school, it is best to call the parents or guardians to confirm that the child has permission to work at the business during the hours discussed. Establishing a good relationship with the parent or guardian can increase the chances younger employees will be dependable and that they do their best. If the applicant is hired, invite the parents or guardians over for a visit or free meal so you can meet them.

Background Checks

Since it would be a waste of money to do a background check for every application that is completed, management should wait to make sure the applicant is hirable before going through the expense of the background check. Professional background checks should be done on every applicant the firm is considering hiring. Failure to do so could endanger employees and customers, plus create a legal nightmare for the firm. The cost of background checks can be as little as $15 to $30 and vary with the size of the firm and the details request. Typical areas covered include:

• **Criminal Background Check**. Any crimes and what type. Violent crimes being the worst, but repeated nonviolent crimes, such as cashing bad check can also be a cause for concern. Because case law changes all the time, an attorney should be consulted to determine which crimes should eliminate the employee from consideration.

• **Civil Records**. Are they suing anyone or being sued? What types of law suits? Do they have a habit of suing past employers?

• **Driver's License**. Do they have excessive tickets or DUIs? Are they responsible? Could they drive a hotel van or deliver pizza?

• **Social Security Number**. Are they are who they say they are?

• **Employment Verification**. A professional verification by an outside firm is often more effective than the business manager calling.

• **Personal Reference Check**. This may or may not yield critically important information, but it can help increase their credibility (e.g., best student in class, Eagle Scout, Black Belt in Karate, raised $3,000 for the local women's shelter, etc.).

• **Educational Verification**. There are many people with fake degrees or who lie about their degrees.

• **Workers' Compensation Claims**. Unfortunately, some applicants are just looking for a job to fake an injury to receive workers' compensation. If done once in the past, management must verify the validity of the claim because there is the possibility of their trying it again. If done twice in the past, the chances are high that they will try it again.

• **Credit Check**. If applicants are not paying their bills, they may represent a risk around cash; and they may not be reliable or responsible. Because of the bombardment of college students by credit card firms, a reasonable amount of bad debt should be ignored.

Interviews—First/Screening and Second/Final

The purpose of the first or screening interview is to prequalify the applicant (e.g., can work certain days/times, desired position and pay, etc.) and to make an initial assessment of the applicant's job qualifications. For some firms, this will be the only interview. For others, this first interview will be acceptable for *conditional hiring*, that is, hired pending the outcome of the background check. Other firms will set up various additional interviews, role-playing, and tests (e.g., job skills, personality, ethics, etc.). In the past, it was common for an applicant to fill out an application form, then be interviewed and hired within 15 minutes—or less. Because of liability issues, increased professionalism, and the need to make sure the employee is a good fit for the company, the interview process is becoming more involved. For hourly employees the first interview can take place when the application is completed at the business, but most often occurs when they are called back for an appointment. If there is no time for an interview when the application is completed and dropped off, the applicant can be respectfully told so and that if there are openings that a manager will call them for an appointment. If there are no openings for the position the applicant is applying for, the applicant should be told as soon as possible.

Prequalifying Questions

The first interview should be a one-on-one interview, during which the completed application is reviewed with the applicant. The interview can be ended quickly under two common circumstances:

1. At the beginning of the interview, management must ask initial qualifying questions to determine if the applicant's needs coincide with the business's needs. For example, what does the applicant want in terms of desired shift, desired position, part-time or full-time work, rates of pay, advancement opportunities, and so on. If the needs of the applicant and business do not coincide, then the interview can be politely ended. If there are no openings for the position the applicant is applying for, tell the applicant, but let the applicant know that the application of those who are hirable will be kept on file in case something comes up.

2. If the applicant is not hirable for reasons other than the above (e.g., poor communication skills, hygiene, or inappropriate habits, such as frequently scratching their nose, etc.), quickly but politely end the interview. For example, "Thank you for coming in, but even though it appears that you have some reasonable skills, we're looking for

someone with more experience," or something else that is appropriate that you feel comfortable with and that would not embarrass the applicant. Each manager will have a different comfort level with telling employees exactly why they will not be considered for employment. Honesty may be a bit shocking to the employee (e.g., "You were picking your nose during the interview."), but the applicant may appreciate it because it will help them in future interviews.

Developing Questions and Assessment Criteria

The core task of management is to determine if the applicant is qualified for a specific position at the firm. This is done through an assessment of the applicant's abilities relative to the **job analysis** (i.e., the duties and tasks of the job) and the **job specification** (i.e., the *personal* and *behavioral characteristics* required for the job). (Each of these were discussed in Chapter Five, The Job Creation Process). The duties will deal with the specifics of the job (e.g., ability to check in a guest at a hotel, ability to work the broiler station in a busy restaurant on a Saturday night, a hotel manager being available 24/7 for emergencies, etc.), while job specifications normally deal with more general characteristics/abilities (e.g., problem solving, pleasant personality, customer service orientation, manual dexterity, etc.). For each duty and each characteristic in the job specifications there should be a corresponding means of assessment—a question or some type of task performance. Case Studies 7.2 and 7.3 at the end of this chapter provide students with an opportunity to learn this skill. For example, the duty, "Treat all customers equally and with respect, regardless of race, appearance, or socioeconomic level," could be assessed in the following ways. Before his/her interview with the manager, have a dishwasher come by and ask the applicant if they have seen the manager. Then, attempt to determine if the dishwasher was treated with respect. Another option would be to learn if the applicant had previously worked in a diverse environment. The applicant's ability could also be assessed by asking them questions or by having them perform a job description task (e.g., A guest comes to the front desk upset about an overcharge on their bill. What would you tell them? or Prepare a béchamel sauce.). For job specifications, math ability could be assessed with a math test, while loyalty could be assessed by seeing how long the employee has stayed at each of their recent past jobs. Once questions and various performance tests are compiled for each position, they should ideally be reviewed by an attorney for compliance with the law. They then can become standard questions or task performances for each applicant for a specific position.

The Employment Interview and Assessment

There are various philosophies on employment interviews. Some managers prefer a casual conversation, while others pepper the applicant with questions in an attempt to create a level of stress similar to what occurs in the actual position (sometimes referred to as a *stress interview*). The ideal interview style is probably somewhere in between or with characteristics of both styles. The challenge of the interview format is that from a conversation, the manager is trying to assess whether the applicant can perform the duties and tasks of the position and meet the characteristics in the job specifications. The interview/conversation is quite valuable and provides insights into applicants' key characteristics, such as personality, attitude, and communication skills. The problem is that there may be a difference between their verbal skills and their ability to do the job. *The most valid and reliable assessment is when the applicant performs a required duty/task of the position.* This could be through role-play with the interviewer or another employee or performing a task that does not require anyone else, such as cooking something or preparing a brief written strategy for solving a marketing problem.

Assessing or judging applicants' responses to questions can be challenging. In normal conversations after someone says something, people normally do one of three things: (1) not listen—something else is on the listener's mind; (2) listen without responding, but at least give it some thought; and (3) give it some thought and respond. Hopefully, in a job interview the interviewer will be doing a combination of options 2 and 3. Sometimes it is appropriate to move on to the next question, other times a response or follow-up question is needed. The challenge is to quickly form an assessment of each response and to learn to do so without extensive training. Since few managers are psychoanalysts, a simple technique that allows average managers/interviewers to increase their assessment ability is to listen for positive and/or negative aspects (e.g., pros and cons) of each of the applicant's responses. For example, an applicant is asked, "What would you do if a customer complained about their room not being cleaned properly." The applicant responds with, "I would immediately contact housekeeping and have it taken care of." The positive is that at least the applicant seems concerned enough to solve the problem. The negative is that the applicant should have first apologized for the problem, asked the guest if he/she wanted another room, acted quickly to resolve the situation, and finally contacted the manager. Case Study 7.4 provides an exercise in learning these skills.

Common Assessment Problems (Bias)

• **Personality versus Ability**. An important factor in the assessment is that applicants have different personalities, communication skills, and different levels of confidence. For example, most people would agree that these characteristics are important in the hospitality industry. However, during an interview, many applicants may be a little nervous and not be themselves, or they may simply have an average personality, communication skills and confidence, but otherwise have great potential. Also, there is not always a direct correlation between these skills and ability (i.e., they could have these skills, but simply lack the ability to do the job or they lack the effort—they can talk the talk, but can't walk the walk). Management must understand these factors to be able to limit bias and errors in assessing an applicant's ability. This can be where task performance can help management learn more about the applicant.

• **Halo Effect**. This occurs when one or more positive perceptions of the applicant weigh too heavily in the hiring decision. While there are many possible reasons for the halo effect, the most common are attractiveness/appearance, interpersonal skills, and having something in common with the interviewer.

• **Devil's Horns Effect**. This is the opposite of the Halo Effect—when negative perceptions weigh too heavily in the hiring decision.

• **Closed Ended Questions**. The most common types of closed ended question is where the applicant can answer with a *yes* or *no*. Since there is often little thought in the response, little is learned from it. Obviously, there will be a few occasions where these are necessary, such as, "Have you ever performed job *x* or *y*?" However, even in these situations, a follow-up question, such as, "How did you do it?" can be asked.

• **Civil Rights Discrimination**. Some managers will consciously or unconsciously illegally discriminate against employees based on race, color, religion, sex/gender, national origin, age, pregnancy, and so forth. Looking at the diversity of the firm's employees may indicate if this form of bias exists.

• **Interviewer Domination**. People like to talk about themselves. Either knowing this or just trying to have a good conversation, the applicant may ask the interviewer many questions. When the interview is over, there have been very few questions asked of the applicant and therefore, little knowledge has been gained. A potential problem with this is that the interviewer, like most people, likes talking about him or herself, and thinks that the applicant has great potential, even though little was learned about them—other than potentially being a good conversationalist. The interviewer must have a strategy going into to the interview of finding if the applicant meets the firm's qualifications. If that is not accomplished, the interview was not successful. This is where set questions or tasks for each applicant can help. Common wisdom is that the balance of talking time should be about 20% for the interviewer and 80% for the applicant.

• **Body Language**. Managers should be aware of applicants' body language. While there are traditional signals, such as crossed arms indicating be closed off, unless there are strange or overt postures or actions, managers should place applicants' body language in context of their overall performance. For example, in an otherwise great interview, crossed arms or less eye contact than desired may be okay. If the applicant has potential, he or she could be told about the habits to get a feeling about whether they can change them. Actions such as frequently scratching one's nose, playing with their hair, avoiding eye contact or extreme nervousness would normally be signals that the applicant is not hirable.

Structured Interviews

Because of the need to increase the validity and reliability of interviews (Wiesner & Cronshaw, 1988) and the increasing frequency of lawsuits for asking inappropriate questions, many hospitality firms are moving to structured interviews. These are a set of questions that each interviewer will ask of the potential employees for any given position. Over time, management will learn that certain traits and skills have either a positive or negative impact on an applicant's potential success. A quality management team or the corporate headquarters will subsequently develop questions that help determine whether an applicant has the appropriate traits and skills. In the structured interview, managers are given a list of specific questions to ask applicants based on the above analysis. They are also trained to know what a good response is for each question and to be ready with suitable follow-up questions based on likely responses. The opposite of a structured interview is the unstructured interview where all or a majority of questions by the interviewers are whatever they feel like asking. As one can imagine, this results in inconsistent hiring practices and potentially illegal questions and discussions with applicants.

Group or Panel Interviews

These can occur in a couple different ways. The most common is when a panel of managers or employees interview an applicant. Please note that it is critical that all interviewers must be trained in both good and bad questions (i.e., valid questions that are legal) or perhaps have specific questions to ask. The justifications are that a group of managers will be able to simulate common situations where several customers are asking for different things from a manager or employee. It also helps management determine the applicant's ability to quickly respond to a variety of questions on different topics. While this is mainly used for managerial positions, there is no reason it could not be used for hourly employee positions. Another type of panel interview that is sometimes used for sales positions is when one or more managers interview a panel of several applicants—at the same time. Another example of its usage is when several applicants are given a problem to solve while interviewers observe how the applicants interact. Because the applicant panel can be uncomfortable for applicants and most firms have little experience with it, it is not commonly used.

Ending the Interview

If after going through the appropriate questions, it is felt that the applicant could be a good employee, the employee should be asked to sign the company *pre-employment waiver form* (referred to above and perhaps already signed as part of the application), and be told that someone from the firm will get back with them within a specified period of time. Depending on the philosophy of the firm, some will tell the applicant that several applications are being reviewed and that the person being hired will be informed in the next week. In other words, only the applicant that is hired will be called back. Other firms state up front that all applicants that are interviewed will be called to let them know if they were or were not hired. Follow-up on this is important. *Conditional hiring*, where a person is hired subject to a background check, is becoming more common. In cases like this, when applicants appear to be well qualified, they can be told that they are being hired pending the background check (calling references, criminal background check, drug test, etc).

Multiple Interviews

Applicants that appear to meet the business's requirements should be interviewed by a minimum of two people, ideally three. Generally, another manager and one of the senior or key employees spend a few minutes with the applicant to provide a second opinion. This not only provides more information to make a better decision, but it also helps morale because management is asking their opinion on an important issue. Applicants for management positions should be interviewed not only by several managers and hourly employees, but interviewed in different situations, such as a reception, lunch, group meeting, and so forth.

Questions Not to Ask

It is illegal to discriminate against a job applicant because of race, color, religion, sex, pregnancy, national origin, age (40 or older), disability, or genetic information. Technically, it is not illegal to ask questions related to these topics, however, doing so could quickly lead to related EEOC charges and lawsuits, not to mention very bad publicity. Asking related questions would also become *prima facia* evidence of discrimination in a lawsuit and be difficult to defend. Because discrimination is illegal, questions related to EEOC laws are therefore also best viewed as illegal. In fact, if there is a remote thought that a question might be considered illegal, it is best not to ask it. Certainly, there are other questions that can help determine if an applicant is qualified. If the applicant brings up a topic related to areas protected by EEOC laws, it would be best to state that it cannot be discussed during the interview process. Additionally, the manager should not make notes on the application, especially those concerning EEOC information that the employee discussed or something else, such as "wants to retire soon, so just wants to work for a year or so." One firm lost a suit when it was found that a manager wrote, "too old" on the application. **Figure 7.2, Illegal and Legal Interviewing Questions** presents examples of what not to ask and what can be asked.

It is permissible to inquire about some of the above topics, but only for (1) job-related reasons (see Business Necessity and Bona Fide Occupational Qualifications in Chapter Four, Employment Law) and (2) if the same question is asked of each applicant. For example, it is permissible to ask about criminal records (convictions, not arrests) that are job related. For the hospitality industry, not having a criminal record, especially a violent one, can be a Bona Fide Occupational Qualification (BFOQ) and is therefore acceptable to discuss. The BFOQ rule is supported because guests reside on our premises; there are knives and other potentially dangerous equipment in our kitchens; and varying amounts of cash on hand in registers. Those convicted of violent crimes or theft could pose an undue risk to guests, employees, and the firm's assets. The second criteria would be critical in this situation. If, for example, managers only asked housekeepers about criminal records and it turned out that most were minority females, the hotel would find it very difficult to defend the practice in court.

Questions to Ask

There are several different types of questions. Prequalifying questions (discussed above), questions to assess specific qualifications, such as situational and behavioral questions, general qualifications (job specifications), and multitasking questions. *Situational questions* are those that give a hypothetical situation, and then ask the applicant how he or she would deal with it. *Behavioral questions* are those that focus on how an applicant acted/behaved in the past when confronted with a certain challenge. Some firms are beginning to focus on behavioral rather than situational questions, as they should ideally represent what the applicant actually did in the past. *Multitasking questions* are

---

Figure 7.2:   Illegal and Legal Interviewing Questions

Gender and Family Arrangements

Illegal Questions: What is you gender? Are you married? What is your spouse's occupation? Do you have children (how many, any children in school)? What type of childcare provisions do you have? Can you get a babysitter on short notice? Any plans for having children? Are you pregnant? Does your spouse have health care through their employer? Who is your closest relative who does not live with you (you can ask this after they have been hired)? How do you feel about supervising men/women? How do you feel about having a man/woman as your supervisor?

Legal Questions: Do you have relatives employed by our firm? Would you be willing to relocate? Can you travel? What hours or shifts can you work? Can you work overtime?

Race and Color

Illegal Questions: Can you please include a photo with your application? Where are you from? Any questions related to the applicant's race or skin color.

Legal Questions: None

National Origin

Illegal Questions: What is your country of origin or nationality? Where were you born? How long have you lived here? Where were your parents born? What nationality is your spouse? Are you a citizen of another country? What is your native language? What is your maiden name? Where is your accent from?

Legal Questions: Do you have the legal right to work in the United States? Do you speak, read, and write English fluently (if job related)? Do you speak any other languages (if job related)? What is your current address?

Religion

Illegal Questions: Do you believe in God? What is your religion? What religious holidays do you observe?

Legal Questions: None directly related to religion. Are you able to work the schedule we have for you? What days are available for work? Can you comply with our dress code?

Age

Illegal Questions: How old are you (except for above legal context)? When do you plan on retiring?

Legal Questions: Are you over 18 years of age? If not over 18, how old are you (there are different employment laws for those that are 14 and 15 and those that are 16 and 17)? What are your long-term career goals?

Disabilities

Illegal Questions: Do you have any disabilities? How severe are your disabilities? Please fill out this form about your family's and your medical history?

Legal Questions: Can you perform the essential functions of the job?

Drugs/Smoking/Alcohol

Illegal Questions: Do you take drugs (illegal to inquire about legal drugs)? Do you smoke or drink?

Legal Questions: Do you use illegal drugs?

Personal

Illegal Questions: How far is your commute? Do you have dependable transportation? Have you ever been arrested? Where you honorable discharged from the military (no questions about the type of discharge are allowed)? Are you a member of the National Guard or Reserves? How much do you weigh? How tall are you?

Legal Questions: Can you arrive at work by 8 a.m. (or other specific time)? Have you ever been convicted of a felony or misdemeanor? What training did you receive in the military that might benefit you here? Can you lift 40 pounds above your waist?

---

situational questions involving several different challenges. They attempt to indicate how applicants deal with complex situations. It also tells something about their memory and ability to follow directions. For example, "You are the only employee working behind the front desk of the hotel, a customer is checking into the hotel, you get a call from a guest that just checked in to a dirty room, and you see that several guests are ready for the 8 a.m. van to the airport and it is 8:08 a.m. How will you deal with this?"

Although there are some questions that focus specifically on Job Analysis information and some on Job Specification information, most will provide information for both categories. For example, a behavioral question about how something was done in the past, would provide information about how the applicant would handle duties and tasks in the Job Analysis, but also about their problem-solving ability for the Job Specifications. The following are typical questions asked in the hospitality industry. Many more questions are included at the end of this chapter in Case Study 7.5.

• Tell me about some of the duties listed in the job description that you've performed?
• Which duties have you had the most experience with?
• Which duties have you had the least experience with?
• Which duties do you think you were strongest at? Why? Weakest at? Why?
• Which did you enjoy most? Why?
• Which did you enjoy the least? Why?
• Are there other positions in the business that you may be interested in for the future?
• What would you do if a guest complained about their housekeeper's attitude?
• Tell me about a time that you dealt with a customer's complaint?
• If a guest at the front desk complains about another employee's rudeness, and a manager is not available, what would you do?
• What did you like best about your last manager? What did you not like about your last manager?
• What do you think are the main attributes of a good employee?
• What types of recognition or rewards are most important to you?
• What frustrated you most about your last job? (Or previous jobs)
• What are the three most important things you look for in a job?
• Why do you want to work in a hotel or restaurant?
• What did you like or dislike in your previous jobs?
• What have you learned from your previous jobs that you feel will help you here?
• What are your goals for the next year, next 5 years?

Written Employee Questionnaire

The more information available about an applicant, the more successful hiring decisions will be. If desired, the applicant can be given questions similar to the following to complete. In some ways, this can take the place of an employment test. Answers may expose the applicant's problem-solving skills, character, and writing ability. Obviously, these questions can be asked verbally in an interview.

• What type of work do you (or did you) perform on an average day?
• What part of your job do you (or did you) enjoy?
• What part of your job do you not (or did you not) enjoy?
• Why are you considering leaving or why did you leave?
• What is your opinion of the managers at your present or last job?
• Based on the previous question, how would you improve conditions at this job?
• What are your career goals and how can a job with us further them?
• How would you describe yourself?
• What are your best qualities? Your worst qualities?
• In what areas would you like to improve yourself?
• Is there anything not covered in the above questions that you would like to comment on?

Employment Tests

Today, most large firms are utilizing formal employment tests of one type or another. The main reason for their increasing popularity is that they appear to help improve the validity and reliability of the selection process. Another reason is that some HR managers are using herd mentality and adopting them because others have done so. The most popular employment test is the Personality Test/Personality Profile. While some firms will use this test to select or eliminate applicants, others use it simply to learn more about the applicant. Many managers feel they can learn more about an applicant's personality by simply sitting down and talking with them. One reason for this perception is that many applicants' responses on these tests are either invalid or not reliable. They appear to answer the way they think the employer would prefer—termed social desirability bias (Berry, Sackett, & Johnson, 2009). Another factor about employment tests is that if a firm uses them, they will need to make sure that the tests do not discriminate against protected groups. The creators of most of the initial employment tests were psychologists who happened to be Caucasian and from upper-middle-class backgrounds. Therefore, the questions were often biased against minorities. Most of these problems have been corrected, however, a few persist.

• **Aptitude or Cognitive Ability**. Ability to think through a problem or challenge. For example, a case study, a series of questions or an aptitude test.

• **Personality**. Whether an applicant is an extrovert or introvert, likes helping people, enjoys researching details, is fast paced or casual, and so forth.

• **Ethics**. How does the applicant value honesty and what has been his or her history related to it? One head of an ethics testing firm said that it is the applicant's past two years that are most important. Some say that the one of the most valuable outcomes of ethics or integrity testing is the reduction of Workers' Compensation claims (Sturman & Sherwyn, 2009).

• **Physical Ability**. Does the applicant have the energy and ability stand on their feet all day or lift whatever weight would normally be required of the position?

• **Drug Test**. Are they drug users—recreational marijuana or regularly shoots up methamphetamine? Many young people occasionally smoke a little pot now and then. On its own this does not make them unhirable.

• **Work Sample**. Having the applicant perform (e.g., role-play) a task that would be part of the job they are applying for.

• **Trial Shift**. Have them work a shift for them to see if they would like the job and for the employer to see if they have the potential to be a good employee. Because of liability concerns, the employee should not do anything that could be potentially dangerous. They should also not do anything that could negatively impact customers. Some firms simply have a potential employee watch what happens for the position they are applying for to see if they feel they would enjoy doing it. The firm's attorney could be consulted about how to best utilize this testing strategy.

• **Assessment Centers**. A business that specializes in placing applicants in various job-related situations and administering various tests to determine if they are suited for the job. These seem to be more popular in Europe than in the U.S.

Ranking Applicants

Some firms use what is termed a *weighted* application form. Through research, the firm knows which factors on the application are closely associated with quality employees who tend to stay with the company for longer than the average tenure. These questions are then weighted more than other questions. Love of the service industry, inclusion of details on the application, and tenure at the employee's last job are examples of characteristics that may carry more weight. The weight multipliers need to total 1 (one). For example, in **Figure 7.3**, average tenure is valued at .2, personality at .2, knowledge of position at .3, appearance at .1, and problem-solving ability at .2, for a total of 1 (.2 + .2 + .3 + .1 + .2 = 1). When the ratings are multiplied by the values, the result is a weighted score for the employee of (.6 + .8 + .9 + .4 + 1 = 3.7 on a 5-point scale).

Figure 7.3:   Weighted Ranking of One Applicant on a Five Item Scale
(Hypothetical characteristics; 5-point scale, 1 = poor to 5 = excellent)
Average tenure at previous jobs (4+ years = 5; 3+ years = 4; 2+ years = 3; 1+ years = 2; less than 1 year = 1)
Rating: 3; Weight: .2 (3 x .2 = .6)
Personality
Rating: 4; Weight: .2 (4 x .2 = .8)
Knowledge of position
Rating: 3; Weight: .3 (3 x .3 = .9)
Appearance
Rating: 4; Weight: .1 (4 x .1 = .4)
Problem-solving ability
Rating: 5; Weight: .2 (5 x .2 = 1)
Weight Ranking: 3.7 (.6 + .8 + .9 + .4 + 1 = 3.7)

Second/Final Interviews for Hourly and Management

For hourly applicants, the hiring decision may have essentially been made after the first interview. The second interview, aside from agreeing on pay and other possible terms of employment, is often the beginning of the employee's orientation. As previously mentioned, some firms may have a series of other assessment devices, such as more interviews, role-plays, and tests before the final decision is made. If there are several applicants for the position, second interviews can help determine which is best suited for the job.

One form of assessment that is gaining in popularity is the *job preview*. Here, an applicant shadows an employee who works in the position they are applying for. For example, an applicant for management could shadow a manager for a few hours to see what the job is like. Assuming the applicant was given the chance to interact a bit with customers, it would also give management a glimpse of the applicant's comfort level and ability to deal with customers. This would also help management determine if the applicant would be a good fit for the culture of the firm. For example, are they highly motivated to please customers, do they interact with employees in a supportive manner, and so forth. Since the applicant cannot be given much responsibility, management must use good judgment when making decisions based on this preview.

Probation Period

This is a safety net for poor hiring decisions. As long as new employees were not placed in a hostile work environment or discriminated against, they can be terminated if: (1) management feels they cannot perform the responsibilities listed in the job description or (2) if they are unable to meet the requirements listed in the job specification. Management must exercise reasonable care during probationary period such as: (1) management assistance and coaching, (2) orientation mentor (generally coworker), and (3) interim informal appraisals from manager and possibly coworkers.

Case Study 7.1: Managers' Favorite Interviewing Tactics

Student Name:_____

Business Name:_____

Ask the manager of a hospitality business the following questions:

1. How long have you been a manager? _____ years

2. What are your two favorite questions to ask applicants for hourly positions? Why?

1._____

_____

2._____

_____

3. What are the two most important judgments you make about an applicant before deciding to hire them? Why?

1._____

_____

2._____

_____

4. Do you have a story about someone you either:

     A. hired and found out you made a mistake; or

     B. Did not hire because you checked out the application and noticed or found out something terrible about the applicant?

_____

_____

Student's Analysis of Management Interviewing Tactics

1. From the manager interview in Case 7.1: Managers' Favorite Interviewing Tactics, do you agree/disagree with the questions asked?

_____

_____

2. Do you agree/disagree with the manager's two most important judgments? Explain your answer.

_____

_____

Case Study 7.2: Assessing Job Description Criteria

Required:

You will be assigned several of the following sample job duties from a hotel manager's job description.

1. Develop an assessment strategy for determining if an applicant has the assigned characteristic or skill.

2. Present it to the class.

3. Ask for advice on how it could be improved.

Hotel General Manager Duties

1. Monitors employee performance and corrects deviations from policies.

2. Trains and/or monitors training of new and existing employees for compliance with applicable company policies. Must be knowledgeable about the duties and tasks of each position in the hotel.

3. Regularly meets with other managers in the hotel to make sure everything is going according to current plans/policies. When things are not going according to current plans/policies, makes necessary corrections or seeks ways of improving how things are done.

4. Sets budgets for each department and monitors implementation of the budget. Performs inventories as appropriate.

5. For hotels without a sales/marketing manager, performs duties of sales and/or marketing manager, including public relations in the city (e.g., works with Convention and Visitor's Bureau, Chamber of Commerce, United Way, etc.), sales calls (in person and via phone), and marketing research (e.g., room rate and occupancy comparisons, business and personal services, and amenities).

6. Establishes competitive room rates.

7. Maintains the building, equipment, furniture, and fixtures with internal maintenance personnel or outside services.

8. Performs daily, weekly, and monthly sales and expenses reports. Makes sure the hotel's accountants have the appropriate information to prepare and file necessary tax forms.

9. Inspects at least five rooms per day and reports findings to executive housekeeper.

10. Except when assigned to someone else, the General Manager must be available 24 hours per day for emergencies.

11. Bank deposits must be made on a daily basis according to company policies.

_____

_____

_____

_____

_____

_____

_____

_____

Case Study 7.3: Assessing Job Specification Criteria

Required:

You will be assigned several of the following sample job specifications.

1. Develop an assessment strategy for determining if an applicant has the assigned characteristic or skill.
2. Present it to the class.
3. Ask for advice on how it could be improved.

Personal Characteristics

1. Education
2. Experience
3. Legal right to work in United States
4. Physical ability/stamina
5. Age (minimum age in the state to deal with alcoholic beverages)

Behavioral Characteristics

6. Positive attitude/enthusiasm/conscientiousness
7. Ethics/honesty
8. Neat appearance/hygiene
9. Written communication skills
10. Oral communication skills
11. Respect for others
12. Responsible/reliable/conscientious
13. Personality/interpersonal skills/friendliness
14. Love of service/passion for service
15. Intelligence
16. Productivity
17. Manual dexterity
18. Willingness to learn
19. Internal/self-motivation/pride in personal performance
20. Potential for accepting external motivation
21. Willingness to work toward company goals
22. Teamwork/cooperation
23. Creativity
24. Math reasoning
25. Decision-making/problem-solving skills
26. Analytical ability
27. Ability to follow directions
28. Memory
29. Loyalty to the firm
30. Composure under pressure
31. Accomplishment of goals
32. Ability to delegate (for managers)
33. Ability to motivate (for managers)

_____

_____

_____

_____

_____

_____

_____

_____

_____

Case Study 7.4: Interviewing Hourly Employees

Assume that you are the recruiter for the hospitality firm of your choosing. Using the following standardized interview format, interview a classmate, having them assume the role of an applicant for any hospitality position. If you desire, you can make this case study more comfortable by having the fellow participant apply for a position they have never worked before thereby creating some hypothetical circumstances.

1. What question did you use to relax them and get them to talk about their work history (II.B.)?

2. A. Rate the applicant's responses for section IV on a 1 to 5 point scale (1 = poor, 2 = fair, 3 = average, 4 = good, 5 = excellent. This is based on your perception of the quality of their response. Quality is determined by how well what the applicant says matches up with the appropriate response from a good employee for that position.

B. Assess the positive and/or negative factors (red flags) in the applicant's responses to each of these behavioral questions. What specific factors stood out in the applicant's responses that would help you determine whether this applicant was more suitable or less suitable for the position than other applicants (i.e., character, attitude, motivation to do a good job, enthusiasm/interest, knowledge, past effort and performance, time to respond, exaggerations/honesty, etc.).

3. What types of information would you give the applicant to help sell them on working for your company (V.)?

Sample Interview Format for Applicants for Hourly Positions

Time: Good candidate, 10–15 minutes; poor candidate, 3–5 minutes.

I. Review the Application (30 seconds)

(Skip this step unless you have an application.)

II. Establish a Rapport (1 minute)

        A. Make person physically and mentally comfortable and make them feel important.

        B. Use "useful small talk" as opposed to trivial talk about the weather (i.e., "I see you have worked in kitchens for five years. What's your favorite recipe?")

III. Prequalifying questions (2 minutes)

        A. What job/position are you applying for?

        B. What days and times are you available to work?

        C. What wage/salary do you expect to receive?

        (If the employees is "definitely" not suited for the job, politely explain why you cannot hire them.)

IV. Gather Information about the applicant's potential ability to meet requirements of job description and specifications—dependability, personality, character, etc.) (10 to 15 minutes)

(This area would be customized for your particular firm and the position you are interviewing for.)

        A. Review Background

            1. Why do you want to be a server (or other position)?

            2. What would your former coworkers tell me about your work performance?

            3. What did you like/dislike about working at your last (current) job?

            4. What qualities do you think are important in a server (or other position)?

        B. What has been your greatest success in your work in hotels/restaurants?

        C. Have you done anything to improve your job performance over the past year?

        D. Describe a problem at your last (current) job that you solved.

        E. Describe a time at work when you were under pressure, you had many things to do and little time in which to do it. What did you do to complete the work?

        F. Why would you be an asset to our hotel/restaurant?

        G. Who was your favorite boss and why?

V. Give information/sell position (2–3 minutes)

VI. Close interview (30 seconds to one minute)

        A. Make the applicant feel good about the interview.

B. Let applicant know when a decision will be made.

1. Option for candidate that may not be hired: "We will make our decision within the next week. We will hire two of the 15 people that have applied. Thank you for applying, and good luck!"

2. Option for candidate that may be hired: "We will make our decision within the next few days. From your application and interview, I think you have a good chance. We still have a few interviews left, so good luck!"

Case Study 7.4:   Interview Worksheet   Name:

IV. A.1	Pos	
	Neg	
IV. A.2	Pos	
	Neg	
IV. A.3	Pos	
	Neg	
IV. A.4	Pos	
	Neg	
B	Pos	
	Neg	
C	Pos	
	Neg	
D	Pos	
	Neg	
E	Pos	
	Neg	
F	Pos	
	Neg	
G	Pos	
	Neg	

Case Study 7.5:   Good Question/Bad Question

Required:

You will be given a number of possible interview questions from the following list (e.g., 1 through 30, 31 through 60, etc.).

1. Select what your group feels are the best four questions. Be prepared to tell why you think each is the best and how you could make them better. Your group should specify whether the question is equally good for applicants for managerial or hourly positions, or better for one or the other. Also explain why your group thinks it is better for one applicant category than the other.

2. Select what you feel are the two worst questions. Be prepared to tell why you think each is the worst, and if there is any way to make it a useful question.

Sample Interview Questions

(These questions are primarily for managerial positions, but most could be used for hourly positions. There are also some very good and very bad questions on the list.)

1.   Why do you want to work here? What interested you most?
2.   What are your current responsibilities?
3.   What responsibilities of your job do you consider most crucial? Why?
4.   On a score of one to ten, with ten being the greatest, how would you rate your overall current job performance? Why? What areas are strengths? Why?
         What areas could you improve on? What have you done to improve?
5.   How do you organize and plan for major projects? Daily activities?
6.   What would you like to be doing five years from now?
         How are you going about making this happen?
7.   What are the two most important things you are looking for in your next job?
8.   Describe a difficult problem you have had to deal with. How did you solve it? Looking back, what would you have done differently with the same problem?
9.   Tell me about a situation when your work or an idea that was criticized.
         Was the criticism merited? Why? Why not?
10.   What do I need to know about motivating you? Demotivating you?
11.   What quality assurance programs are you currently working with or have you worked with in the past? What were obstacles in implementing them?
         How did you manage to achieve the results you desired?
12.   What type of decision is the most difficult for you? Why?
         Give an example of the last one, Outcome?
13.   What type of people are the most difficult to work with? Why? What have you done in the past to work with them?
14.   What are the primary factors needed for you to stay with a company?
15.   Discuss a time when your integrity was challenged.
         How did you handle it?
16.   What would you do if someone asked you to do something unethical?
17.   Have you ever experienced a loss for doing what is right?
18.   Have you ever asked for forgiveness for doing something wrong?
19.   In what business situations do you feel honesty would be inappropriate?
20.   If you saw a coworker doing something dishonest, would you tell your boss?
         What would you do about it?
21.   What brings you joy?
22.   If you took out a full-page ad in the *New York Times* and had to describe yourself in only three words, what would those words be?
23.   How would you describe your personality?
24.   What motivates you most?
25.   How would you describe your performance at your past positions?
26.   Do you consider yourself a risk-taker?
         Describe a situation in which you had to take a risk.

27.   What kind of environment would you like to work in?

28.   What kinds of people would you rather not work with?

29.   What kinds of responsibilities would you like to avoid in your next job?

30.   What are two or three examples of tasks that you do not particularly enjoy doing? Indicate how you remain motivated to complete those tasks.

31.   What kinds of people bug you?

32.   Tell me about a work situation that irritated you.

33.   Have you ever had to resolve a conflict with a coworker or client?
      How did you resolve it?

34.   Describe the appropriate relationship between a supervisor and subordinates.

35.   What sort of relationships do you have with your associates, both at the same level and above and below you?

36.   How have you worked as a member of teams in the past?

37.   Tell me about some of the groups you've had to get cooperation from.
      What did you do?

38.   What is your management style? How do you think your subordinates perceive you?

39.   As a manager, have you ever had to fire anyone? If so, what were the circumstances, and how did you handle it?

40.   Have you ever been in a situation where a project was returned for errors? What effect did this have on you?

41.   What previous job was the most satisfying and why?

42.   What job was the most frustrating and why?

43.   Tell me about the best boss you ever had.
      Now tell me about the worst boss.
      What made it tough to work for him or her?

44.   What do you think you owe to your employer?

45.   What does your employer owe to you?

46.   Tell me about an objective in your last job that you failed to meet and why.

47.   When is the last time you were criticized? How did you deal with it?

48.   What have you learned from your mistakes?

49.   Tell me about a situation where you abruptly had to change what you were doing.

50.   Tell me about a situation where you "blew it."
      How did you resolve or correct it to save face?

51.   If you could change one (managerial) decision you made during the past two years, what would that be?

52.   Tell me of a time when you had to work on a project that didn't work out the way it should have.
      What did you do?

53.   If you had the opportunity to change anything in your career, what would you have done differently?

54.   When was the last time you "broke the rules" (thought outside the box) and how did you do it?

55.   What have you done that was innovative?

56.   What was the wildest idea you had in the past year? What did you do about it?

57.   Give me an example of when someone brought you a new idea, particularly one that was odd or unusual. What did you do?

58.   If you could do anything in the world, what would you do?

59.   Describe a situation in which you had a difficult (management) problem.
      How did you solve it?

60.   What is the most difficult decision you've had to make? How did you arrive at your decision?

61.   Describe some situations in which you worked under pressure or met deadlines.

62.   Were you ever in a situation in which you had to meet two different deadlines given to you by two different people and you couldn't do both? What did you do?

63.   What type of approach to solving work problems seems to work best for you?
      Give me an example of when you solved a tough problem.

64.   When taking on a new task, do you like to have a great deal of feedback and responsibility at the

outset, or do you like to try your own approach?

65. How do you measure your own success?
66. What is the most interesting thing you've done in the past three years?
67. What are you short-term or long-term career goals?
68. Why should we hire you?
69. What responsibilities do you want, and what kinds of results do you expect to achieve in your next job?
70. What do you think it takes to be successful in a company like ours?
71. How did the best manager you ever had motivate you to perform well? Why did that method work?
72. What is the best thing a previous employer did that you wish everyone did?
73. What are you most proud of?
74. What is important to you in a job?
75. What do you expect to find in our company that you don't have now?
76. Is there anything you wanted me to know about you that we haven't discussed?
77. Do you have any questions for me?
78. What have you done in the last year with your own time and money that would make you more valuable to our company?
79. What have you done that has demonstrated a high level of initiative?
80. What have you done since you were hired on your last job to be a more effective performer?
81. Where do you want to be in five years?
82. What are short-term and long-term career objectives?
83. How will this job enable you to reach your long-term career goals?
84. How do you feel about the progress you've made in your career to date?
85. What career objectives have been met?
86. What aspects of your career have not lived up to your expectations?
87. What do you feel it takes a person to be successful in your field?
88. What type of rewards are most meaningful to you?
89. What's most important to you in a job?
90. When have you felt fully appreciated for your contribution?
91. How does this affect the effort you make on the job?
92. What aspect of your work life do you feel passionate about?
93. What project has made you really excited?
94. What are you looking forward to?
95. If we hire you, how long could we expect you to stay with our organization? (typically gets response "as long as it's challenging")—How do you define challenge?
96. What do you feel you can achieve at this company you can't elsewhere?
97. Of the various work environments you've experienced at your different jobs, which was the most productive for you, why?
98. Which work environment was least productive for you, why?
99. What would you definitely like to avoid in your work-life?
100. Tell me about a time people you were working with weren't being as honest or sincere as you would have liked. What did you do?
101. When have you felt the most pressure to compromise your personal integrity?
102. Have you ever had to put your job on the line for something you believed in?
103. Describe for me a situation where self-centered behavior produced bad teamwork that was expensive for the company. If you were the supervisor and wanted to solve the problem, how would you have done it? How would you have described the problem to the individual?
104. What do you feel makes for good teamwork and morale?
105. Tell me about a time when you pulled the team together. How have you built morale?
106. Describe your present coworkers, and briefly, their strengths and weaknesses.
107. What problems have you encountered with them?

        (Listen for pattern in responses that lays blame on others.)

108.   What do you feel makes for good teamwork and morale?

109.   Tell me about a time when you pulled the team together.
        How have you built morale for the team?

110.   How do you feel about your workload?

111.   Tell me about a situation where a crisis developed to meet a deadline requiring long hours of extra effort. What happened, and how did you handle it?

112.   What things have you had to do in your professional life that were particularly unpleasant?

113.   Describe for me a difficult political situation you faced.

114.   What type of problems frustrate you most?

115.   When was the last time you felt really angry on the job?

116.   What was the toughest emergency you've ever faced?

117.   How do you feel your personality changes working under pressure?

118.   What have you done under extreme pressure you later wish you hadn't?

119.   What have you changed about yourself as a result of criticism?

120.   What have you been criticized for that you've heard from more than one source?

121.   When was a request for support you felt was important denied by a superior? Why was it denied?
        How did you deal with it? (see how in touch they are with the big picture)

122.   What was your favorite job?

123.   What made your favorite boss so good to work for? Was he/she your mentor? What were the traits of your least favorite boss?

Chapter Eight: Orientation

Strategy Review: Prepare a strategy review for this chapter (See back of Chapter One).
Case Study: 8.1: Developing an Orientation Program
Case Study: 8.2: Giving an Orientation
Chapter Objectives: After reading this chapter you should understand and be able to do the following:
1. Define orientation and discuss its importance.
2. Differentiate between orientation and training.
3. Discuss two primary types of orientations—general property and job specific orientations, and describe what is covered in each.
4. Discuss the concept of what the business has to offer the employee.
5. Discuss why certain information in the employee handbook is critical.
6. Describe some typical problems with orientations.
7. Describe the purpose of new employee paperwork and list some examples.
8. Explain why the orientation checklist is important.
9. List the five responsibilities of employees (see the employee handbook) and understand their purpose.
10. Explain the importance of a careful review of the employee handbook.
11. Discuss important topics in the employee handbook.
12. Explain the employee handbook disclaimer.

Overview of the Orientation Process

Orientation is the formal introduction of new employees (also known as orientees) to the firm, its history, culture, and traditions, plus a review of general policies and an overview of their position. It sets the tone for the employees' entire future with firm. A proper orientation can instill confidence and direction in new employees, increasing the effectiveness of their efforts. It is one of the first ways that management lets employees know it is concerned with their welfare and that they are important to the business. It also communicates the importance of the business's policies and that the business is organized enough to ensure a stable future.

The cliché of having one chance to make a first impression is true. If fact, it might better be said that the orientation is the firm's first *and* last chance to make a good first impression. There is often stress associated with anything new, and a new job is no exception. In the orientation, new employees have a chance to get acquainted with managers and other employees and have their questions answered. This questioning not only helps the orientee understand their new environment, but it helps them build positive relationships and learn the value and cultural norms of the business and its employees. The orientation helps new employees become productive faster. The more comfortable they feel with their new surroundings, the better able they will be to focus on their training. A thorough orientation can prevent misunderstandings, lower turnover and hiring costs, and help the long-term success of the organization.

For some firms, the orientation begins after the applicant has agreed to the basic terms of employment (e.g., position to be worked, pay, benefits, shifts to be worked, starting date, etc.). For example, the orientee may be provided an employee handbook to take home to review and asked to complete the payroll processing form. Others may even review the employee handbook. This is likely a little too much too soon. The norm is to have the new employee return another day for the orientation. Orientations for managers generally take place in two different ways. One is to have the new manager visit corporate headquarters for several days to learn about the company, meet various corporate managers, select benefit packages and so forth. Another is to have the orientation at the property the new manager will be working at.

Orientation versus Training

Where orientation deals with general information the employee should know before they begin their work with the company, training deals with the specific duties the employee will be responsible for in their position. Orientation also helps the employee transition into their training program.

Socialization (culture, values, norms/normative behavior)

Socialization primarily concerns relationship building and giving new employees a sense of belonging and a chance to get to know their new co-workers. Though much of socialization is accomplished in a quality orientation, management must make sure that activities, such as meetings with managers and fellow employees in a comfortable, non-business, or at least, less formal environment takes place. Examples include having lunch, sitting down and casually talking about how things are done at the business, employee picnics, company-wide volunteering, and so forth.

The Need for an Orientation Program

Management must be convinced of the need for a proper orientation program. A proper orientation will take time from a manager's already busy schedule and the employees must be paid during the orientation. Therefore, the commitment from management for time and money is required. Many managers have a 10- to 20-minute orientation for signing paperwork and reviewing basic policies—or simply saying, "Here's the employee handbook." This is obviously a mistake. Others spend anywhere from several hours to several days on their orientation program. Full-time employees will work 2,080 hours in one year. Four hours is less than one-fifth of 1% of the employee's first year with the company (i.e., 1/5 of their first year's pay). This is a very small investment, considering the importance of an effective orientation. The reality is that a quality orientation program can pay off for the firm on the new the employee's first day when he or she provides a customer with an exceptional experience.

Orientation Program

An orientation program is generally a two-step process consisting of a *general property orientation* and a *job specific orientation*. Each should have input from management, new employees, some of the longest tenured employees, the human resources department, and supervisors and/or employees from departments for which the program is being prepared. If there is no HR department, then management will have to suffice. Input from the department is important to learn the types of information that need to be communicated during the orientation and to make sure they are effective and legal.

General Property Orientation

This is information about the business that will help the new employees become comfortable with their new surroundings, make them feel that they are an important part of the business, and inspire them to do their best to fulfill their responsibilities.

• **History and traditions of the business**. Most businesses have inspirational stories about someone who mortgaged their home to get enough money to open a restaurant, and now they have 20 locations and are opening a new restaurant each month. To some, this may be just words, but to most this means that people have put their heart and soul into the business—"This isn't a job, we're on a mission."

• **Values the business stands for and examples of how they are upheld**. The values that are important to the business and employees should be written down and clearly communicated to employees. Examples of what management and employees have done to uphold the values will provide clear messages of what is important. For example, how the firm and its employees helped an elderly lady paint her home will inspire all but the coldest hearts.

In training, the employee will focus on the duties and tasks of their position. Though this is certainly valuable to them, it does not provide answers to everything they will need to perform their jobs to the height of their ability. The extra information that is needed, the difference between good and great, is the new employee's ability to incorporate the values of the firm in their decisions as early in their tenure with the firm as possible. For example, a new employee may not have been told/trained to help an elderly customer to his or her table, but knowing the firm's values will provide the missing information needed, guiding them to assist the customer.

• **What the business has to offer the employee**. Every hospitality firm has some benefits it provides its employees. It could be limited to social security, workers' compensation, and unemployment, but whatever it is, it should be communicated. Many employees do not know they have these benefits or realize what they are worth. Also, many employees believe that the position they start out at is where they will stay, at least for the one year they plan on staying. Opportunities for advancement are one of the greatest benefits of working in our industry. A promote from within policy will reinforce this statement.

One of the challenges of the hospitality industry is that our pay is not great and we ask employees to work hard to satisfy our customers. As we ask them to do this for us, we need to have something to offer them. That something is the opportunity to learn the habits of success, habits that they can take with them when they go back to school and to everything they do in life. The habits of success are perhaps the greatest gift any manager, friend, relative or teacher can pass on to employees.

• **Information about their new surroundings**. A tour showing new employees where the various departments are in the business will limit their chances of getting lost. It will also help them to assist customers who have questions. There may be stories of various features in the building such as paintings or the room where the President stayed.

• **How various departments work together and knowledge of other departments**. In the hospitality industry practically every department is connected in some way to every other department. For example, people at the front desk will coordinate their efforts with housekeeping and answer questions about the hotel's food service. A host in a restaurant must coordinate the seating of customers with the ability of the servers to take care of guests, the busser to clean the tables, and the cooks to prepare the food. They may also be asked if a certain type of meal could be prepared, such as without ingredients a customer is allergic to. Historically, in the hospitality industry there has tended to be friction between different departments. Problems between cooks and servers are not uncommon. If employees are told early on in their employment that cooperation is critical, this will hopefully minimize these problems.

• **At least some management and staff should be introduced to the orientees**. It is most helpful if the General Manager of the property takes some time to introduce her or himself and even have lunch with the orientees. One philosophy is that if the orientees are on a first name basis with the highest-ranking person in the company, they will feel more comfortable with everyone else. Before introducing new employees to the staff, it is critical for managers to make sure that current employees realize the importance of a warm welcome.

• **Review of the employee handbook (i.e., employee policy manual)**. Employees have the ability to read the manual, but the information is too important to leave to chance (See Sample Employee Handbook later in the chapter). Every employee should have a reasonable understanding of how things at the business work. Things such as expectations of employees, the goals of the company, pay periods, schedules, open door communications, and so forth should be carefully reviewed. Some firms go so far as to have tests over their employee policies. If the manager states that certain information is important, there is nothing like a required test to reinforce it.

      Critical Employee Handbook Information. Most everything in the handbook is important; however, the following can be critical to the success of the new employee, the firm, and for safety.

• The *Welcome* is important because this helps make the employee feel that they are valued and provides a broad overview of how they fit into the organization.

• The *Goals of the Business* gives new employees a short lesson in how to run a successful business.

• The *Five Responsibilities of Employees* condenses the hours and many pages of new information into a short list of things they need to remember. This helps soften the information overload that tends to overwhelm new employees, and especially employees at their first job.

• Information on how the *Bulletin Board* is used can be critical. It is one of the most effective and efficient means of communicating to employees who work varying schedules that they need to be aware of something.

• *Personal Grooming and Hygiene* for hotels and restaurants is obviously important. The problem is that people develop habits that may be difficult to change. If employees know that something will not be tolerated, they will be less likely to continue it.

• *Safety* should be reviewed in detail. Most managers simply review safety procedures with employees stressing the importance of being careful. Another philosophy is to frighten new employees a bit by telling them about accidents that can happen when people disregard safety rules. For example, "The slicer is a four pound razor blade spinning at several thousand revolutions per minute. It can easily cut your fingers off if you're not careful."

• Reviewing the concept of *Performance Appraisals* along with a copy of the form that will be used helps employees learn how they will be judged and helps teach them how to be viewed as a good employee.

• Understanding *Discipline* lets the new employee know what happens when policies are not followed. Whether at school or at home, young people may not fully understand that there are consequences for improper behavior.

• *Paid Vacations* are one of the most effective means of motivating employees to stay with the company. If every employee stayed long enough to earn vacation time, payroll costs would rise by about 2%. On the other hand, if turnover was high, payroll costs would rise even higher, not to mention related problems, such as poor customer service, low productivity, and so forth. Historically, few firms offered them to hourly employees. Today, most do.

• *Employee Meals* are one of the best short-term motivators. The cost of soup and bread or a sandwich is around $1. The average employee (part-time and full-time) earns around $250 per week. Therefore, the food cost for employee meals for the week is around 2% of payroll ($5 ÷ $250 = .02). Most employees have little spare time, spare money, and they are almost always hungry. Also, most employees appreciate a free meal. Assuming that other things in the business are satisfactory, the cost of the meal will be returned many times over in improved morale, productivity, and customer satisfaction. Some firms charge enough to cover the cost of the meal; others unfortunately try to make money from it.

• **Current goals of the company**. Perhaps the company is trying to franchise or open a new location someplace. Growth, even to a high school student, is exciting. Everyone wants to be part of something successful.

Job Specific Orientation

• **An overview of the position including an explanation of major duties**. Since people learn in stages, providing them with a good overview is a critical step in the learning process. This allows the brain to begin assimilating the necessary information they will need to learn and achieve their full potential. Understanding the major duties at the beginning of their employment will also increase their confidence that they can do what is required. Questions about what to do and doubts about one's abilities are not productive thoughts for new employees.

• **Management expectations related to general responsibilities**. If management has hired the right employee, a key question in the new employee's mind will be, "How can I be a good employee?" and "How can I meet management's expectations of me?" Seeing a 100+ page training manual and knowing that you are responsible for its contents can be quite daunting for a new 18-year-old employee. The challenge here is to find a way to reduce the 100+ pages down to key responsibilities that the new employee can easily remember. These are referred to as the *Five Responsibilities of Employees*. They will be discussed further in the *Sample Employee Handbook* later in this chapter, but they are: (1) Dependable, (2) A Pleasant Personality (Good Attitude) and Customer-Service-Orientation, (3) Teamwork, (4) Performance, and (5) Personal Grooming and Hygiene. Learning these basic traits of a good employee—what is expected of them—will simplify the challenge ahead of them.

• **The most important aspects of their new job**. While the *Five Responsibilities* includes general expectations, this area will focus on one or two specific and critical aspects of their new job. For example, for cooks—cleaning as you go and follow the recipes; for servers—make sure each customer is happy with their experience and be aware of each of your customer's needs; for front desk agents—take ownership of each customer's request, and verbally acknowledge guests that pass within 5 feet of the front desk. Obviously, there is more to doing a great job than any one or two requirements, but giving the new employee something important to focus on early will speed their learning curve. Also, as new employees hear this critical aspect from others during their training, it will help them become more comfortable with their progress (e.g., "I think I'm catching on.").

• **An introduction to their trainer and a review of training program**. The trainer will generally be the most important person in the life of a new employee. Yes, the training program is the foundation for learning, but the trainer's ability to teach and inspire cannot be overemphasized. The review of the training program should focus first on the Job Description (i.e., the duties and overall summary of what the job entails) and that the trainer is there to support them and help them become a great employee, then on what will be done each day. If the orientee seems to have a general understanding of the Job Description, the Job Analysis or some specifics of the training manual can be reviewed.

• **Opportunities for promotion and personal development based on performance**. A major opportunity to maximize new employees' enthusiasm and motivation to do their best may be lost, or certainly minimized, if no one talks to them about opportunities for promotion or the ability to achieve their potential. Quality new employees not only want to be successful at their new job, but need a dream, a target, to aim for.

Problems with Orientations

Each applicant will feel differently about new circumstances. Of course, the biggest problem with an orientation is the lack of one. Assuming there is one, management should attempt to make the applicant feel as comfortable as possible—have something for them to drink and maybe a snack of some type, making sure the applicant understands everything or asking if there are any questions. Being sensitive to the cultural or psychological needs of each individual is also important.

Sometimes there can be an emphasis on completing the various forms, plus an information overload. Completing various new employee forms, insurance, payroll, and other forms is important. It should not, however, be the focus of the orientation. A key for most employees is that they get help in completing the forms. Having someone methodically reviewing the forms with the new employee, explaining what is important and where to sign will minimize frustration and help get the employee through the potentially tedious task. Another option is, rather than give all required paperwork to employees at one time, to have them complete the forms at different times during the orientation. If a large position manual is provided, management or the person responsible for the orientation must take the necessary time to review it. Handing a new employee a 100+ page manual and telling them to read it and be ready for a test is no way to make the orientee feel comfortable.

There are some firms that have an orientation once per month. This is fine if it is the first day for any employees taking part in the orientation. However, if an employee has already been working for up to several weeks before the orientation, then, while still important, much of its potential usefulness has probably been lost. For example, what is the point of a warm welcome to the company, when the employee has already been working for several weeks? Why explain the general policies of the firm if the new employee has already learned them through trial and error and making mistakes and then being told so by many other employees. There is nothing wrong with having a monthly orientation for all employees hired during the month as long as it is each employee's first day of work.

There are both positive and negative aspects of every job. It is good to discuss both. It communicates that the business is being honest and not trying to paint a false picture of the new employee's future (unrealistic job previews were discussed in Chapter Six, Recruiting).

New Employee Paperwork

The following paperwork is commonly completed when a new employee is hired. The decision of what to include will be made by management, the firm's accountant, payroll processing firm, attorney, and other entities.

• **Orientation Checklist.** Each employee agrees that the topics/company policies on the checklist have been adequately reviewed with them and to work according to them by signing the checklist. This protects the business from potential lawsuits. This applies to all employees.

• **Employee Records File.** Start a personnel folder for each employee containing information and forms, such as the employee application, employee processing form, the orientation checklist, a completed W-4 form, a completed 1-9 form, completed tests, performance appraisals, disciplinary reports, performance record, and any other applicable information. The personnel folders should be kept in alphabetical order, but can also be divided into separate categories for each position—also in alphabetical order.

When an employee voluntarily or involuntarily terminates, store his or her entire file as follows:

• **Voluntary Terminations**. The Equal Employment Opportunity Commission requires that, when an employee quits, their personnel folder must be kept on file for a minimum of one year. These folders should be kept together for a one-year period (for example, January 1 through December 31), and then discarded one year later (December 31 of the following year).

• **Involuntary Terminations**. The Equal Employment Opportunity Commission requires that these applications also be kept on file for one year after the termination. However, because these employee files may be required to help defend lawsuits, they should be kept for longer periods of time. Some firms retain them for 10 years. For excellent firms there will be very few involuntary terminations, so it is not the storage problem that some may perceive it to be. Whatever length of time is chosen, files for involuntary terminated employees for each should be kept together in a dated folder or container.

• **Employee Processing Form.** This becomes the cover sheet for the employee's personnel file. Record most noteworthy information about the employee here (e.g., social security number, address, phone number, person to notify in case of emergency).

• **Employees Withholding Allowance Certificate, W-4**. This applies to all employees.

• **Employment Eligibility Verification, Form 1-9**. This is needed to verify that an employee has the legal right to work in the United States. It applies to all employees upon being hired. There are federal penalties for failing to properly administer these forms.

• **Payroll Information Sheet.** This includes all information necessary to place the new employee on the payroll. The sheet should be forwarded to the payroll department when completed.

• **Tip Credit Policy.** The current Federal Minimum Wage as of the date this book was published was $7.25. Federal law allows employers of tipped employees to reduce the hourly wages paid to these employees by $5.12 (the tip credit), or to $2.13 per hour as long as specific conditions are met. It must first notify the employees in writing that the tip credit is being taken, the tipped employee's total hourly income must be at least $7.25 or equal to or greater than the minimum wage, and the tipped employee must receive at least $30 per month in tips. Many states have established lower tip credits to allow tipped employees to have greater incomes. Federal law also requires that employees accurately report their tips to their employer for each payroll period, on their tax return, and be able to prove their tip income if their tax return is questioned. This applies to all tipped employees, such as those that share in pooled tips (e.g., busser, hostperson, cooks, etc.). IRS Form 4070A can be used by servers to keep a daily record of tips. If tips are pooled or shared, the business must notify employees in writing of the process and amount. The percentage of the shared tip cannot be more than 15% of an employee's earned tips for the shift (or whatever is customary and reasonable for the area). Each business should have a written Tip Credit Policy that is signed by each employee that receives tips, explaining the firm's policies regarding tips.

• **Employee Handbook.** The handbook includes company and employee goals, policies of the business, and other information deemed important to the company. The policies included in the handbook in this chapter are generally accepted standards in the hospitality industry; however, like anything a company adopts, it should be reviewed by an attorney before implementation. If adopting the policies for a particular firm, they may be changed or omitted, and additional policies can be added. Suggested additional policies are listed in the employee handbook options, following the handbook.

Supplemental Position Information

Each employee handbook can include the applicable position information, the information may be included in a separate packet, or it may be placed on the firm's web site. Examples of supplemental position information include job descriptions, menu descriptions and abbreviations, and other specific policies that employees will need to help them learn as quickly as possible to perform their assigned tasks.

Orientation Checklist

An orientation checklist is helpful for the following reasons (see: **Figure 8.1: Sample Orientation Checklist**):

• Few managers can remember to cover over 30 different topics.

• Both the manager and employee know that the items were covered.

• Checking off items after they are communicated and understood gives the employee confidence that they have a decent grasp on the topic. It also puts pressure on managers to make sure they are effectively communicating the information for each new employee. Some new employees will need more help than others, so patience is critical.

• If there is a question in the future about whether something was communicated, there is proof. This could minimize the chances of a lawsuit.

Figure 8.1:   Sample Orientation Checklist

Employee_____

Applicable new-hire paperwork completed, W-4 (Withholding Certificate) _____, 1-9 _____,
Tip Credit Policy _____, Employee Processing Form _____, Payroll Information Sheet _____, etc.

The following must be reviewed with new employees: (Employee initials line below after each topic is reviewed)

History and traditions of the company	
Market position	_____
Restaurant goals	_____
The five responsibilities of employees	_____
Pay and pay periods	_____
Attendance and working hours	_____
Workers' compensation insurance	_____
Health card requirement	_____
Paid vacations	_____
Employee meals	_____
Holidays	_____
Parking	_____
No solicitation policy	_____
Telephone usage	_____
Care of equipment and furniture	_____
Family and Medical Leave Act	_____
Personal appearance, health and hygiene	_____

Safety rules	_____
Performance appraisal	_____
Discipline	_____
Recordkeeping	_____
Equal employment policy	_____
The employee handbook is not a contract	_____
Where to clock in	_____
Bulletin board for schedules and other information	_____
Emergency procedures for injuries and fires	_____
Robbery procedure	_____
Training schedule	_____
Review of position guidelines	_____
Tour of restaurant	_____
Introduction to staff, especially in the new employee's department	_____

Management has reviewed the above information with me.
I understand it and agree to work according to the goals and policies of the restaurant.

_____   _____   _____   _____
Employee's Signature   Date   Manager's Signature   Date

Sample Employee Handbook

The Employee Handbook is one of the key aspects of the orientation, and as such, should be thoroughly reviewed with the new employee. (This sample is for a restaurant. The vast majority of policies would be the same for a hotel.)

WELCOME FOR NEW EMPLOYEES

We are proud of our business and hope you will be proud to work here. Our success is based on a sincere desire to satisfy our customers and our commitment to provide employees with a positive work environment where they can develop the skills necessary for a better future.

You may be working here temporarily, perhaps as a student, or waiting until an opening comes up in your chosen career. You may not know what career path you will take, or you may have chosen a career in the hospitality industry. Whichever the case, we want your time spent here to be fruitful for both of us. Whether you work here for six months or six years, it is our hope that you will be better off because of it.

You will be trained for your position and asked to learn about our policies and procedures. Your success and that of our business depend on your ability and effort to learn our methods.

The one thing we ask from you, more than anything else, is that you show enthusiasm in everything you do. Being enthusiastic will serve you well in the future and help you to achieve the goals that once were only dreams. "Act enthusiastic, and you'll be enthusiastic!"

THE GOALS OF THE BUSINESS

Customer Satisfaction

Customer satisfaction is our number one goal. It is the result of giving each customer a quality dining experience, good food, courteous and efficient service, and high standards of cleanliness that pleases customers enough to make them want to return. The regular customer is the most valuable asset a business can have. Each employee must do everything possible to promote customer satisfaction.

Product Quality

All food and beverages must be the highest quality possible. This is assured by preparing all products according to the restaurant's recipes and procedures. We must be proud of everything we serve.

Service Quality

The attitude of employees must be warm and congenial enough to make customers feel they are truly welcomed. This is evidenced by smiling faces and every employee's efforts at doing whatever necessary to make each customer's experience a pleasant one.

Cleanliness and Sanitation

We have a moral responsibility to provide customers with healthful food and beverages in a clean and sanitary environment. All employees must learn to uphold the business's standards of cleanliness and sanitation.

Personal Development

You will be given the opportunity and encouragement to grow to the peak of your abilities. We will do whatever possible to facilitate the career advancement of all employees through cross-training (after you reach a level of excellence at your present position), performance appraisals (both oral and written), and career guidance.

Profit

Profit assures the long-term success of the business. It is the direct result of reducing waste of any kind and increasing the number of satisfied customers. Profit gives us the financial resources to offer better working conditions, job security, and opportunities for advancement for all employees. Many more manager and supervisor positions are created when profits are used to open other restaurants.

Communications and Open Door Policy

It is our goal to keep you abreast of everything that goes on in the company. Likewise, we want to hear from you if you have thoughts about anything affecting you or the company. This means we want to hear your suggestions for: improving anything, work-related problems, personal problems, or concerns.

THE FIVE RESPONSIBILITIES OF AN EMPLOYEE
(Each employee needs to memorize the five responsibilities—titles only and understand the concepts behind them.)

1. Dependable (i.e., good ethics and character)

Show up for work on time, perform the work you were hired to do. Be ethical in your dealings with others. If you develop a reputation for getting things done and being someone people can count on, you and the business will be assured of a great future.

2. A Pleasant Personality (Good Attitude) and Customer-Service-Orientation

You should have a sincere smile for everyone associated with the business—customers, guests, other employees, and suppliers, and a love of service. Your attitude conveys to the customer your thoughts about working here. If the customer feels you do not enjoy your work, he or she will not enjoy the meal. Avoid letting personal problems interfere with your work.

3. Teamwork

We expect you to cooperate with your fellow employees and management. Helping others when they need it will create a friendly atmosphere that will make your work easier and more enjoyable and will allow the business to function at its highest level.

4. Performance

Through the firm's training program, you will acquire the *knowledge* and develop the *ability* to perform each required task up to the standards of the business. Subsequently, you must put in the appropriate amount of *effort* to make sure you are doing your best. You should have a sense of urgency and take pride in everything you do, especially in all customer-related work. The goal of your performance is to be able to say, "I'm proud of my work and so is my manager!"

5. Personal Grooming and Hygiene

You are the business's personal representative for our customers. Your appearance and hygiene should instill confidence in the business and our standards. Employees should avoid habits of poor hygiene, such as body odor, bad breath, picking one's nose, etc.).

General Employee Policies
(The following are examples of policies utilized by hospitality firms.)

Pay and Pay Periods

New employees' starting pay will be based on their experience and the prevailing wages in the area. Raises will be given according to performance, time on the job, and the success of the business. Your rate of pay is a private matter and should not be discussed with other employees.

Pay periods are from _____ to _____. Payday is _____. Paychecks will be deposited directly into your bank account. Employees may not cash payroll checks at the business. If you lose your paycheck, a new check can be issued only after payment is stopped on the first check. The cost of stopping payment will be deducted from your pay.

Attendance and Working Hours

For the business to operate effectively, you must be at your station, ready to begin working at the time posted on your schedule. If you will be more than ten minutes late, call your manager (Tardiness or absence should be a rare occurrence.). If you will not be able to show up for work for any reason, call other employees to get someone to cover your shift. If you are feeling ill, please begin finding a replacement as early as possible, preferably the day before your shift. Only a serious illness (e.g., flu or worse) or family emergency should keep you from working your shift.

Schedules will be posted each _____ for _____ through_____. If you need to have a certain day off, let the manager know in writing (schedule request book) at least one week before the schedule is posted.

It is your responsibility to see that the hours you have worked are properly recorded. Management must approve (preferably in writing) any hours that do not correlate with your schedule, such as clocking in early, clocking out later than your scheduled shift, or working a shift you were not scheduled for. When your shift is over, the manager, an assigned employee/supervisor, or both will verify that all your work was completed.

Workers' Compensation (Disability Insurance)

If you are injured as a result of your work, you may be eligible to receive benefits under the State's Workers' Compensation Laws. These funds will pay for medical expenses and, in some cases, partially reimburse you for time off the job. This benefit is paid for by the company. When employees are injured, Workers' Compensation costs go up and profits go down. Do your best to do everything in a safe manner.

Holidays

The business will be closed on the following days:

[List the days here.]

We may close on other days, depending on business conditions. Employees are not paid during holidays.

Parking

Employees may not park directly in front of the business or in front of any neighboring businesses. Park far enough away from the business so that you do not interfere with customers attempting to park close to the entrance. If it is dark and you cannot find parking in a highly visible area, have someone watch or escort you from the building to your car. The business may have additional policies regarding where you can park and how you can safely getting to your car.

No Solicitation Policy

Employees may not conduct personal business or solicit other employees or customers for donations, membership in any organization, or distribute any type of literature in the business at any time. Outside persons are likewise prohibited from soliciting employees or customers for any purpose. When you see someone violating this policy, immediately get the manager. If a manager is not available, tell the person, "I'm sorry, but we do not allow solicitation of any kind either inside or anywhere on the business's property." If the person persists, the manager should call the police.

Telephone

Answer the telephone *within* three rings in a warm, congenial manner, as follows: "Hello. (Name of business), (your name) speaking. May I help you?" If you are on one line when another line rings, immediately tell the person you are talking with to please hold and answer the other line. Get back to the first caller as quickly as possible. Never make a customer in the restaurant wait while you are on the telephone. Tell the caller you have customers that you have to take care of and that you will call them back. Of course, ask for their phone number.

Alternatively, if you feel you would be away from the phone for just a minute ask them if you can place them on hold while you quickly help someone.

Business Phones. Our telephones are important to the business. It is necessary to keep our lines open for customers, suppliers, and others who must contact us. Do not make any calls when the restaurant is busy or that cause you to neglect a customer or your work. Incoming or outgoing personal calls must be limited to emergencies. Please keep these calls to a minimum in length and number. If there is a critical situation in your life, please notify the manager.

Personal Phones. No cell phones can be used at work, unless there is an emergency.

Care of Equipment and Furniture

Equipment and furniture; such as cooking equipment, ice machines, refrigerators, tables, chairs, booths, china, silverware, and glasses, are expensive and should be handled with care. When equipment is not properly cared for, it will not work the way it should, which will make your job more difficult, increase maintenance costs, and hurt customer satisfaction. Notify your manager if there are problems with any equipment or furniture.

Bulletin Board

All employees are responsible for reading all information on the business's bulletin board that pertains to them. Review the board daily.

Family and Medical Leave Act of 1993

An up to 12-week leave of absence, without pay, may be granted to full-time employees with a minimum of one year on the job (1,250 hours or more for the year). This allows you to retain benefits and your job (or one as close as possible to the one you had before you left) when you return. A leave of absence may be granted for a legitimate personal or family emergency, such as pregnancy or serious illness. If a husband and wife work for the same restaurant, it is lawful to limit their combined leave of absence to 12 weeks. The leave of absence must be in writing and approved by the manager.

Note: Many firms will have policies that allow for longer periods of leave time and perhaps additional benefits. This is acceptable as long as the firm's policies include greater rights than applicable federal and state laws.

Uniformed Services Employment and Reemployment Rights Act of 1994 (USERRA)

This law requires that upon their return, service members must be reemployed in the job that they would have attained had they not been absent for military service (the "escalator" principle), with the same seniority, status, and pay, as well as other rights and benefits determined by seniority. Advanced written or verbal notice must be given to their employer unless for justifiable reasons it is not possible. The cumulative time that a service member can be absent is 5 years. Disabled veterans who are convalescing from military service or training have up to 2 years from the completion of their service to return to or reapply for their civilian job.

Personal Health and Hygiene

The products we sell, food and drinks, are the most closely scrutinized products sold. No other product goes through the same examination process and then is placed in the mouth like food purchased in a business. This process involves trust in the sanitation standards of the business and in particular, the employees who maintain those standards. This trust is broken when the personal hygiene of an employee is questioned because of unwashed, uncombed hair; dirty fingernails; a sloppy appearance; continuous coughing or sneezing; bad breath or body odor; or anything else that might concern the customer. Few things are more offensive to a customer than seeing such an employee preparing or serving food. This is the quickest way to lose customers. You should take care of your health to help avoid contaminating food and, thereby, people, with germs.

You must observe the following personal hygiene rules:

1. Wash your hands before you start work, after eating or drinking, and after using the restroom. When leaving the restroom, if you must touch the door with your hand, use the paper towel you dried your hands with to open the door. Wash your hands after touching your face, nose, and hair, and after performing any nonfood tasks, such as handling money, opening boxes, cleaning anything, and throwing out trash. A high percentage of foodborne illnesses have been caused by employees who did not wash their hands often enough.

2. Never report for work with a fever, constant coughing or sneezing, or any illness that might be potentially hazardous to the customers' or other employees' health. If you must cough or sneeze, turn away from people and food and cover your mouth with your hands, arm, or a tissue or paper towel. Wash your hands immediately. Do not cough or sneeze into a towel or cloth used for other things. The business cannot allow an employee who is continuously coughing or sneezing to remain on duty.

3. Never touch your face, nose, or hair, or scratch any part of your body in front of customers.

4. Take pride in your appearance. You should be well groomed, with neat and clean hair, a trimmed beard, and clean and trimmed fingernails. Employee's clothes—uniforms or personal clothes worn for work—should be clean, reasonably free of wrinkles, and in good condition, with no holes or obvious worn areas.

5. Hair restraints of some type must be worn by all food prep employees. Any employee whose hair is shoulder length or longer must tie it back.

6. Bathe before coming to work or at least daily. Anyone having an offensive odor will be counseled about it. "Bathe daily and use a good deodorant."

7. Because of the many negative aspects of smoking, employees may not smoke in or around the business.

Safety Rules

Safety is the responsibility of everyone working at the business. It is the policy of this business to make each employee aware of the importance of safety and to provide every reasonable safeguard available. Safety rules are for your protection and should be observed at all times.

First Aid

A first-aid kit is available in the manager's office or other specified location in the building. Management must check it weekly to make sure it is properly stocked.

Foot Traffic

1. Be aware of what is going on around you. Most accidents can be prevented if you think before you act and watch where you are going.

2. If there is a corner you need to pass around but you cannot see people coming from another direction, swing wide to lessen the chances of running into someone.

3. If you are walking behind another employee, especially in an aisle, let him or her know you are there by saying "behind you." This is critical if the employee in front of you is carrying something, especially a tray of food.

Handling of Knives

1. You must not use knives or operate any equipment with sharp blades without being properly trained.

2. When working with knives, or any equipment with sharp blades, proceed with caution and give it your undivided attention.

3. When using a knife, never cut directly toward your hand or body.

4. When walking with a knife, point it toward the floor, especially when rounding a corner.

5. If you drop a knife, do not attempt to catch it. Stand back and let it fall.

6. Do not use a knife to open cans or boxes. A box cutter (if needed) is used for opening boxes.

7. Clean the knives after using them, then store them in their proper place. **Never** place a knife in the sink for someone else to wash.

8. No one is permitted to sharpen a knife without being properly trained.

Power Equipment

1. You must not operate any power equipment without being properly trained.

2. Do not operate power equipment when wearing long sleeves, a tie, or loose clothing.

3. Do not reach into the opening of any grinding or chopping equipment.

4. Do not distract anyone who is using potentially dangerous equipment such as knives, cutting, slicing, grinding, or mixing equipment.

5. Never leave a machine running unattended.

6. Unplug power equipment before you clean it. If any equipment is directly wired, turn it to the slowest speed and be very careful not to turn it on when you are cleaning it. Reassemble equipment immediately after cleaning it.

7. Never reach into the grinding chamber of a garbage disposal. Keep all glass, china, bones, plastic, paper, and metal objects out of the disposal.

Heavy Objects

1. Do not attempt to lift anything that could put a strain on your back. Fifty pounds (or less, depending on your size and strength) is the authorized limit for one person. If you need to pick up a container that weighs over 10 pounds or so, lift with your legs, not your back. To do this, bend your legs and keep your back as straight as possible as you lift. Use a hand truck, dolly, or cart when possible.

2. Never place heavy objects on shelves above waist level.

Fire Safety
1. Know where the fire extinguishers are and how to use them.
2. At the first sign of a fire, get the nearest fire extinguisher and spray it at the base of the fire. For very small fires, use salt. If you are unsure of exactly what to do, immediately get someone to help.
3. Immediately notify manager if a fire has started in or around the restaurant. The only exceptions are flame-ups in broilers and other cooking equipment that may commonly occur in the kitchen. If the manager cannot be found and the fire cannot be put out immediately, *calmly* tell customers and employees that the building needs to be evacuated.

Cleaning Products and Chemicals
1. Carefully read the labels on all cleaning products before using them. If you have not been properly trained to use any product, ask an experienced employee or the manager. Too strong a solution can be harmful to your skin or the objects you are cleaning.

!!!!!!!!!! **DO NOT MIX BLEACH WITH AMMONIA** !!!!!!!!!

It creates deadly chlorine gas. The restaurant should not have both on the property.
2. Never put cleaning chemicals or other poisons in drinking glasses or cups.
3. Store cleaning products in a completely separate area from food products.

When to Alert Management
1. To prevent injuries, point out all potential dangers, such as defective equipment, broken furniture, shelves, and doors to management and other employees immediately.
2. Report all accidents, such as cuts, falls, and injuries, to management immediately.
3. See Fire Safety.

Miscellaneous Safety Rules
1. If you must leave a pan on the stove unattended, turn the handle away from the aisle side of the range.
2. Clean all spills on the floor immediately. If it cannot be cleaned up immediately, either place a "wet floor" sign in front of it that is visible to everyone walking by or have someone there to warn people about spill until it can be cleaned and dried.
3. Do not put broken glass or china in a trashcan. It must be placed directly into a box labeled "broken dishes."

Robbery Policy
    In the event of a robbery, remain calm—all the robber generally wants is money. The robber may have a knife or gun, but this is only to show that he or she means business. If an employee loses control, a robber who may be drunk or on drugs may use the weapon in reaction to the excitement. Therefore, cooperate with the robber by handing over the money. Do your best to get a description of the robber without being too obvious. Look for unique features such as scars, accents, clothing, mannerisms, type of walk, facial hair (a beard or mustache), type of car, license plate number, or anything else that may help police identify the robber. After the robber has left and is out of view, call the police.

Employee Performance Appraisal
    Your manager will regularly evaluate your work performance to let you know how you are doing and what you can do to improve your performance. The appraisal can help you increase your chances for higher wages and advancement within the business. You will receive written appraisals at least every six months, and oral appraisals as management sees the need for them. If at any time you would like to know how you are doing, ask your manager (preferably away from other employees and definitely not around customers).

Discipline
    When you do not act in accordance with the goals and standards of the business, you will be made aware of the improper action to limit the chances of it happening again. Disciplinary procedures are in writing so that you will know what response to expect for any of the actions listed in the categories below (see **Figure 8.2: Disciplinary Actions**). Each employee's time on the job, performance, and any circumstances pertaining to the action will be taken into consideration by management when deciding what action to take.

    Right to Appeal. You may appeal any action brought against you if you feel you have been misjudged or terminated unfairly. Your first appeal should be to the supervisor or the manager who disciplined you. You may appeal to succeeding levels of management if you are not satisfied. Any appeal should begin within two weeks of the disciplinary action.

Figure 8.2: Disciplinary Actions

	First Offense	Second Offense	Third Offense
Category 1	Termination		
Category 2	Written Warning	Termination	
Category 3	Oral Warning,	Written Warning	Termination

(Note: Many firms have a *suspension* between the Written Warning and Termination. They give the employee a day off with or without pay—must be the same for everyone. The employee then has a meeting with the manager to determine if continued employment is in the best interest of the employee and the firm. If not, the employee can be given the opportunity to quit, rather than being fired.)

CATEGORY 1

1. Gross insubordination or any flagrant act, including fighting, intimidation of other employees or customers, refusing to cooperate, not showing up for an assigned shift, or poor conduct, that reflects seriously on the business or hinders the ability of the business to operate smoothly.

2. Willfully destroying or damaging property.

3. Use of alcohol or illegal drugs while on duty.

4. Theft or other acts of dishonesty, such as giving away food, stealing from the business or anyone associated with the business such as employees or customers, and falsification of such items as time cards, guest checks, or inventory reports.

5. Possession of a weapon or anything that represents a danger to employees or customers.

CATEGORY 2

1. Not complying with the business's uniform policy.

2. Negligent waste of any business item such as food, beverages, dishes, or silverware.

3. Misuse or abuse of the business's equipment or furniture.

4. Ignoring safety rules.

5. Reporting for work under the influence of alcohol or illegal drugs, or when your ability is impaired by its use.

6. Use of offensive or abusive language around customers or employees.

7. Any action that negatively affects the reputation of the business.

8. Reckless noncompliance in working toward company goals.

9. Not complying with the alcohol service policy.

CATEGORY 3

1. Not complying with general company policies.

2. Working in a disorderly or unsanitary manner.

3. Not properly performing assigned duties, after being trained and counseled.

4. Nonproductive use of work time.

5. Carelessness in the performance of tasks.

Recordkeeping

The federal government requires the business to keep current information on all employees. Notify management if there is a change in any of the following.

    1. Address or telephone number.

    2. Person to be notified in case of an emergency.

    3. Your legal name.

    4. Number of income tax deductions.

Equal Employment Policy

Based on the Civil Rights Acts of 1964, 1991, and related laws, the company prohibits discrimination based on race, color, national origin, sex (gender), age, religious beliefs, pregnancy, disabilities, and other categories as covered by Federal or State laws. The government agency that administers Equal Employment Opportunity (EEO) is the Equal Employment Opportunity Commission (EEOC). This law applies to applicants and all other terms and conditions of employment, including pay raises, promotions, and termination.

<u>**Miscellaneous General Policies**</u>

1. Refer requests for employee applications to the manager.

2. There is a locked suggestion box in the restaurant. If you have any ideas that would help make the business a better place to work or improve the food or service, write the idea down and submit it. If your idea is used, you may be eligible for a cash bonus. Management is open to new ideas and is willing to try to improve any situation. Unsigned suggestions or problems with other employees or business policies will be given serious attention.

3. The business's hours of operation should be included in the handbook.

4. Any changes in the schedule must be recorded in the shift change book (a bound book with numbered pages) and approved in writing by the manager as follows.

    a. Record the shift, including time, position or station, day, and date.

    b. The scheduled employee and the replacement employee must both sign, verifying that both are aware of the change.

    c. Circle the name of the employee picking up the shift, denoting that he or she is responsible.

    d. At this point, ask the manager to approve the change.

    e. Once a change has been approved, the replacement employee is fully responsible for the shift.

5. Employee telephone numbers may not be given out to anyone not employed by the business.

<u>Optional Policies</u>

Specific policies not included in the employee handbook will be posted on the bulletin board or available in the manager's office.

Paid Vacations

(Paid vacations for all employees are highly recommended. If every employee who worked for the business earned vacation time, labor costs would increase by slightly more than 2%. Because of turnover this figure is closer to 1%. The cost of training new employees can be between 2% and 5% of labor costs, not including product waste and reductions in product quality, service quality, and customer counts.)

Policy: All employees are eligible for paid vacations after one year of continuous work. Hourly employees will be paid their normal hourly rate times the average number of hours worked per week. Servers will be paid their guaranteed hourly wage or minimum wage, whichever is higher, times the average number of hours they work each week.

Hourly personnel will receive paid vacations as follows:

1. First year of continuous employment—one week

2. Two or more years of continuous employment—one week plus one additional day per year, up to a maximum of ten days.

3. You must take earned vacation time before your next anniversary date or risk forfeiting it. You must request vacation times at least two month's in advance. Management will make every possible effort to accommodate each employee's vacation request. Seniority and the needs of the business will be considered when scheduling vacations.

4. Employees who resign (voluntary termination) will receive earned vacation pay, provided they give two weeks' notice. Employees who are fired (involuntary termination) will receive earned vacation pay, provided the termination was not the result of a Category 1 violation.

Employee Meals Option

Most hotels and restaurants have an employee meal benefit of some type. The following three alternatives are most commonly used:

1. All employees eat for half price.

2. Kitchen personnel eat certain menu items free of charge; all other personnel pay half price. (Most common in full-service restaurants.)

3. All employees can eat certain menu items free of charge during their shift. (Most common in quick-service restaurants.)

4. A special meal is provided free of charge for all employees each day.

An additional benefit is to allow each employee and up to one friend to eat at half price when the employee is off duty. Employees normally pay happy hour prices whenever they order alcoholic beverages (two drink maximum for off duty employees of legal drinking age). Some restaurants prefer to charge full price to discourage employees from drinking.

Uniform Policy Option

Since uniforms and uniform policies vary, you must write your own policy. If uniforms are not issued, call the policy a dress code. An example of a dress code might be that servers should wear pastel, long-sleeved oxford shirts, khaki slacks, and brown shoes. If uniforms are issued, have employees sign an agreement stating that they have received them, are responsible for wearing them in a certain manner and condition (i.e., wrinkle-free, shirt tucked in, etc.), and any conditions for returning them (e.g., upon voluntary or involuntary termination). If employees are required to purchase uniforms, the business must provide free uniforms to those employees who are paid minimum wage because no required business expense can reduce an employee's wage below that minimum. Servers who work under the tip credit law are considered minimum-wage employees.

Tuition Option

Paying tuition for employees can reduce turnover. There must be a limit on the amount and it should be equally available to all employees who want to further their education.

Tuition

We consider education important to your future. Therefore, the business will reimburse you for college or vocational courses under the following terms:

1. You must be employed by the business for six months before requesting any funds.

2. Reimbursement will not be made for courses that began before your first six months with the company.

3. The maximum benefit amount is $_____ each year.

4. You must present a receipt as proof of payment.

5. Tuition reimbursement will be made once you provide proof of satisfactory completion of the course (a certificate of completion or a grade of C or better).

Off-duty Employees

When you are in the restaurant and off duty, do not disturb or distract employees who are working.

If you are off-duty and eating at the restaurant as a customer, behave like a customer. Do not walk through areas that are off limits to customers or overly fraternize with other employees. Since regular customers may recognize you as a restaurant employee, please conduct yourself in a mature manner.

There is a two-drink limit (liquor, beer, or wine) for off-duty employees who are of drinking age.

On-duty Employees

Never sit with customers while on duty. (Some companies like their servers to sit next to customers while taking an order.)

Do not graze—that is, eat a little of this and a little of that in the kitchen, food pickup areas, and, especially, in any areas where you can be seen by customers.

Suspicious-Behaving Customers (versus Suspicious Looking)

If a customer is acting suspicious, get the manager. In court it is viewed as discriminatory to associate race or ethnicity with suspicion.

If you suspect a customer of walking a check—that is, leaving the restaurant without paying—get the manager. Do not attempt to handle this situation yourself. There are serious legal consequences for accusing an innocent person of walking a check (in some cases, even a guilty person). This could easily cost the business a thousand times more than the check they did not pay.

Health Card

All employees must maintain current health cards (or other certifications as required by local or State ordinances or codes).

Addendums to the Employee Handbook

See *New Employee Paperwork, Supplemental Position Information*, for other items that can be provided to employees.

Disclaimer

This employee policy handbook is not an employment contract and, as such, may be changed by management with or without notice to employees. Employees are responsible for abiding by whatever policies are included in the current handbook. (Check with an attorney when preparing the handbook and this disclaimer.)

Case Study 8.1: Developing an Orientation Program

You are a management trainee for a relatively new independent luxury hotel chain (i.e., Ritz-Carlton, Four Seasons, etc.). Though the hotel has excellent employee policies, including job descriptions, job specifications, employee manuals, and so forth, there is no organized orientation process.

Required:

Prepare an orientation program for housekeepers or any position assigned by your instructor. This should include a relatively detailed list of what should be done for both a general property and job specific orientation.

_____

_____

_____

_____

_____

_____

_____

_____

_____

_____

_____

_____

_____

_____

_____

_____

Case Study 8.2: Giving an Orientation
Required:

1. Select a company that you either currently work at or have worked for in the past.

2. For a hotel, assume that you are the Director of Human Resources. For a restaurant, assume that you are the General Manager.

3. Select one position.

4. Based on your knowledge of the firm and general knowledge of the position, conduct an orientation with a classmate as the orientee (the new employee). Review the following outline with employees.

• Welcome the employee (See Welcome information at beginning of Employee Handbook).

• Provide some information about their new surroundings.

• History and traditions of the company.

• Company values (If you need help, see Four Seasons Hotel and Resorts Corporate Values in Chapter Two.).

• What the business has to offer employees (See General Property Orientation in this Chapter).

• How departments work together (teamwork, cross-functional coordination).

• Review and stress the importance of the five responsibilities of employees:

       1. <u>Dependable</u> (Show up for work on time, perform the work specified in your job description, and maintain high ethical standards.)

       2. <u>Personality and customer-service orientation</u> (Be friendly to everyone.)

       3. <u>Teamwork </u>(Help other employees as you have time.)

       4. <u>Performance</u> (a combination of knowledge, ability and effort)

       5. <u>Personal grooming and hygiene</u> (neat appearance, bathe daily and use deodorant)

• Safety rules (Something related to their position.)

• Performance appraisals (How often and a brief overview.)

• Discipline (We have a four tiered/progressive disciplinary process):

       1. <u>Oral warning</u>, 2. <u>Written warning</u>, 3. <u>Suspension</u>—if the employee has potential with

         the firm, but has made a few mistakes, 4. <u>Termination</u>

• Briefly explain how the various departments work together, in particular the department that the orientee will be working in.

• Where to clock in

• End with a "welcome," a "thank you," and let them know where they go next. Example: "Thank you for your time. I'm now going to turn you over to your department head (or supervisor). If I can ever help you with anything, please let me know."

Orientee is to evaluate the orientation based on:

1. Establishment of rapport.

2. Made me feel important.

3. I have a reasonable understanding of what is expected of me, at least as far as what was reviewed in this exercise.

4. I feel confident about going to work for this company.

_____

_____

_____

_____

_____

_____

Chapter Nine: Training

Strategy Review: Prepare a strategy review for this chapter (See back of Chapter One).
Case Study 9.1: Designing a Training Program
Chapter Objectives: After reading this chapter you should understand and be able to do the following:
1. Explain the purpose of training.
2. Discuss the similarity between a hospitality manager's main responsibilities and that of routine training.
3. Discuss the benefits of training.
4. List the types of training.
5. Describe training needs assessment.
6. List and explain the four components of a training program.
7. Design a training program for any job.
8. Explain how people learn.
9. List and explain the four steps of the job-instruction-training process.
10. Describe various on-the-job and off-the-job training methods.
11. Discuss typical content of training manuals for any position.
12. Explain how a training schedule is created.
13. Assess the competence of a trainee.
14. Understand the logic behind the knowledge/ability hierarchy for training.
15. Describe the traits of a good trainer.
16. Evaluate the effectiveness of a training program.

The Basics of Training

Training provides employees with the *knowledge* and the *ability* to perform their duties and tasks at the highest reasonable level. Additional benefits include improved morale and efficiency (i.e., cost control), greater opportunities for employee advancement and personal growth, ability to deal with unique managerial challenges, reduced supervision, improved safety, and enhancing the firm's reputation. Its proper execution is one of the most important elements in a business's success. Metaphorically, it has been said that the job of the manager is to turn lumps of coal into diamonds. That is, to take people with minimal skills, but good potential, and turn them into great employees. Once employees are trained, it is then the responsibility of management and the employee to make sure that employees put forth the appropriate *effort* to continue to maximize the knowledge and abilities learned during the training process. Unfortunately, many businesses pay little, or at least not enough attention to training because it is time consuming, another task to take care of in a manager's already busy schedule, costs money, and is not a revenue-producing activity. More unfortunate is the fact that any savings in time or money from minimizing training is a false savings because as one intuitively might suspect, training improves performance and profit (Luthans, Avey, Avolio, & Peterson, 2010; Paul & Anatharaman, 2003).

Training in the hospitality industry has historically focused on on-the-job training for a certain number of days, followed by actual job performance (often referred to as soloing). Over the past several decades through increased competition and more astute customers, our industry has become significantly more sophisticated. This has forced firms to upgrade their training programs. A typical training program now includes off-the-job training such as: classes to learn about specific responsibilities of the job and to review what has been learned; testing over information presented in training manuals; computers that show how things are supposed to be done and can either test employees or have them participate by stating, for example, what the employee should have done when the customer complained about the steak; videos that can show both the right and wrong way to do something; and role-playing that allows the employee to practice without their efforts affecting a customer's experience. As labor cost increases, more firms are attempting to put much of their training on computer programs (Liddle, 2008). It is important that this strategy be cautiously considered. Since so much of what is done in the hospitality industry is labor-intensive and people-oriented, effective training cannot be accomplished without interaction with others.

<u>**Routine Training and the Hospitality Manager's Job**</u>

Depending on one's perspective, the most important responsibility of management is to make sure the business shows a profit. Profit is based on sales being high relative to expenses. Sales are kept high by making sure that customers are satisfied. Managers make sure customers are satisfied by having employees follow company policies. Therefore, the majority of managerial success is based on the manager's ability to train employees to perform their duties and tasks at an acceptable level of competence. Supervision, what managers spend much of their time doing, is how they verify that employees are continuing to perform as they were trained. Therefore, the ability to effectively train others and oversee the results is one of the most important responsibilities of the manager.

Benefits of Training

Training has many benefits. The key is to do it properly and professionally to achieve the following benefits.

<u>**Knowledge and Control**</u>

Since management cannot properly train an employee without knowing what needs to be done and how it should be done, training forces management to analyze in detail all routine activities of the business (duties and tasks). Management can then decide whether employees are working at levels that meet the standards of the business and therefore can know who needs more training and who does not.

<u>**Improved Efficiency**</u>

A good training program is the most economical way to teach new employees what they need to know to make a contribution to the business. Subsequently, experienced employees do not need to help new employees as much. This allows the experienced employees to work with fewer interruptions, thereby increasing their productivity and morale. When employees are properly trained, less time is needed to accomplish each task, increasing worker output (production capacity) and thereby, sales potential.

<u>**Improved Morale**</u>

Training improves employee morale by letting employees know that management is concerned enough about them to spend the time to train them. Employees who are properly trained have more self-confidence, are happier with themselves, earn more, and stay on the job longer. Morale also improves because they are also maximizing both their ability and compensation.

<u>**Greater Opportunity for Advancement**</u>

Training increases employees' opportunities for advancement because, once an effective training program has begun, people will develop more rapidly in their present positions by increasing their knowledge and performing better.

There are also opportunities for becoming a trainer. The majority of corporations have trainers for all levels of employees. There are unit level trainers, such as server trainers; trainers for new locations, where excellent employees are invited to help with the opening; ongoing training performed by unit-level trainers and managers; and corporate training of various types, such as for new managers, new locations, and so forth. One benefit of being a corporate trainer is a more traditional schedule, generally 8 a.m. to 5 p.m., Monday through Friday; however, travel is usually required.

<u>**Versatility**</u>

Training facilitates cross-training (also known as rotation), making employees more versatile and therefore, more valuable to the business. It is easier to complete an employee schedule when employees are trained for two or more positions.

<u>**Vehicle for Change**</u>

When it becomes necessary to change the way something is done, a training program provides a built-in vehicle with which to make the change. It also makes new tasks easier for employees because the tasks can be properly communicated and implemented, rather than being informally passed on from one person to another.

<u>**Reduced Supervision**</u>

Training makes management easier because it reduces the need for supervision. Rather than coping with the problems caused by improper training, management can concentrate on the little things that increase customer satisfaction or other ways of increasing sales.

Improved Safety

Proper training reduces the number of accidents and injuries for employees and customers. This in turn can have a major impact on Workers' Compensation claims. Injuries not only cause physical pain, but also psychological pain as employees perceive the business to be a risky place to work. Because the employees now know what to do, training can also lead to increased confidence in cases of crises, such as fires or robberies (Williams & Thwaites, 2007).

Cost Control

Proper training can reduce product waste, inefficient use of employee time, and lead to increases in productivity.

Improved Reputation

Much of a business's reputation is based on consistent quality. Effective training improves the likelihood of customers having a great experience each time they patronize the business.

Types of Training

There are six basic types of training in the hospitality business. These include the following:

Pre-Opening Training

Unless a business that had significant problems was being taken over, pre-opening training for opening a new business is the most challenging training situation. Virtually none of the employees know what to do, the potential business volume is unknown, and duties and tasks may not have been fully tested. Some employees may have experience at other businesses, but they must still be trained for their new job.

Training of new Employees for an Existing Business

This is the most common type of training. Each new employee that is hired must be trained to perform up to certain standards.

Ongoing Training

Training must be continuous to make sure that all employees are performing up to or above the standards of the business. Some question the need for this, but look at professional sports teams that teach fundamentals to athletes with many years of experience. This would generally focus on training for specific requirements of a position or could be focused on common aspect of all jobs, such as customer service training.

Cross-Training or Rotation

This involves training employees who work in one position, such as front desk agent, and in another position, such as server in the hotel's restaurant. It is most effective when employees are cross-trained in areas where some of their present skills can be used. For example, front of the house employees, those working in the dining room and bar area, can be cross-trained in other front of the house areas. Those who work in the kitchen (sauté, fry, pantry, broiler, pastry, etc.) can be cross-trained in different kitchen areas. This practice allows for flexibility of scheduling, filling positions in emergencies, maximization of employee abilities, and reduction of boredom. This way when an employee does not show up for work or extra help is needed in another area of the business, cross-trained employees can help.

New Policy Implementation

Training with the objective of implementing new policies or procedures. Although skills, such as that of a housekeeper, will rarely undergo extensive changes, some changes for each position are inevitable.

Personal or Professional Development

As opposed to training for a specific position in the business, development refers to education that helps employees improve their opportunities for personal growth and advancement. Topics could include traditional business subjects, such as management, marketing, and accounting or topics like diversity, personal finance, communication, creativity, literacy, and crisis training. The format can vary from 30-minute meetings at the business, seminars outside the business, to classes offered in college. The goals are to help employees increase their personal and business competence and subsequently, to provide the business with future managers and leaders, and to help the business improve its performance (e.g., ideally set higher standards) (Costen, Johanson, & Poisson, 2010).

Training Needs Assessment

There must be various means of assessing the need for training. As with most anything in business, the key means of identifying problems should be the control component of the planning process. For example, are we meeting our objectives in customer satisfaction of 4.6 on a 5-point scale? If not, the cause must be found—perhaps training, perhaps not. There are also management assessments of strategies related to training, such as employees seem to be unhappy with the current training program; managers having to frequently correct employees; or customers complaining more than usual. Other related methods include manager meetings (in larger hotels referred to as executive committee meetings), employee advisory groups (e.g., housekeeping or some other group of employees discussing the training program), poor performance appraisals being linked to poor training, regular competence testing of employees, and guest comment cards and surveys. The above examples are referred to as operational controls—that is, achieving the firm's objectives and the implementation of effective strategies and tactics to achieve the objectives.

Another category is strategic controls, which identifies changes in the firm's situational analysis—the internal and environmental analyses. For example, has the ability of the HR department to prepare effective training programs diminished (internal analysis)? Are competitors providing better quality service based on a superior training program (environmental analysis)?

One of the first topics covered in this book is that of symptoms and causes. Management must make sure that when it identifies a perceived need for more training, that this is in fact the case. For example, when managers see employees that are not following policies—the symptom, rather than the cause being poor training, it could be low morale, poor scheduling, lack of effective equipment, and so forth.

Developing a Training Program
Any training program is based on the sequential process of first determining what employees will be trained to do (i.e., The Job Analysis or duties and tasks); next, how they will be trained (i.e., training methods); followed by, the timing for their training (e.g., the schedule, Day 1 this is done, Day 2 that is done, etc.), and finally, the level of competence expected before employees can work on their own (see **Figure 9.1: Developing a Training Program**).

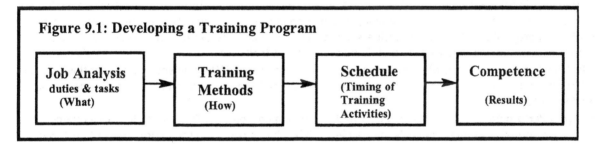

Figure 9.1: Developing a Training Program

| Job Analysis duties & tasks (What) | → | Training Methods (How) | → | Schedule (Timing of Training Activities) | → | Competence (Results) |

Job Analysis
A job analysis for the position is needed to show the details of how things should be done (e.g., the duties and tasks, see Chapter Five, Job Creation Process). This is what the employees will be trained to do. Before management goes further, it must determine if the duties and tasks for the position are accurate and effective. Sometimes, such as for new businesses that have not opened to the public, this may be very difficult. In such cases, management must simply prepare the best duties and tasks lists that it feels it can. Generally, each position will have a position manual (also referred to as a training manual) that includes the job analysis information for the position, plus other relevant information (e.g., menu abbreviations, bar abbreviations, how to use the property management system or point-of-sale terminals, and general information, such as an articles on the characteristics of excellent service, how to upsell rooms, motivation tools, etc.).

Training Methods
Training methods consist of knowing how people learn—auditory, visual, and kinesthetics (AVK); job-instruction-training (JIT); job training methods (OJT); and the organization of the training program.
How People Learn
Managers need to consider the cognitive learning patterns of trainees and how best to utilize those patterns in their training. Individuals have differences in how they learn best. Some learn best by hearing (*auditory*), some by seeing (*visual*), and some by doing (*kinesthetic*), hence, AVK. Virtually all training should begin with auditory and

visual learning methods, such as a lecture or discussion of what the trainee will be doing. Because most hourly employees are paid to *do things* (e.g., checking in guests, cooking, cleaning, etc.), their training should be significantly focused on various types of kinesthetic training. Since managers are primarily paid to think, much of their training can be focused on visual and auditory training (e.g., case studies—what would you do in this situation?). No manager could be fully trained without some kinesthetic training, being in the restaurant or hotel supervising employees and performing other managerial duties.

Job-Instruction-Training (JIT)

The following four-step training program is the most common generic format for training employees. Like many things done in business, it was developed by ancient military trainers thousands of years ago. It is applicable for all types of training.

Step 1. Prepare the Employee/Trainee. Training involves learning new tasks or changes. Since this can cause anxiety, it is important to put the trainee at ease by talking about neutral topics such as past jobs, school, and career goals.

A. Describe the job. Briefly review the basic duties and tasks of the position, emphasizing key points, such as safety, accuracy, customer service, following policies, cleanliness, and sanitation.

B. Find out what the employee knows about the job requirements (duties and tasks) for the position. If a trainee for the front desk has for example, worked at the front desk of another hotel for four years, then training can often progress quicker than for someone without any experience.

C. Interest the employee in learning the task by explaining how it would benefit him or her personally, such as better chances of advancement, better tips, pride in his or her work, and that the business expects all employees to perform their tasks properly and according to specific standards.

Step 2. Present the Task. Demonstrate the task(s) one step at a time. Verbally explain the process, emphasizing key points. Establish eye contact to make sure the trainee is paying attention and appears to understand what has been shown.

A. If the trainee is inexperienced, make sure he or she understands each task before moving on to the next. If the trainee is experienced, review all pertinent training information because the trainee's previous experience may not necessarily be appropriate for the current business. Be forewarned that some experienced employees tend to ignore much of their training because they feel they "already know it all."

B. Ask the trainee questions about what he or she has been shown or told: "What do you think about this?" or "Do you understand this?" Encourage the employee to ask questions. Tell him or her "the only dumb question is the one you don't ask."

Step 3. Tryout Performance. Let the trainee perform the duty or a portion of it. This is best done as a role-play so it will not affect normal customer service. Some trainees will be able to complete the entire duty/tasks without problems. Others will need to have it divided into smaller portions to make it easier to understand and perform.

A. Have the trainee explain the key points. A cook could explain what he or she is doing while performing a new task. A front desk agent could sit down with the trainer and explain the process of checking in a guest.

B. Have the trainee ask questions about his or her performance. At this point the trainee knows enough about the task to ask questions that will help achieve a more complete understanding of the duties and tasks.

C. Confirm that the trainee understands the duty/tasks. Ask questions such as, "What does our Bigburger have on it?" or "What is the hotel's cancellation policy?"

D. Have the trainee repeat the task until he or she can perform it at a satisfactory level (up to the standards of the business, perhaps except for speed, but do not expect perfection at this stage).

E. Customer contact during this stage? If trainees are able, they can perform a few duties and tasks for customers under very close supervision. This should be done at first during slow periods, then, as the trainee's performance improves, during busier periods (i.e., greater volume). Closely monitor the trainee's performance during the tryout performance. In some businesses there may be positions or activities that only the very experienced or talented can perform (e.g., broiler, sauté, concierge, etc.). Trainees can attempt these tasks under close supervision, but they should not be a major requirement of the job at this point. Be supportive and let the trainee know that the particular task is very difficult and that he or she will get better with practice.

F. Praise the trainee's proper performance, constructively correcting areas where improvement is needed.

Step 4. Follow up. At this stage the employee should be able to perform *most* assigned tasks without direct supervision.

A. Have someone available at all times in case the trainee needs help or wants to ask a question. All employees should know that they are expected to help trainees in any way they can.

B. At first, check the trainee's performance frequently, then taper off to normal employee supervision. Continue to monitor the trainee's performance with praise and counseling as needed.

Management should verbally critique or coach each employee's performance on a regular basis, preferably weekly or twice a month. This way management keeps track of each employee's performance and employees know that they are being monitored and supported. This gives them the opportunity to get positive feedback if their performance is good, or counseling if they need improvement.

Job Training Methods

Managers need to determine how they will teach the employee to perform the duties and tasks in the job analysis. There are two general options, off-the-job and on-the-job training. Both AVK concepts and JIT methods can be used for any training methods.

• **Off-the-Job Training**. The primary examples of off-the-job training include role-play, lecture, lecture combined with discussion and case studies, videos, computer, simulations, and virtual reality. For hourly employees, role-play is by far the most effective and efficient means of training. It consists of having trainees perform a series of tasks just as employees would in the actual job, except that they perform it for another employee, rather than for a customer. Prior to role-play beginning, the trainee should have the tasks thoroughly explained to them and have a reasonable understanding of what will be done. They should also have the opportunity to try it out to gain a little confidence. For example, after the review of customer service in a restaurant, a server trainee could practice taking orders off the menu from a trainer, inputting the order into a point-of-sales system (in the training mode), then serving the trainer (either real food or just empty plates). If food were used, submitting the order to the kitchen and picking it up could be added to the role-play process. As can be seen, this method comes as close to approximating the actual activity of serving a customer as possible—without risking customer satisfaction. Other benefits include reducing the stress on the trainee and improving the ability of the trainer to constructively make suggestions during or after the training session. An excellent option that increases the reality of role-play is to have the trainee serve another employee in the dining room during an actual meal period. A one-table station with regular customers who know they are being served by a trainee, is another option. In this case, the customer's meal could be complimentary.

Forty years ago the vast majority of college students were taught mainly by lecture. Interaction with the professor or with other students was rare. Today, straight lecture is rare and has been replaced by a mix of lecture, discussions, and in-class case studies—a much more effective method for students *and* trainees. The reason for the change was that straight lecture rarely engages students' minds and is therefore minimally effective. Sitting in class (college or training) for an hour or so and simply listening and taking notes is little better than having the trainee skip the class and read on their own. Since a video can combine both lecture and action, it can be better than a straight lecture, but it depends on the quality of the video. Too many times, the video is out of date and may seem more comical than a serious learning method. Computers can be excellent, *if* they are interactive. As the video or script is being shown to the trainee, there should be questions about what has been covered (e.g., Dishes should be removed from the A. right, B. left, C. right or left). This way the trainee is actively involved, training topics are reinforced through questions, and management, via the test results, knows whether the trainee has learned what was presented. Simulations generally consist of a relatively complex case study with groups of participants competing with other groups to find the best solution. Because of the expense of the software and the time needed to learn to use them, in the few cases when they are used, they are generally used only for management trainees. Virtual reality software, while rarely used at this time, would be almost perfect for training, as actual scenarios could be provided to trainees who would then respond to them. Their responses could be graded by the software or by a trainer who is monitoring the session. The results could be compared with others who have completed the training. As the prices of virtual reality software and hardware come down in price, it will probably one day be a commonly used format for hospitality training.

• **On-the-Job Training (OJT)**. The primary examples of on-the-job training include shadowing, task performance under close supervision, and coaching. *Shadowing* is popular because, as with role-play, the trainee is generally not doing anything that will risk negatively impacting the customer's experience. In shadowing, the trainee simply follows the trainer as he or she performs routine tasks of the job. Because much of what a manager does is supervisory in nature (i.e., walking around and making sure everything is going okay), shadowing is a great training method for managers. When possible, such as in housekeeping, the trainer could explain what is being done during the session. While shadowing is very popular, there is a downside. Some trainees are not comfortable standing and watching, especially in front of customers. For example, a server trainee has just been introduced to a table of four customers in a restaurant. While the trainer is taking the order, the trainee must stand next to them for several minutes with nothing to do or say. This discomfort can be minimized somewhat by trying to involve them verbally or physically in the activity, such as writing down the order. Once the trainee has been shown how to perform their required tasks and has practiced them competently in role-play, they may be ready for *task performance*. Here, the trainee performs the job as a regular employee under close supervision. *Coaching* is done not only for trainees, but for all employees. Even the most experienced employee will occasionally need a suggestion on how to improve. A lesson from sports is that even the best athletes in the world have coaches to help them improve their performance. Hospitality employees should be no different.

Organization of the Training Program

A training program should be set up for each position in the hotel or restaurant. The program is structured around a training manual for each position. Each manual could include a training schedule, job description, a daily breakdown of major activities, necessary tests, a copy of the trainer's checklist, and any other written information related to the position. These manuals will standardize the training process, make it easier for management to train employees, and make it easier for the trainer and trainee to understand their respective responsibilities. The trainer could consider reviewing the manual with the trainee each day during the training period.

Training Manuals

The following are sample Tables of Contents for training manuals for a few positions.

Manager's Training Manual

- Training schedule
- Job description (general responsibilities)
- Job analysis
- Manager's daily tasklist
- Management paperwork (daily sales report, food cost controls, labor cost controls, and new employee paperwork)
- Tests: The manager must complete each test given at the business.
- Trainer's checklist
- Employee manual

Front Desk Agent's Training Manual

- Training schedule
- Job description
- Job analysis
- Using the property management system
- Register checkout procedure
- Tests: Property Management System, Check-in and Check-out Procedure, and Employee Policy
- Trainer's checklist

Kitchen Worker's Training Manual

- Training schedule
- Job description
- Job analysis
- Menu abbreviations and descriptions
- Prep lists
- Recipes
- Menu assembly guidelines
- Station setup
- Daily kitchen tasklist
- Closing checklist
- Weekly cleaning schedule
- Tests: menu abbreviations, menu descriptions, kitchen procedures, kitchen personnel, employee policy, and others, if applicable
- Trainer's checklist

Server's Training Manual
- Training schedule
- Job description
- Job analysis
- Menu abbreviations and descriptions
- Drink prices, brands, and abbreviations
- Server sidework
- Writing the order
- Using the point-of-sales terminal
- Server checkout procedure
- Tests: menu abbreviations, menu descriptions, alcoholic beverage, alcohol service policy, server, and employee policies
- Trainer's checklist

Schedule

A schedule must be prepared detailing what the trainee will be doing each day during training. This entails taking the chosen OJT training methods and breaking them down in a way that best allows the trainee to learn how to perform the duties and tasks. Each of the training methods/concepts reviewed above (AVK, JIT, OJT) can be used for training employees or anyone for virtually anything.

There is no one best way to prepare a training schedule. The general rules are to work up from simple duties/tasks to more complex; to allow for repetition of important and difficult duties/tasks; and to assess the trainee's performance after each duty/task is attempted to learn if it was done correctly and if the trainee is ready for the next task. It is also important (at least ideal) for management to meet with the trainee for at least a few minutes at the beginning and end of each training day to ask the trainee how he or she thinks the training is going; show that management is involved in the process and is concerned that the trainee is having a good experience; and to discuss areas where the trainee, trainer, or company could improve.

The following are sample training schedules for the positions of manager and server. Each business will have varying training requirements, so specific training schedules must be developed to effectively coordinate the process. Once approved as policy, the schedules must be diligently followed during each employee's training. Some variations may be required, such as when employees learn quicker than scheduled or need more time.

Manager's Training Schedule (Hotel or Restaurant)

The manager should be trained at each position in the business, according to those positions' specific training schedules, as well as be trained to perform all duties and tasks in their own job analysis or training manual. The length of time devoted to training for each position will depend on the experience of the trainee, his or her progress, and the opinions of the trainer and managers.

It is important to train managers in all areas of the business. Frequently, the area receiving the least attention during training very often will cause the most trouble later. The areas that are most often neglected are cleanliness and sanitation, safety, security, energy management, and equipment management. The trainee should read the manager's position manual thoroughly and use it as a training guide and supplement to on-the-job training.

During the management portion of the training program, give the trainee increased responsibilities and authority to perform each task. At the end of a designated period (based on the size and complexity of the operation), the trainee should be able to perform all management tasks with minimal assistance. At the end of a second designated period, the trainee should be able to perform all management tasks at a satisfactory level with further improvement expected as tasks are repeated.

Administer tests at convenient times. For each test, a score of 85% is considered passing. The tests may be retaken two times. If a score of 85% or better is not achieved on this or any test, then the general manager must determine if it is the best interest of the trainee to remain with the firm, or if there is an alternative solution.

At the end of the training, the manager, the trainer (the trainer is likely a manager), and the trainee should evaluate the trainee's progress and review the manager's training checklist. The manager and trainer decide whether the trainee is ready to work on his or her own.

DAY 1 (Manager's Training Schedule)

1. The trainer reviews the manager's training schedule with the trainee.

2. The trainer and trainee review the manager's training manual, concentrating on the manager's job description. The trainee receives his or her own copy of the manager's training manual.

3. The trainee shadows (follows) the trainer throughout the day and the trainer explains each task as it is completed.

4. At least four times during the day, the trainer and the trainee sit down and review what has happened up to that time and what will happen next.

5. The trainer and trainee have a question-and-answer period at the end of the day.

DAY 2 AND THEREAFTER

The trainee will be trained at each position, based on the respective manuals, for the amount of time indicated. The following is for a midscale hotel:

1. Front desk, four shifts

2. Night auditor, two shifts

3. Housekeeper, two shifts

4. Maintenance, two shifts

5. Human Resources, five shifts

6. Marketing Department, 10 shifts

7. Manager (routine oversight of the hotel), approximately one month, depending on how the trainee is progressing and the complexity of the responsibilities

The following is for a casual-dining restaurant:

1. Kitchen, 3 weeks or up to one week at each major kitchen position (e.g., broiler, sauté, pantry, fry, set-up)

2. Dishwasher, 2 shifts

3. Expeditor, 3 shifts

4. Busser, two shifts

5. Host, one shift

6. Server, one week

7. Manager (routine oversight of the restaurant), approximately one month

Server's Training Schedule

The server trainee should memorize all the menu abbreviations and be prepared to take the menu abbreviations test on the first day of work.

DAY 1

1. The manager on duty meets with the trainee and the trainer to welcome the trainee, makes sure everything is okay, and has a general discussion of what will happen for the day.

2. The trainee takes the menu abbreviations test. A score of 85% is considered passing. The test may be retaken two times on successive days.

     For most tests: If a score of 85% or better is not achieved on this or any test, then the general manager must determine if it is in the best interest of the trainee to remain with the firm, or if there is an alternative solution.

3. The trainee works in kitchen helping with prep, cleanup, and setup for lunch.

4. The trainee shadows from the pickup side of the serving line, observing tickets going into the kitchen, orders being cooked or plated, food being assembled for pickup, and food being picked up by the servers.

5. As things slow down, the trainee can help cooks in each station prepare a few items (e.g., salad, broiler, fry, etc.)—only things that are not potentially dangerous (e.g., no knife use without proper training, etc.).

6. The trainee can help with cleanup in the salad station—only things that are not potentially dangerous. Cleanup in the hot food station may be too dangerous for someone who is not properly trained.

7. The trainee, trainer, and manager meet to review how things went for the day. Any applicable reports such as checklists, evaluations, and assessments can be completed at the end of the day.

Day 2

1. The trainee, trainer, and manager meet for a general discussion of what to expect for the day.

2. The trainee takes the table numbers test. A score of 100% is required. The test may be retaken two times on successive days.

3. The trainer reviews the server's training manual with the trainee.

4. The trainer thoroughly reviews the server position guidelines with the trainee and solicits and answers questions.

5. The trainee works with the host during the busiest period of the shift, for between 30 minutes and one hour. The host teaches the trainee the location and purpose of the table sections, how to seat customers, and other basic responsibilities of the position.

6. The trainee works with the busser during a slower period of the shift for between 30 minutes and one hour.

7. The trainer shows the trainee how to use a tray and tray jack, how to serve and refill beverages, and how to pre-bus a table.

8. The trainer shows the trainee how take orders and ring them up.

9. The trainee, trainer, and manager meet to review how things went for the day. Any applicable reports such as checklists, evaluations, and assessments can be completed at the end of the day.

DAY 3

1. The trainee, trainer, and manager meet for a general discussion of what to expect for the day.

2. The trainer reviews the server's training manual with the trainee and solicits and answers questions.

3. The trainer should set up a role-play exercise to teach the trainee how to serve customers. The closer the role-play can be to actual food service, the better.

4. The trainee shadows (follows) the trainer through an entire shift. As the shift progresses, the trainer should allow the trainee to perform each of the duties and tasks during slow periods.

5. The trainee rings up all of the trainer's guest checks.

6. The trainee presents and refills beverages.

7. The trainee learns how to garnish alcoholic beverages (if applicable).

8. If a "runner system" is used (e.g., any server that is close to the pass thru when food is ready, delivers or *runs* the food), the trainer explains the system, shows how it is done, and lets the trainee run the order for one two-top.

9. The trainee begins to learn how guest checks are issued and how to complete the server's checkout report.

10. The trainee, trainer, and manager meet to review how things went for the day. Any applicable reports such as checklists, evaluations and assessments can be completed at the end of the day.

DAY 4

1. The trainee, trainer, and manager meet for a general discussion of what to expect for the day.

2. The trainee takes the menu descriptions test. A score of 85% is considered passing. The test may be retaken two times.

3. Guest checks are issued to the trainee.

4. The trainee shadows the trainer, working one or two tables (as capable) in the trainer's station for the entire shift.

5. The trainee rings up his or her own guest checks and those of the trainer.

6. The trainee helps with sidework.

7. The trainee completes the server's checkout report with assistance from the trainer.

8. The manager, trainer, and trainee meet to review how things went for the day, evaluate the trainee's progress and decide where emphasis should be placed. Any applicable reports such as checklists, evaluations, and assessments can be completed at the end of the day.

DAY 5

1. The trainee, trainer, and manager meet for a general discussion of what to expect for the day.

2. The trainee takes the alcoholic beverage and alcohol service policy tests (if applicable). A score of 85% is considered passing. The test may be retaken two times.

3. Guest checks are issued to the trainee.

4. The trainee completes the necessary sidework.

5. The trainee works two tables in the trainer's station for the entire shift.

6. The trainee pre-checks his or her own guest checks and those of the trainer.

7. The trainee completes the server's checkout report with assistance from the trainer.

8. The trainee, trainer, and manager meet to review how things went for the day, evaluate the trainee's progress and decide where emphasis should be placed. Any applicable reports such as checklists, evaluations, and assessments can be completed at the end of the day.

DAY 6

1. The trainee, trainer, and manager meet for a general discussion of what to expect for the day.
2. The trainee takes the server and employee policy tests. A score of 85% on each is considered passing. The tests may be retaken two times.
3. Guest checks are issued to the trainee.
4. The trainee completes the necessary sidework for the assigned station.
5. The trainee works a two- or three-table station (depending on their progress) next to the trainer's station with indirect supervision from the trainer.
6. The trainee completes the server's checkout sheet.
7. The manager, trainer, and trainee evaluate the trainee's progress and complete applicable portions of the server's training checklist. The manager and trainer decide whether the trainee is ready to work on his or her own. Any applicable reports such as checklists, evaluations, and assessments can be completed at the end of the day.

Assessing Competence

Assessment of the level of competence is generally determined through various judgments by the trainer or manager and, as appropriate, by the trainee (i.e., I feel/do not feel confident in my ability). The key to assessing competence is to make sure trainees can work up to the company standards for the specific duties and tasks being learned. That is, can they properly perform the duties and tasks on their own? If customer satisfaction could potentially be compromised, then the trainee is not ready. Different firms have differing philosophies on how competent trainees should be before they can work on their own. This is why some firms have one or several week training programs, while others train their employees for a couple of hours, and unfortunately, in some cases, less.

Training and assessment are normally done in stages. For example, has the trainee mastered various duties and tasks, so they can move on and be trained in the next set of duties and tasks? A front desk agent should be trained to use the hotel's property management system (PMS) before being trained to greet and check in a guest. If competence, or something close, had not been achieved for using the PMS, going on to the next stage of training may not be fruitful.

Quantitative and Qualitative Assessment. There are two general categories of assessments, quantitative (i.e., very objective/minimal subjectivity) and qualitative (i.e., very subjective). These concepts were discussed in Chapter Five, Job Creation Process, and will be covered again in Chapter Ten, Performance Appraisals and Discipline (i.e., how to assess qualitative and quantitative duties and tasks). Their use here in training assessment is essentially the same as in performance appraisals and discipline. Judging the trainees' performance for quantitative duties and tasks is relatively simply. They either did it or did not do it. For example, they completed or did something (e.g., used the guests' names when they checked in); they completed something in a certain amount of time, or completed a certain amount of something within a certain amount of time (e.g., cleaned 12 rooms to the hotel's standards in one eight-hour shift). Qualitative assessments for performance criteria, such as courtesy, respect, personality, and problem-solving skills, can be very subjective. These assessments should only be performed by trainers and managers who have been specifically trained to determine if the trainees' performance is acceptable. For example, without thorough knowledge of what is expected, two different trainers or managers could have differing views on an employee's customer service orientation. However, if each is trained in what to expect, then the evaluation of each trainee's performance on qualitative criteria will be more consistent and accurate.

Knowledge/Ability Hierarchy for Training

This model (see **Figure 9.2: Knowledge/Ability Hierarchy for Training**) provides a theoretical view of the progression of a new employee from virtually total incompetence to a high level of competence. In the first quadrant, *subconsciously incompetent*, employees have not internalized what they are supposed to do, that is, the firm's policies or the standards of how things should be accomplished. It naturally follows since they do not know what they are supposed to do, that they cannot yet perform up to the firm's standards.

Next, employees are *consciously incompetent*; they know what to do because the trainer reviewed the training manual and they have had some training, but the new employees cannot yet perform up to the standards of the firm. Firms at the lower end of the service scale, such as quick-service restaurants and budget hotels will often stop initial training someplace between conscious incompetence and conscious competence. The reasons being that these firms have fewer policies that trainees need to learn and their customers are generally less demanding than concepts with more services and/or higher standards. Customers want the core product offering, the food or the room, and do not expect high levels of service (Reich, Xu, & McCleary, 2010). The obvious question that must be asked is, if firms with lower customer expectations would train their employees at a higher level, would they be able to improve customer and employee satisfaction to a high enough level to be able to afford the extra training costs? Hopefully, the answer would be yes. There is also an interim solution where employees would begin their work at the consciously incompetent level, but be given reduced responsibilities in areas where they are competent. Subsequently, their responsibilities would progressively increase until conscious competence was reached for each of their duties and tasks.

Figure 9.2:   Knowledge/Ability Hierarchy For Training

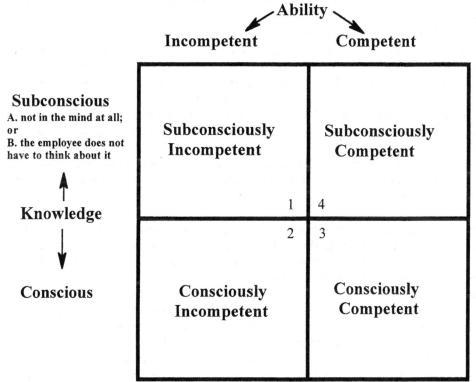

1. Subconsciouly incompetent. At first the information is not in the employees' subconscious (or conscious) mind. (i.e., employees do not know what they are responsible for) and they cannot perform up to company standards (incompetent).

2. Consciously incompetent. After some training, they know what they are responsible for (i.e., they are conscious about it), but cannot yet perform up to company performance standards (incompetent). This will take additional training and performance.

3. Consciouly competent. They can now perform up to company standards (competent), but must think through each step (i.e., consciously think through each step). These employees are somewhat less efficient than their colleagues. If the goal for a certain task was 20 seconds, employees at this stage take take 25 or 30 seconds. If a server had to consciously think through everything that had to be done, it would probably not be possible to deliver excellent service to everyone.

4. Subconsciously competent. The goal of training is to have employees complete most tasks without having to consciously think through each action. This not only makes them more efficient, but reduces their stress levels (i.e., it reduces the number of times they need to worry about what to do next).

Adapted from: National Restaurant Association Supervision Seminar. 1977.

After some practice at their position, employees become *consciously competent*. They can perform most tasks up to the standards of the firm; however, since they must think through each step, they are not as efficient or effective as they should be. For example, newly trained servers may be capable of doing a good job with two tables, while those with more experience can handle four tables. As the new servers are able to more quickly recognize the many things they are responsible for without stopping to think of each of them, they can progress to more tables. The key here is that many restaurants will give new servers who are capable of providing good service to two tables, a four-table station. The result is poor service. Examples of firms that stop initial training at this level are those in the middle of the service scale, such as most full-service hotels and casual-dining restaurants. These firms have policies (i.e., standards) that allow them to provide services that meet a moderate level of customer expectations. As time goes on, the employee will move toward subconscious competence, but it may take a while.

The last stage of training is *subconsciously competent*. Employees know how to perform their duties and tasks and can do many of them quickly and naturally, without thinking through each step or needing to stop and consider what to do next. Another way to express this is that they can multi-task (i.e., do many things at once) at a reasonably high level. An observer watching a subconsciously competent server would see him or her flow from one task to the next, seemingly without thinking—and without missing customer needs, such as an empty water glass, plates that should be removed from the table, a tables that is ready for its check, and a dessert that was ordered that needs to be picked up. Firms at the highest level of the service scale, such a luxury hotels and fin-dining restaurants, have extensive policies (i.e., very high standards) that new employees must become competent in and very demanding customers. The cost of additional training is minimal compared to losing one or more customers that spend $10,000 or more per year at the restaurant or $30,000 or more at the hotel. Therefore, the firm can justify training employees somewhere between consciously competent and subconsciously competent. Why not train each employee to be subconsciously competent? Because the length of time to go from consciously competent to subconsciously competent can be considerable, so the best that can usually be achieved during initial training is somewhere in between.

Tests

To ensure that trainees have acquired the knowledge necessary to properly perform their job, they should be tested on what they were taught during training. These initial tests are given to determine if the trainee is making a good effort in learning critical details of his or her position. **Form 9.1: Hostperson Test** is a sample of the type of test that can be given. Other tests, such as one for the point-of-sales or property-management-systems, check-in procedure, menu abbreviations, and so forth can also be given. Additionally, since the test are administered during the employee's probationary period, if the trainee does not do well on them, management can determine if it is in the best interest of the firm and the employee to continue with training. Tests can be administered on an annual or biannual basis to see if employees have retained information. The need for tests can also be assessed by monitoring various indicators of the need for improvement, such as changes in customer satisfaction scores, customer complaints, mistakes, productivity, employee morale, turnover, and any other factor related to employee performance. The objective of any one test, whether during initial training or as part of ongoing training, is to ask questions that reveal employees' knowledge or lack of knowledge of their work. Of critical importance is that when the results of these ongoing tests are known, that employees are helped to improve, rather than chastised for questions that were missed. Occasionally, very good employees may be very bad at written tests, so management must use good judgment and be supportive when assessing test outcomes. If management sees a direct association with the results of the test and the employee's performance, then something must be done.

Types of Assessment (Assessment Forms)

The following are typical types of assessments used in training. Each can be adopted for any position. **Figure 9.2: Server's Training Checklist** is an overall record of the trainee's progress. **Figure 9.3: Server Trainee Evaluation** is completed each day during training to have a record of the employee's performance and daily progress. It is reviewed with management so it can be aware of the trainee's progress and with the next trainer so he or she will know what to focus on. At the conclusion of training, the trainee and trainer should complete the applicable portions of a training assessment form (see **Figure 9.4: Training Assessment**). This assessment will give management insight into the effectiveness of its training program and information on how it can be improved. This can be a list of the various duties and possibly tasks the trainee is responsible for, along with a rating scale (e.g., 1 = Poor, 2 = Fair, 3 = Average, 4 = Very Good, 5 = Excellent) for the evaluation. It can also include general information on the quality of the training program. To see if progress is made in weaker areas, the manager should review the Training Assessment prior to the employee's first written performance appraisal.

Figure 9.1   Hostperson Test (Sample)

Employee _____   Date _____

1. What is the restaurant's dress code for customers?

2. What is meant by "rotating stations"?

3. Give two reasons why seating customers in rotating stations is important.
   1.
   2.

4. Why is it important to welcome the customer at the door with a warm, congenial attitude, a pleasant greeting, and a sincere smile?

5. If all tables are occupied, what procedures do you follow?

6. Before you seat customers, the table must be (please complete sentence).

7. What do you say to the customer to direct them to their table?

8. Why should you converse with the customers on the way to the table?

9. What are your sidework duties?

10. What is the restaurant's policy on seating incomplete parties?

Figure 9.2: Server's Training Checklist (Sample)

Trainee _____   Date _____
                                                              (first day of training)

√		Date of Completion and Comments:
	Review of server's guidelines	
	Menu abbreviations test passed	
	Menu descriptions test passed	
	Alcoholic beverage test passed, if applicable	
	Alcohol service policy test passed, if applicable	
	Table numbers test passed	
	Employee policy test passed	
	Server test passed	
	Writing an order	
	Pre-checking or ringing up an order	
	Drink delivery	
	Assembling an order	
	Food delivery	
	Customer check-backs	
	Pre-bussing	
	Service during the meal	
	Offering and serving dessert	
	Check delivery	
	Adequate knowledge of sidework	
	Successful solo during slow shift	
	Successful solo during medium shift	
	Successful solo during busy shift	
	Teamwork, cooperation	
	Approved for employment status	

To be signed by the primary trainer and manager when training is completed.

Trainer _____ Date _____   Manager _____ Date _____

Comments:

Selecting a Trainer

Generally, the best person to train a new employee is an experienced employee whose performance meets or exceeds the standards of the business. The trainee will be more relaxed with an employee rather than a manager and will benefit from their daily hands-on experience. The employee-trainer can often tell faster if a new employee will succeed because a lazy trainee will be more revealing to another employee than to a manager. If the training program has been set up properly, training will take very little of management's time. For consistency, the same trainer should be responsible for the trainee through the entire training program. If not possible, it is not a problem. There may be some benefits to different perspectives on how things can be done—as long as each trainer follows company policies.

Selecting an employee to be a trainer is a good way to recognize and reward experienced employees. To make it a positive experience, equate being chosen a trainer with a promotion. In situations where the trainer provides one-on-one attention, they could receive higher wages. In areas such as the kitchen, each employee will generally help train the trainee in some activity so across-the-board raises would not be necessary. In this case, make sure that the trainer (such as broiler, pantry, or fry cook) has been properly trained and has the qualifications to train someone else. Have a designated kitchen trainer, usually the kitchen manager or chef, oversee the training.

The performance of the trainer as well as the trainee should be monitored because the trainee's ability to become a qualified, contributing employee is directly related to training. The business's best employees may not be the best trainers. Some employees do not have the patience to work at the slower pace required to train someone. The methodical employee with average or better speed is often the best trainer.

Qualifications for Being a Trainer

• Job performance that meets or exceeds the standards of the business.
• The ability to teach—to express him or herself clearly so the trainee can understand.
• Patience with inevitable trainee mistakes.

• Knowing how to constructively correct and to avoid accidentally or purposefully ridiculing a trainee by choosing the wrong words.
• A pleasant personality and an ability to get along well with others.
• The trainer must be sincere or the trainee will feel like a nuisance and therefore feel neglected.
• The trainer must set a good example by exhibiting pride, enthusiasm, and loyalty to management and the business.

Figure 9.3: Server Trainee Evaluation (Sample)

(To be completed each shift during training)   Date _____   Shift # _____

Check applicable performance	Poor	Fair	Average	Very Good	Excellent
Menu abbreviations					
Menu descriptions					
Alcohol abbreviations					
Liquor, beer & wine selection					
Alcohol pricing					
Acknowledging the customer					
Writing the order					
Pre-checking					
Drink delivery					
Food delivery					
Customer check-back					
Pre-bussing					
Delivering the check					
Customer relations					
Employee relations					
Teamwork					
Checkout procedure					
Attitude					

Comments for the next trainer
(Specific areas where improvement is needed.)

_____ Trainer's signature   _____ Trainee's signature

Figure 9.4   Training Assessment (Sample)

Trainee _____   Date: _____

1 Do you feel confident that you can or will soon be able to perform at your position in a satisfactory manner?
Yes / No: For Yes or No responses, why do you feel this way?

2 What areas of your performance do you feel confident in?

3 What areas of your performance do you feel you need more training or help in?

4 How can we help you to improve?

5 Do you feel your taining program was adequate? How can it be improved and what are your recommendations?

Trainer: _____   Date: _____

1 What are the trainee's strengths and weaknesses?

2 How can we help the trainee to improve in weak areas?

3 Is the trainee ready to solo?

Manager's Signature _____   Date _____

Training the Trainer

Each employee who is chosen to be a trainer must be educated on the importance of training, the qualifications of a trainer, and the proper methods to be used. This can be accomplished by assembling a trainer's manual that includes topics, such as training benefits, types of training, the trainer's test, the Knowledge/Ability Hierarchy, an overview of how the training program is set up (Job Analysis, Training Methods, Schedule, and Competence), the list of qualifications for being a trainer, and so forth.

Evaluate the Training Program (Control)

• **Formative Evaluation**—Was the program effective and efficient?
The training program is evaluated by seeing how the trainee and the trainer are doing during training, asking employees involved in training process about what was and what was not effective, and asking management their opinion of the training program.
• **Summative Evaluation**—After training, how has the performance of employees changed?
This is evaluated by viewing the new employee's performance after training and drawing conclusions about the relationship between the training program and post-training performance. The overall best indicator of training quality is the customer satisfaction score.

Case Study 9.1: Designing a Training Program

Your restaurant's (or hotel's) service quality has been steadily declining over the past six months (a symptom). Turnover is higher than your competitors and overall morale is lower (additional symptoms). After interviewing employees to find the cause, management determined that it was the business's training program. The main problem was that since there was no organized training program (no training manual), each trainer decided how he or she would train new employees. This fact resulted in major inconsistencies in the way each new employee was trained. A few new employees did well, but even these employees did not always follow company policies.

Required:

1. Select a position in a hospitality firm (or you will be assigned one by your instructor), create two duties and the related and detailed tasks for the position. You select the type of restaurant or hotel for your case study or your instructor will help.

2. Prepare a basic and very brief training manual for that position including:

   A. Three training methods (on-the-job, off-the-job training, or a combination) for each duty (and related tasks) and be able to explain why each training method will be effective;

   B. Include the number of days of training for those duties and tasks and a relatively detailed breakdown of what will be covered on each day;

   C. Specify some specific level/measure of qualitative or quantitative competence for each of the duties before a trainee can go solo (work on their own). Basically, specify your desired level of competence (e.g., qualitative: effectively solved the hypothetical customer complaint, was very personable during the check-in role-play, quantitative: all orders out in 10 minutes or less without errors, no complaints, food presentation according to policies, each guest checked in according to the eight listed tasks, each guest is directed to a clean and properly set table, given a menu after they are seated, and politely told to enjoy their meal or some other similar comment).

   D. If assigned: Select two or three managerial duties (as assigned by your instructor) from Figure 5.5: Hotel General Manager Job Description in Chapter Five, The Job Creation Process), then set up a training program including the above requirements.

Chapter Ten: Performance Appraisals and Discipline

Strategy Review: Prepare a strategy review for this chapter (See back of Chapter One).
Case Study 10.1: Role Play - Performance Appraisal
Case Study 10.2: Designing a Performance Appraisal System
Case Study 10.3: Compassionate Conservatism
Chapter Objectives: After reading this chapter you should understand and be able to do the following:

1. Describe the concept of performance appraisals, including the phrase, policies should be in writing, communicated, and enforced.
2. Give some reasons why managers neglect performance appraisals and disciplining employees.
3. Explain the primary reasons for the performance appraisal.
4. Describe what is measured in a performance appraisal.
5. Describe the importance of the manager/employee relationships to the appraisal process.
6. Explain the Sandwich Approach to performance appraisals and why it must be used with caution.
7. Discuss various forms of bias in performance appraisals.
8. Differentiate between informal and formal performance appraisals.
9. Discuss direct and indirect forms of informal performance appraisals
10. Discuss some steps in preparing a performance appraisal.
11. Describe the 360-degree performance appraisal.
12. List the advantages of the self-appraisal and describe how it can be implemented.
13. Differentiate between appraising quantitative and qualitative duties and tasks.
14. Discuss some basic steps in disciplining an employee.
15. Describe the three (and four) tiered disciplinary system (progressive discipline).

Performance Appraisals and Discipline

The concepts of performance appraisals and discipline focus on the assessment and management of human performance in organizations. Assessment is the measurement and evaluation of employee performance. Management of performance consists of the recognizing deviations from company policies/standards and correcting them in a way that motivates employees to improve. Harry H. Pope, one of the first restaurant operators to apply scientific management principles to the industry, said that policies should be "in writing, communicated, and enforced" (Pope, 1972). The job creation process puts policies in writing, that is, how things should be done (i.e., duties and tasks). Training is how managers communicate them. Enforcement is accomplished through performance appraisal and disciplinary actions of the manger. The vast majority of firms have reasonably detailed policies, such as training manuals for each position. A fewer number have quality training programs and unfortunately, fewer still effectively enforce or uphold their policies/standards.

Managers are very busy people with literally hundreds of things to focus on each day. An old related saying is, "You can't see the forest for the trees." When managers have many things to think about and take care of, they tend to neglect those that *seem* least important. Many managers focus on the *big picture* (e.g., do customers seem to be happy, are things flowing smoothly, etc.), but neglect the details of what helps make the *big picture* work—each employee following the policies for their position. The next most common reason for managers' avoidance of upholding standards is the fact that telling people they are not doing what they are supposed to be doing is not the most pleasant task in the world. Consequently, many managers will simply ignore employees' mistakes, justifying it by thinking that employees are doing their best or that they can be told later about their subpar performance. Of course, the problem is that later may never come and not correcting minor problems prevents the firm from achieving excellence.

Alternatively, managers need to know the difference between burnt toast and tragedy. No one is perfect. Employees will make minor errors throughout the day. Managers must be able to recognize when they need to say something and when they do not. If the problem impacts customer satisfaction, then quick remediating action is required. If the problem does not impact customer satisfaction and is simply a one-time event, then perhaps nothing needs to be said. If the event is a bit more serious, that is, not impacting customer satisfaction, but keeping the employee from following policies/standards 100%, then something should be said. When correcting deviations from policies, great managers do so in a way that will instills self-confidence in their employees so they will make fewer mistakes in the future.

A critical note here is that many new managers are afraid of the concept of terminating or firing someone. Don't be! Good managers rarely need to fire anyone. When you hire good employees, train them well and provide them with a positive work environment, termination is a rare event. As the author, I have included few personal notes, so understand that this one is important. I worked in the hospitality industry for about 20 years before entering the teaching field. First, I have never terminated an employee that I hired. Also, in all that time I had to terminate employment for two employees and three managers. In each case, the terminated employees and managers essentially terminated themselves through bad attitudes or serious cases of not following company policies (e.g., fighting, drinking on the job to the point of being drunk, bringing a weapon to work, and blatant disregard for company policies). In other words, I was not terminating someone with a good attitude who was trying to do his or her best; I was terminating someone who was essentially asking to be fired. In several places in this book, attitude was discussed as one of the most critical characteristics of those working in this industry. When employees or managers have a good attitude, they are almost always capable of doing most any job in our industry. When a good attitude is not enough to help them succeed in their current position, then there are either other positions in the firm they can be transferred to or they can be helped to find employment in an industry where their skills can be better utilized. Rather than allow employees with a good attitude to progress through the disciplinary process to the point of potential termination, it is best to work with them to find a solution that helps them, rather than hurts them. Firms in the habit of terminating employees suffer from higher unemployment taxes, low morale, and a significant competitive disadvantage.

Reasons for Performance Appraisals
Uphold Standards
The manager should evaluate the performance of all employees on a regular basis. All managers should have their performance evaluated by their supervisor. Informal performance appraisals should be a daily process so that praise and appreciation can be given for employees' efforts and problem behavior can be corrected immediately. Most businesses conduct a formal performance appraisal after the first month of employment, at the end of an employee's probationary period, and every six months or one year thereafter.

Employee Development
Performance appraisals should also let employees know what they can do to improve their general performance, their chances for advancement, and their general ability as an employee or manager. The following are more specific examples of employee development:

• **Assess value of employee**. Decisions regarding the completion of the probationary period, compensation decisions, promotion, or disciplinary procedures.

• **Assessment of training and development needs**. How are employees' actions matching up to their job description? Are there areas, such as communication or prioritization, where they could improve?

Validation of Recruiting and Hiring Process
If employees overall are doing a good job, then the recruiting and hiring process was likely successful. Of course, there is always the possibility that recruitment and selection was marginal, but was compensated for by excellent training and supervision (i.e., performance appraisals and discipline).

Protection from Suits or Having to Pay Workers' Compensation Claims
Having a record of helping employees develop in their positions and in their general abilities can minimize the chances of lawsuits. For example, employees will perform better, which lessens the likelihood of employee and customer injuries. Having employee development efforts in writing also limits the ability of a lawyers stating that their client was not trained or treated properly.

Opens Lines of Communication Between Employees and Management
Ideally, managers should be talking to each on-duty employee on a daily basis. When this does not occur, the process of effective informal and formal performance appraisals forces managers to communicate with them.

What Is Measured in a Performance Appraisal?

Performance of Duties and Tasks (Job Analysis)

Performance appraisals must focus on the employee's performance—the duties and tasks of position. That is, if a duty has five accompanying tasks, the manager would make an assessment of the employee's performance on those five tasks and informally or formally (the written performance appraisal) communicate this to the employee.

Job Specifications

There are two issues here. One is whether the employee has exhibited the characteristics listed in the job specifications. For example, are they dependable, have a good attitude, able to solve customer problems, and so forth? Another goal here is to learn if the job specifications for the position are accurate. For example, if employees whose performance on duties and tasks is excellent, also matches up well with the position's job specifications, and those whose performance is poor do not match up well, then the specifications may be accurate. In scientific terms, the job specifications have been validated (i.e., shown to work, shown to be valid).

Management by Objectives (MBO)

Many managers will set specific objectives for employees and managers to work towards. For employees, objectives are most often related to quantitative duties and tasks. For example, in upselling at the front desk, the agent would carry out the duties and tasks related to upselling and have a measureable objective (e.g., at check-in upsell 10% of guests). Because qualitative duties and tasks are more challenging to measure, they are normally not used for an MBO program. Typical objectives for managers include sales, profit, labor cost, food cost, and customer satisfaction scores.

What Is Not Measured in a Performance Appraisal

An employee's personal life should not be mentioned, unless it is affecting the employee's performance. In such cases, the problem should generally not be confronted directly, but indirectly through questions such as, "Is something bothering you?" as opposed to, "Are you taking drugs?" or accusations, such as "You seem to be hanging out with a bad crowd?"

General Guidelines for Appraisals and Discipline

Manager/Employee Relationship

A key factor in any appraisal or disciplinary action is the relationship between the manager/supervisor and the employee. If the relationship is a good one, then the anxiety of the situation is eased and there will be less resistance to what the manager is communicating. "We need to get the silverware to the table before the guests sit down" comes across a lot less intimidating from someone that employees talk to on a regular basis and who has an interest in their personal lives, than from someone who knows nothing about them and seems not to care.

Objectivity of What Is Being Measured

The objectivity of the appraisal can be improved by increasing the number of quantitative (i.e., objective) measures relative to qualitative (i.e., subjective) measures. Examples of quantitative measures include, completing check-ins within one minute, the broiler cook completing all orders within 15 minutes, a $19.00 check-average for a server, number of times a cook had a problem getting orders out on a 300 entrée night, using a guest's name twice during check-in or checkout. Qualitative measures include criteria, such as overall performance, dependability, attitude, and respect for guests. This is discussed further later in this chapter in Qualitative and Quantitative Appraisal Forms.

Employee Knowledge of Performance Criteria

Employees should have an understanding of *what* is being evaluated, *why* it is being evaluated, and the *reason* for each rating in their evaluation. This makes them a better manager of their own performance and, theoretically, should make supervision easier. It also increases both customer and employee satisfaction.

Sandwich Approach

Most managers use the sandwich approach to criticism—first, positive comments; second, areas for improvement; finally, end with positive statements. When using this approach, make sure that the employee does not leave with the idea that improvement is not necessary or important, especially when there are significant areas for improvement. This must be left to the judgment of the manager, but ending an appraisal or especially a disciplinary procedure with only positive statements may not be as productive as ending with something positive along with a statement of where improvement is needed. Again, the severity of any areas for improvement should dictate how the conversation is ended.

Bias in Performance Appraisals

Bias is defined as any conscious or subconscious distortion of reality—"looking at everything from his or her personal slant, or point of view" (Gibbons & Kleiner, 1994, p. 10). Reality in this context is a rational and accurate consensus of performance. The conscious intent of management bias can manifest itself in four primary forms: (1) an ethical attempt to interpret reality (i.e., an ethical attempt to minimize bias); (2) glossing over minor or major deficiencies in an attempt to protect one's self or coworkers, or to somehow gain an advantage (e.g., a bonus, promotion, or positive recognition); (3) to maintain morale; and (4) a malicious attempt to denigrate individuals or groups within the organization (Juran, 1992). In the case of the subconscious use of bias, the mind is too complex for anyone to be aware of the thousands of influences that go into the rating of a specific performance. The predominant subconscious causes include defense mechanisms, ego gratification, poor self-image, and a lack of understanding or knowledge (Jung, 1969). These subconscious flaws were described by Jung (1969) as the Shadow—elements of the subconscious that people are not willing to deal with. Management must realize that human judgment entails elements of bias and those elements must be minimized.

The following are the primary types of bias observed in hospitality situations (Woods, 2002). When any of these types of bias are utilized, the effectiveness of the performance appraisal is minimized to the extent of the bias. As one could imagine, providing employees with a truthful and accurate assessment of their performance is critical. When bias plays a role and the assessment is based on the manager's personal opinion of the employee, overall firm performance will decline.

Halo Errors/Bias (Devil's Horns Effect)

The Halo Effect occurs when the manager lets positive feelings about the employee influence them to minimize or ignore areas for improvement and to maximize positive attributes of the employee. An example could be a manager who likes an employee because they have something in common, like playing golf or being from the same city or state. Devil's Horns Effect is the opposite of the Halo Effect and exists when negative feelings influence the manager's thoughts and/or actions. The Halo and Devil's Horns Effects are the most common types of bias and can play a role in each of the remaining categories in this list.

Leniency Bias

Being too nice when describing areas where the employee could do better. Giving them a 4 on a 5-point scale when they deserved a 3. A frequent example of leniency bias is ignoring areas where improvement should take place. It is impossible to be a good manager without the ability to recognize areas for improvement, communicate the problem, and then help the employee improve. The most common reason for leniency bias is that most people find criticizing others to be uncomfortable. Rarely do people criticize others in their everyday lives. For this reason, of the three types of rating bias (leniency, severity, and central tendency errors), leniency bias is by far the most common.

Severity Bias

Being too harsh when communicating areas for improvement. Giving employees a 3 on a 5-point scale, when a 4 or 5 might be appropriate (e.g., no one gets a five because no one is perfect). Since most people are not mean and do not enjoy being mean, severity bias is the least common of the types of rating bias. An additional reason for it not being common is that when a low score is given, the manager will need to justify it—or at least should justify it. If there are several different managers that provide appraisals, some with leniency bias and others with severity bias, several problems will ensue. First, employees will be apprehensive about their upcoming appraisal and whether they will get the nice manager or the mean one. If pay raises are provided, then it is not only their feelings that may get hurt, but also their wages. The end result will be low morale, which will quickly lead to poor customer satisfaction scores and high turnover.

Central Tendency Errors/Bias

Some managers rate most employees as average. Causes vary, but include saving the time necessary to perform an effective appraisal (i.e., being lazy) and indecisiveness.

Rating versus Ranking

While the vast majority of performance assessments are based on ratings of an employee on a specified scale, some businesses rank employee performance relative to other employees. This is still commonly and successfully used in sales, however morale can suffer when it is used for other positions. For example, someone that is consistently ranked about fourth out of 20 employees may be upset that he or she cannot receive a higher ranking.

<u>**Recency Errors/Past Anchoring Errors**</u>
Recency errors occur when the manager lets something that happened recently or many months ago (past anchoring) weigh heavily in the performance evaluation.
<u>**Political Bias**</u>
Virtually every firm has some level of political bias. Political bias is a form of Halo or Devil's Horns bias, but it is a bit more complex, overt, and unfortunately conniving. Managers will play favorites, giving some employees special treatment—positive or negative, when it is not deserved.

Informal Performance Appraisal Basics

Informal performance appraisals are the daily supervisory tasks of a manager. Through effective training, the employee should know the proper method of performing their tasks. Informal performance appraisals are simply the enforcement of what the employee has learned in training—the follow-up (step 4 of the job-instruction-training process, presented in Chapter Nine, Training). This is what managers spend much of their time doing—walking around to see how things are going. Unfortunately, the most common response to a manager's seeing a problem is to do nothing. The reasons vary, but include being intimidated when faced with having to talk about negative things, and legitimately putting it off until later, and then forgetting to discuss it with the employee. At the other end of the spectrum are managers that overreact. It's human to make mistakes. Management's objective is to minimize mistakes and to keep them from occurring again—not to micromanage employees, making them feel incapable of doing a good job.

There are essentially two primary means of performing an informal performance appraisal (correcting behavior during the work day), *direct* and *indirect*.
<u>**Direct Performance Appraisal**</u>
The direct method consists of talking to the employee about their performance. This should normally be done in private and as tactfully as possible. When privacy is not possible, it should be done in a very supportive manner. "You seem to be making mistakes all the time!" is no way to instill confidence in an employee and will likely not motivate them to improve. Effectiveness of the direct method is heavily based on the relationship between the manager and the employee. A good relationship might allow for something like the following: "Joey, my grandpa is faster than that!"
<u>**Indirect Performance Appraisal**</u>
The indirect appraisal can be accomplished in a variety of ways. The two most common are: (1) to simply help the employee with whatever they are having a problem with (this should obviously not be done in a demeaning way), and (2) discussing the problem at a *shift meeting*. Shift meetings are usually held sometime before employees begin taking care of guests. It is an excellent tool that can be used to pass on general or specific areas for improvement. The advantage of the shift meeting for letting employees know how they can improve is that employees do not need to be singled out and will hopefully be appreciative of the manager's tact in helping them and the team.

Formal Performance Appraisal Basics

The formal performance appraisal is the periodic written review of employee performance.
<u>**Preparation**</u>
Management should take whatever time is necessary to prepare an objective appraisal. The performance appraisal is a great opportunity for managers to help employees improve. If little thought or effort is put into the process, then the opportunity will be missed. Additionally, the employee's morale may suffer due to an obviously poor understanding of what the employee has been doing for the appraisal period. Since rarely will each manager work with an employee for all of the employee's shifts, it is good to consult with all managers who worked with the employee. Ideally, each of the managers could participate in completing the performance appraisal form. A practice helpful in preparing an objective evaluation is to regularly keep a record of excellent, average, and poor examples of each employee's performance over the appraisal period (See Performance Record Form below). This is best kept in the managers' office in a designated folder for the employee.

Managers must be aware of the various forms of bias (previously noted). The most common is leniency bias, to reduce the anxiety of the appraisal, where there is a tendency to rate employees higher than what they deserve. This can defeat the appraisal's purpose and allow a continuance of existing problems.

Performance Record Form

Since the performance appraisal takes place only once about each six months, some means of keeping track of each employee's performance during this time is needed. A page in the employee's file, termed a performance record form, where positive and negative behaviors by the employee are recorded allows managers to keep track of individual employees and to see what other managers have written about the employee. This helps ensure a more accurate appraisal of his/her overall performance over a potential six months to one-year appraisal period. This form can be completed as necessary, daily, and at least periodically as the manager feels something should be recorded. Some firms use a critical incident form to record either only negative behaviors or both negative and positive behaviors.

The Beginning

It is important to remember that the purpose of the appraisal is to improve performance, not to simply give the employee a laundry list of areas where improvement is required. Therefore, managers must consider how different employees accept criticism and how they feel going into the appraisal. Most employees are tense during a formal appraisal, so initially it is best to make a positive statement, such as "Your speed has been picking up lately" or "I'm happy with the job you've been doing." If the employee is not deserving of a positive statement, perhaps the manager can give the employee hope, by saying something like, "Your performance has not been good, but perhaps we can figure out a way to make this work."

The Appraisal

Once the employee is relaxed, or as relaxed as reasonably possible under the circumstances, discussions can begin on the specifics of his or her behavior. The key focus of the appraisal is the discussion of the rating for each item in the appraisal, the justification or reason for each rating, and how the employee can improve. For example, "The reason you received a 4 out of 5 for customer service at the front desk is that several customers commented that you were not able to answer their questions about the various services at our resort." During the discussions, the employee should be asked for their thoughts of the various ratings and manager comments. While most employees perform up to company standards (policies), practically every employee has one or more areas where improvement is possible. The basic reason for the appraisal is to reinforce good behavior and to help the employee correct poor or unsatisfactory behaviors. If an employee is doing well in a particular area, let him or her know that you appreciate it. In areas that need improvement, constructively let the employee know what he or she can do to improve.

The End

The appraisal should end with attainable expectations for the future. If appropriate, a series of successively more challenging goals can be set up with input from both the employee and the manager (or management and their supervisor). So that both parties will know when the goals have been achieved, they must be written, be measurable, and have a date for achievement. For example, a cook's goal might be to successfully work the broiler without assistance on Wednesday night (goal 1), on Thursday night (goal 2), then on Friday night (goal 3) by January 5, 20XX. A front desk agent could have similar goals for successively busier periods of time. A server could be assigned successively more difficult stations or higher check average goals.

The performance appraisal should be a positive event, or at least as positive as possible for the employee and the manager. If the employee leaves unhappy or with questions about the way he or she is perceived, management has not accomplished its task. At the end of the appraisal the employee should feel motivated to perform better both personally and as a team player, and be willing to mesh his or her personal goals with those of the company. It is important to let the employee have plenty of time to explain their feelings about the appraisal.

360-Degree Performance Appraisals

The standard method of conducting a performance appraisal is for the manager to complete the appraisal form and review it with the employee. When the appraisal includes the utilization of several different measurement/evaluation options, it is termed a 360-degree performance appraisal. For example, in addition to the appraisal by management/supervisors, there could be some combination of a self-appraisal by the employee, a peer appraisal by those who work with the employee, subordinates of the employee or supervisor being appraised, customer comment cards or surveys, and mystery shopper audits (Oh & Berry, 2009). The purpose of this strategy is to bring in additional information and to help increase the objectivity of the overall appraisal, especially, qualitative criteria.

The *self-appraisal*, where employees evaluate their own performance, is rapidly increasing in popularity.

Each area traditionally covered in the performance appraisal form and the employee's opinion of his or her performance would be discussed. This approach can reduce the confrontational feelings associated with traditional performance appraisal methods and allows for, but does not guarantee, a rational discussion of where the employee's performance can be improved. Historically, the average employee will rate themselves lower than their manager. The reason for this is typically that employees do not want to put themselves in the position of saying that they are great at something in areas where they feel the manager may not agree. The upside to this, at least for well-prepared managers, is that it gives the manager the chance to tell the employee that they are doing better than they thought, which will hopefully help their morale and motivation. One option for the self-appraisal is to have the employee complete the appraisal (i.e., the manager would not complete one), then the employee and the manager would review it, discussing the employee's ratings.

Peer evaluations can be beneficial because they provide additional opinions and, if effectively implemented, forces employees to think like managers. For example, peers need to know what the employee is supposed to be doing before they are able to assess his or her performance. The main disadvantage is that it can be difficult to implement without varying degrees of bias. Asking employees at the front desk to rate one of their colleagues could result in the Halo Effect from those that like the employee being rated, the Devil's Horns Effect from those who do not like him or her, leniency from those who do not want to be too hard on the employee, and any of the other forms of interview bias. Proper training can reduce bias by employee raters, but eliminating it may be all but impossible. If management is interested, they could try it to see if the results are similar to managements' opinion or if new information or perspectives are gained.

Subordinate evaluations, where employees evaluate their manager, can provide good information. Among the positive aspects are that employee feedback can highlight where managers are doing a good job and where they can improve. Like the peer evaluation, to implement it properly, employees must be trained to assess their manager's performance. Theoretically, this training should increase employees' awareness of the responsibilities of managers and, for some, help them to think like managers and become another pair of eyes to make sure things are going as planned. For example, for employees to respond to the question, "Does your manager help out at the front desk when needed?" they must be able to assess when help is needed and when employees should be able to handle things on their own. On the downside is the possibility that employees will feel pressured into giving the manager a good review for fear that it could affect their future with the firm. Various forms of bias, primarily the Halo and Devil's Horns Effect will also be possible. As in many situations, the manager's personality and popularity, or lack thereof, will likely influence evaluations. As evaluation time comes near, employees may find it easier to receive certain favors, such scheduling preferences, free food or other perks, and less stringent policy enforcement.

Customers, through *comment cards* and *formal surveys* can not only help locate where the business is doing well and where it can improve, but also how individual employees are doing. Because the customer's opinion could be valid or completely wrong, managers need to use caution when disciplining an employee because of what was written on a comment card. Several comment cards with similar information generally help to increase their validity. It is important to make sure that employees cannot either complete their own comments or have only highly satisfied customers complete them. One firm experienced an exodus of quality employees because shift preference was based on comment cards and unethical employees would complete comment cards that praised their own performance.

Qualitative and Quantitative Appraisal Forms

Figure 10.1 Employee Appraisal Form below can be used for most any hospitality business and position. This appraisal form is known as a *qualitative appraisal* because each of the criteria is assessed based on the judgment of the appraiser, rather than something that can quantitatively be measured (e.g., assessed with a yes or no, or a specific quantity or time) (See the discussion on quantitative and qualitative duties and tasks in Chapter Five, The Job Creation Process). The main advantages of this type of appraisal form are that both managers and employees are used to them and they are easy to complete—simply record management's rating for the employee. The two main disadvantages are first that they are highly open to subjectivity and bias, primarily halo effect and devil horn's affect. Associated with this is the fact that since each manager may have a different opinion, how should the management team go about recording the fairest and most accurate response? Second, because the forms are easy to complete, they can be done in a few minutes—often without much thought. This promotes laziness and inaccurate appraisals that do not reflect employee performance and do not live up to the intention of the appraisal—to help the employee improve.

Management first rates employees from poor to excellent on the various *General Criteria* (i.e., Dependability to Personal Appearance and Hygiene). For *Specific Criteria for the employee's position*, management can add factors they feel employees of that position should be evaluated on. For example, the following could be included for a reservation agent: politely answers the phone, uses proper greeting, full details of reservation are repeated back to guest, reservation agent made suitable attempt at upselling, and ends conversation by sincerely thanking guest. If the ratings were quantitative, then the scale of Poor to Excellent may need to be changed. For the next section, *Reasons for ratings of fair or poor*, management can include specific information to help the employee understand the reason for the rating. This also forces management to think about how they will justify the rating to the employee. *Manager's comments* can include information on how the firm will help the employee improve, goals for improvement, and so forth. In the employee comments section, it is important that employees write something about their perception of the appraisal, how they intend to improve, and anything else they would like to state for this permanent record. The same type of appraisal form could be used for managers. The primary difference would be the addition of items in general and specific criteria (e.g., relationship with employees, ability to motivate employees, product quality, service quality, cost control, etc.).

Figure 10.1: Employee Appraisal Form (Sample)					
Employee:			Date:		
Date hired:		Position:			
		(Check pertinent category.)			
General criteria:	Poor	Fair	Good	Very G.	Excellent
Dependability					
Pleasant personality					
Positive attitude					
Sense of urgency					
Teamwork					
Performance					
Follows instructions					
Personal initiative					
Cleanliness of work area					
Works toward company goals					
Personal appearance and hygiene					
Specific criteria (e.g., duties) for position:					
Reasons for ratings of fair or poor:					
Manager's comments: (e.g., what can be done to improve, goals for employee, how management will help, etc.):					
Employee's comments: (e.g., fairness of appraisal, goals for future, etc.):					
Employee's Signature:			Date:		
Manager's Signature:			Date:		

Figure 10.2: Hotel Checkout Appraisal is a sample portion of a *quantitative appraisal* that focuses on Hotel Checkout, but could focus on any area that can be quantitatively assessed. This includes the majority of duties and tasks for most positions in the hospitality industry. The key criteria that are more difficult to quantitatively assess include items, such as courtesy, respect, personality, interpersonal skills, working toward company goals, problem-solving ability, food quality, initiative and so forth. A criterion is quantitative because responses will be (or should be) the same for any appraiser—the employee either did or did not perform the duty or task or it was done in a certain time or amount. Whether or not it was up to the standards of the business will sometimes require a

qualitative assessment. The objective in the quantitative appraisal is to take out subjectivity—the personal opinion of the appraiser. As was seen in the previous appraisal form, the appraisal of each criterion was based on the appraiser's opinion of the employee's performance. The main challenge in using this type of performance appraisal is that to represent an employee's performance over a certain period of time (e.g., six months), the same activities must be assessed several times (See AP#1, AP#2 and so forth below). Since management is obviously responsible for each employee's performance over the long-term, this should not be an impediment to its implementation. From the employee's perspective, this is fairer than the common qualitative appraisal because the employee knows that even though personal opinions play a role in the appraisal, they are at least minimized. Very few firms currently use the quantitative performance appraisal. Its advantages should result in an increased usage.

Figure 10.2: Hotel Checkout Appraisal (Sample)	AP#1		AP#2		AP#3
Duty/Task	Yes	No	Yes	No	>
When the guest approached the front desk were they verbally acknowledged in a pleasant manner?					
Was the front desk agent wearing a name tag?					
Was the front desk agent wearing a clean and pressed uniform?					
Did the front desk agent ask how the guest's stay was?					
Did the front desk agent review the guest's charges with them?					
Did the front desk agent present the guest with a $0 balance folio?					
Did the front desk agent thank the guest for staying at the hotel?					
Did the front desk agent use the guest's name during the checkout procedure?					
Totals for Yes and No Appraisals:					
For each appraisal, if there are areas where the employee did particularly well, explain why you thought the appraisal went well.					
For each appraisal where the employee received a No on the appraisal, explain why the employee received the No response.					

Discipline

Each business must have rules covering all major tasks and most possible activities of employees. When employees disregard these rules, they must be made aware of the improper action so it is not repeated. If an employee does not change the undesirable behavior, management must take further disciplinary action. The goal of discipline is virtually the same as for performance appraisals, to correct the behavior in a way that motivates the employee. The difference is that, in discipline, the negative behavior has reached a point of concern and is hurting the business. This fact makes discipline a serious managerial concept that cannot and should not be taken lightly. Even though each manager within an organization has his or her own managerial style and style of discipline, to be fair with each employee, all managers should use the same disciplinary procedure and be consistent in its application.

Basic Disciplinary Procedures

Disciplining employees can be a delicate matter and, when done improperly, opens the door for legal problems or even violence. While managerial style will influence what each manager does, the following steps should be adhered to when approaching a disciplinary problem.

Identify the problem

Do not begin any disciplinary action without a clear understanding of the problem. Often what is recognized as a problem is only a symptom of a problem. Trace the perceived problem back to any possible cause. For example, what a manager thinks is an employee working too slow at the front desk, may only be the symptom of the fact that the hotel's property management system is outdated and very slow (i.e., the cause of the problem).

Identify who is responsible

Do not jump to conclusions. It is quite possible that management is responsible for the problem—whether because of poor communication, inadequate training, or the absence of a written policy. A problem such as cold food may be the fault of equipment, methods of operation, cooking and assembly methods, the server, the cooks, or a combination of all of the above.

Personally see the problem

In most cases, management must see the problem behavior for themselves. Disciplinary actions or reprimands are too serious to be based on hearsay. In cases where management did not personally see what the employee did, they should be very careful with what they say or do and no direct accusations should be made. In serious cases where the behavior was not seen by management, the employee generally should not be fired, but placed on a paid leave of absence pending an investigation.

Decide what action should be taken

Most problems, such as when an employee is doing his or her best but makes a mistake, can be corrected as they occur with help from management or experienced employees. More serious problems may require an oral warning/reprimand, a written warning, or termination. **Figure 10.3: Employee Disciplinary Report** is typical of what is used for written warnings or terminations.

Be prompt

Management must correct problems as quickly as possible to make sure they are not repeated. This also serves to let employees know that management is in control and sets an example for other employees. Saving up disciplinary actions, then unloading them during a performance appraisal once every six months, clouds the problem behavior(s) managers are trying to correct. The employee being disciplined may not hear what he or she has done wrong, only the barrage of complaints, which may seem like a personal attack. This can result in resentment toward the manager, rather than correction of the problem.

Disciplinary action

1. Ask for a meeting (private) where other employees cannot hear what is being said. Have another manager or senior employee/supervisor with you as a witness and deterrence for violence.
2. Explain facts and the seriousness of the situation.
3. It is better for management and the employee to concentrate on one behavior at a time.
4. Allow employee to express his/her view.
5. Determine action to be taken.
6. Attempt to get agreement with employee on what should be done.
7. Establish specific guidelines with time frames for improvement (e.g., attitude must improve immediately, time to clean a room must be lowered to 20 minutes each within two weeks from today)

It is generally best not to criticize an employee on a personal level

For example, "I appreciate your efforts, but there are a few areas of your performance that need to be improved" comes across better than, "You haven't been following company policies." This way, employees will not feel they have to defend themselves and build up negative attitudes toward management. Also, they will be more likely to concentrate on their behavior, rather than the chastisement. Let them know what they did wrong, how you feel about it, what they can do to correct it, and that you appreciate them. The exact statement will depend on one's managerial style. The style matters less than its effectiveness. In other words, whatever the manager's style, management's main responsibility is to motivate employees to uphold policies. Too often, managers are overly concerned about being liked and consequently neglect to take appropriate disciplinary actions. The common result is that employees will disrespect managers that do not correct improper behavior just as they would a basketball or football coach that did the same.

Criticize in private, praise in public

This typical adage in discipline is a cliché for a purpose. In the vast majority of cases, it works quite well. Embarrassing an employee in front of other employees or especially customers, is not good for anyone. On rare occasions where the manager has tried everything else and nothing has worked, asking the employee to come back to the office in a stern manner in front of other employees may be a last effort to try to salvage the employee.

Follow up with the employee

Since the reason the employee is being disciplined is to change his or her behavior, management should reinforce the employee's actions by praising improvement and giving additional counseling, if and as required. If the employee's performance does not improve, then take whatever action is necessary to uphold the standards of the business (i.e., further discipline, if necessary).

Figure 10.3:   Employee Disciplinary Report (Sample)

Employee	Date

Time of Offense	Date of Offense	Witness if available

Written Warning/Termination
(circle one)

Company remarks:

By:

Employee's remarks: (The absence of any statement on the part of the employee indicates his or her agreement with the report as stated.)

For written warnings, corrective action to be taken:

Written warning: I have read this report, I understand it and agree to the prescribed corrective action to be taken.

Termination: This report was presented and explained to me.

Employee:	Date:

Management:	Date:

Post disciplinary analysis and exit interviews

Since the disciplinary situation is a failure on someone's part, management should take the opportunity to find how it can be avoided in the future. If the fault lies with management, then apologies to the employee may be in order and the employee should be given reasonable help to improve.

Management should ask itself: Did the employee receive an appropriate orientation and was he or she properly trained and supervised? Has everything reasonable been done to help the employee succeed? This could also be the first step in uncovering a larger problem. If one employee was not appropriately treated, were there others? If the employee has very little or no chance of remaining with the company, management should ask itself why the employee was hired in the first place. Perhaps there is a flaw in the hiring process.

Ideally, each employee who voluntarily or involuntarily leaves the firm should be interviewed to see what could have been done to make the experience a better one. The same basic concerns in the two preceding paragraphs would be reviewed.

The Three (or Four) Tiered Disciplinary System (Also Referred to as Progressive Discipline)

The following disciplinary policies are examples of guidelines typically used in disciplining employees. The list of disciplinary categories should be included in the employee handbook so that employees are aware of the consequences of their actions. As with virtually anything in writing that the firm provides employees, an attorney should review it to make sure it is acceptable.

When deciding what action to take, take into consideration the employees' time on the job, performance, and any circumstances pertaining to the action.

Four Tier Disciplinary System

Many firms have a *suspension* between the written warning and termination. They give the employee a day off with or without pay—this must be the same for everyone. The employee then has a meeting with the manager to determine if continued employment is in the best interest of the employee and the firm. If not, the employee can be given the opportunity to quit, rather than being fired.

CATEGORY 1

First Offense: Termination

1. Gross insubordination or any flagrant act, including fighting, intimidation of other employees or customers, sexual harassment, refusing to cooperate, not showing up for an assigned shift, or poor conduct that reflects seriously on the business or hinders the ability of the business to operate smoothly.
2. Willfully destroying or damaging business property.
3. Use or sale of illegal drugs while on duty. Unauthorized use of alcohol while on duty.
4. Theft or other acts of dishonesty, such as giving away food, stealing from the business or anyone associated with the business such as employees or customers, and falsification of such items as time cards or guest checks.
5. Possession of a weapon or anything that represents a danger to employees or customers.

CATEGORY 2

First Offense: Written Warning

Second Offense: Termination

1. Not complying with the business's uniform policy.
2. Negligent waste of any item such as linen, amenities, food, beverages, dishes, or silverware.
3. Misuse or abuse of the business's equipment or furniture.
4. Ignoring safety rules.
5. Reporting for work under the influence of alcohol or illegal drugs, or when the employee's ability is impaired by its use. In cases such as this, no accusations should be made. The employee's behavior should be the focus. An attorney should prepare a policy for situations such as this that comply with current state and federal laws.
6. Use of offensive or abusive language around customers or employees.
7. Any action, on or off the business's property that negatively affects the reputation of the business.
8. Not complying with or working toward company goals.
9. Not complying with the company's alcohol service policy.

CATEGORY 3

First Offense: Oral Warning

Second Offense: Written Warning

Third Offense: Termination

1. Not complying with general company policies.
2. Working in a disorderly or unsanitary manner.
3. Not properly performing assigned duties, after being trained and counseled.
4. Nonproductive use of work time.
5. Carelessness in the performance of duties and tasks.

Case Study 10.1: Role-Play: Performance Appraisal

You will be given a performance appraisal form. It may have information about an employee's performance already recorded, or you may be asked to record some hypothetical information.

Required:
1. Assume the following:
       A. the form provided is your firm's standard performance appraisal;
       B. All employees have previously been appraised with this form (they understand each component);
       C. You are this employee's department head and are well aware of her/his performance in all areas.
2. Depending on the circumstances and your managerial style, begin with a positively slanted statement about the employee's overall performance.
3. If termination is a possibility, positively address the employee's *potential*, and be honest about their overall performance.
4. Review the specifics* of the employee's performance. Be constructive.
       *(You should write the specifics on the PA form before you begin your appraisal.)
5. End with:
       A. an overall assessment (appraisal); and
       B. an objective for the future.
       The objective should focus on a specific area discussed in your performance appraisal. You can write this on the form before you begin your appraisal.

Role-Play: Employee's Assessment
1. Do you feel:
       A. motivated to do a better job;
       B. A lower stress level, knowing that your performance is either very good or capable of being very good;
       C. You will remain with the company (as opposed to this job *@•*@s);
       D. That management cares about you;
       E. That the appraisal was fair.
2. Did the appraiser make you feel comfortable?
3. How could the experience have been better for you?
Discuss your responses to the above criteria with your appraiser.

_____

_____

_____

_____

_____

_____

_____

Case Study 10.2: Designing a Performance Appraisal System

You are responsible for setting up a performance appraisal program for a hotel or restaurant (or any specific firm requested or approved by your instructor). You must justify each decision (i.e., why you made each decision).

The average tenure for employees of your firm is one of the following:

4 months/7 months/one year/three years (If a time period is not assigned, you can select one.)

Turnover calculation: If average tenure is below 1 year, divide 12 months by the tenure in months, then multiple by 100 (e.g., 12/9 mon. = 1.33 x 100 = 133%). If average tenure is above one year, you can either divide 12 by the tenure in months (e.g., 12/60 = 20%) or divide 1 (one) by the tenure in years and tenths of a year (e.g., 1/5 = 20%).

Firm:_____

Required:

Your instructor will assign one or more of the following requirements:

1. Prepare a performance appraisal form for one position of your choosing.

2. What is your firm's turnover rate? _____

3. The appraisal form must include at least eight criteria for evaluation. At least three of the criteria should relate to the job description, and three to the job specifications. Of these, at least two of the criteria must be qualitative. The rest can be quantitative or qualitative.

> Example of a highly subjective (qualitative) criteria:
>> 1. The employee exhibits a pleasant personality <u>1</u> 2 <u>3</u> <u>4</u> <u>5</u>
>
> What or who determines that an individual has a pleasant personality?
> Example of a highly objective (quantitative) criteria:
>> 2. Can the broiler person prepare all assigned food items within the
>> 12-minute time requirement on a 250-dinner evening?   Yes/No (circle one)

4. Each item must have an accompanying scale.

> Example: Poor = 1 Fair = 2   Good = 3   Very Good = 4   Excellent = 5; Yes/No; Exceeds expectations, meets expectations, does not meet expectations; and so forth.

> You must state why you feel your scale is appropriate. If you choose, you can use different scales. Some responses can be open-ended if you feel it is appropriate. Open-ended is when the appraiser can write whatever he or she thinks as opposed to simply giving numerical rating.

5. A. Create a performance appraisal program that will decrease the subjective or qualitative characteristics of most individual appraisals (i.e., a manager stating, "This is what I think of your performance … ") Some of your options (along with a good appraisal form) could include removing qualitative assessments or changing a qualitative assessment into a quantitative assessment, self-evaluations, management evaluations (most appraisals are performed by managers), peer evaluations, subordinate evaluations, customer evaluations, mystery shopper audits/evaluations. Multiple evaluations are referred to as 360-degree appraisals and are explained in this chapter. Justify your decisions.

   B. How realistic is the removal of subjectivity in a performance appraisal?

6. How often will you give performance appraisals (e.g., every 3, 4, 6, 12 months)? Justify your response.

7. How do you create a comparable rating system throughout the business? One where a housekeeper whose performance is average will receive the same overall rating as a reservationist's whose performance is also average. Is this an important issue? Why?

8. You must justify the cost of the evaluations. That is, can you state that the benefits of the performance appraisals (e.g., better performance) outweighs the cost? Use the following averages: time to complete an evaluation form—30 minutes; manager discussing the evaluation with employee—30 minutes (completing a manager's performance appraisal form and evaluation would take twice this long); cost per employee hour—$10; cost per manager hour—$30. You must specify a logical number of employees and managers for your firm.

Restaurant: The average number of employees for a full-service casual-dining restaurant is 80. Hotel: The average number of employees for a full-service hotel with restaurants and banquet service is .5 per room (average rooms, 300), without restaurants and banquet service, the number for hotels drops to about .3 employees per room.

9. How will you monitor the effectiveness of your performance appraisal program? That is, can it improve individual and business performance, can it be fairly administered, can it be used for things other than simply telling people how they are doing (promotions, personal development, etc.)?

_____

_____

_____

_____

_____

_____

_____

_____

_____

_____

_____

_____

_____

_____

_____

_____

Case Study 10.3: Compassionate Conservatism

You are the Director of Human Resources. Because of the following customer comment card, the front desk supervisor is sending an employee to visit with you:

Today as I was checking out after staying in your hotel for 3 days and spending over $500, one of your guest services agents (GSA), Benny Arnold, bluntly pushed my bill (folio) in front of me and said "sign here!" There was no review of the bill, the GSA had no expression on his face, and did not thank me for staying at your hotel. This is not the level of service I expected from what I consider to be a well-run hotel.

Benny has been written up (warned) for similar problems before. Other than this, he is very accurate with his work, always completes his assignments, has never missed a day of work, willingly fills in for other workers, and has been with the hotel for 10 years. Your hotel has excellent disciplinary policies.

Required:

1. What is the first step will you take to ensure that you develop the best possible solution? This step applies to any situation where a decision, especially a disciplinary decision, must be made.

2. Assuming that your firm has a relatively strict disciplinary policy, what would you do in this situation?

3. Would there be other situational factors to consider before finalizing your disciplinary program? Each of these could have varying degrees of importance/relevance on your decision.

4. As the Director of Human Resources, should a situation like this be consistently handled, or are there exceptions to policies?

5. Could the front desk manager deal with this on her own or should she consult the HR department? Explain your answer.

_____

_____

_____

_____

_____

_____

_____

_____

_____

_____

_____

<u>Human Resources Functional Plan Guidelines</u>
<u>Course Project</u>
Overview of Project

These guidelines explain the requirements of the project, how it will be graded, and includes a brief example of what you will need to do for each section. The major written portion of the project is a minimum of about six pages. The balance is primarily lists or brief statements, such as a SWOT Analysis, objectives, strategies, and tactics. The total pages for the project will be a minimum of about 15. The average length is about 20 pages. By the time you have a page or two for the different sections, length should not be a challenge. Quality is more important than quantity.

 Reading the entire guidelines before you begin your project will make preparing the project easier and quicker, and it will save you many hours of redoing sections.

 <u>Individual/Group</u>. This is an individual project, or if your instructor approves, a group project. If group projects are allowed, they must have a *minimum* of ten pages per member.

Purpose of a human resources plan (or any functional plan):

An organized process geared to selectively narrowing the number of possible alternative actions to those that the company can most effectively, efficiently/profitably, and ethically pursue.

To help you understand the project, PLEASE read the following:

Overview of Plan

Planning is simply identifying situations that need to be addressed/changed, setting a goal or objective that if accomplished will successfully address the situation, then determining how you will achieve your objective. That's it! The reason for the length of these guidelines is to give you the information you need to do a better job of it, essentially a chapter on planning, and to show you examples of how it is done (See Chapter One, Making Human Resource Decisions, Figure 1.8, page 14, for a copy of the model you will follow).

 When you work for a company, you may not realize it, but you are helping them implement their plan. By learning how to prepare the plan, you will be better prepared to work in management because you will know how the plan was prepared, how to monitor its implementation, and the basis for changing it. The following paragraph will include a little more detail to help you understand the main components of the plan.

 First, you prepare your **Situational Analysis.** This includes the **Internal Analysis**, information about company performance and abilities—mainly HR, but also other functional areas—marketing, finance, operations, administrative management) and the **Environmental Analysis**, information about the environment the firm operates in—customers, potential employees, competitors, etc. The **SWOT Analysis** is next. This is a summary of the Strengths and Weaknesses from the Internal Analysis and the Opportunities and Threats from the Environmental Analysis. You then analyze the SWOT to see which factors are most important to act on—the **Key Factor Analysis**. For each key factor, you set an **objective** that, if accomplished, will successfully address the Key Factor, that is, the particular Strength, Weakness, Opportunity, or Threat in the Key Factor Analysis. For example, for a key factor such as low pay, an objective might be to increase pay for all deserving employees by 20% within the next three months. Once you have the objective, you then set the **Strategies**, what you will do, and **Tactics**, how you will do it—the specifics of implementing the strategies. For each strategy and its related tactics you will establish some type of **Control** system to measure, monitor, and correct deviations from the tactics or objectives. You might also monitor your Situational Analysis to see if something has changed that would impact your key factors, objectives, strategies, or tactics.

General Guidelines:
Project Topic.

Unless a specific project is assigned, you can study/analyze any existing hotel, restaurant, or related hospitality business. A single unit would be easier than a chain and perhaps better for this assignment. Depending on the consistency of a chain's implementation of strategies and tactics, you can often make moderately accurate generalizations of the chain's performance from its individual units' performance.

 <u>Optional Topic</u>. If you decide that you want to pursue another career path and as long as the instructor approves, you can prepare the plan on the business of your choosing.

You can use your imagination as much as you like. The primary concern is that you get some experience with writing an HR plan, because it will prove invaluable to you when you enter the business world (and hopefully in the some of your other courses). The thought process for completing an HR plan is the same used to solve most any business/functional problem (i.e., Human Resources, Operations (kitchen, dining room, front desk, housekeeping), Marketing, Financial, and Administrative Management). As described above, you prepare a situational analysis, then set objectives, strategies/tactics, and controls. Implementation, which takes place between tactics and controls, is not normally addressed in the plan, except through the specifics in the tactics and how implementation will be controlled (i.e., in controls, the tactics are measured and monitored, objectives are either met or not met, deviations are then corrected).

Format

A. Use a 12-point font (new Times Roman and Calibri are currently the most common—this is Calibri).

B. Double-space between lines for business reports, especially drafts. This makes it easier for people to make changes or include notes.

C. To save money and the environment, please **do not turn in a folder for your plan.** In the real world or if you are doing the project for a company, you should have a simple folder of some type.

Content

The following HR planning model will be used as an outline for your project. **Type this outline in your computer, then fill in the appropriate information.** Exclude the notes in parentheses. Use the numbering format below. See each applicable section for specific requirements.

Outline of the Human Resources Plan that you will turn in.
(You need to use this outline. Copy it into your computer, then begin adding information.)

Cover Page

1. Executive Summary

2. Internal Analysis (Internal and Environmental Analyses = Situational Analysis) (This is only a heading, i.e., no information is required for the Internal Analysis heading. Of course, there is required information for other sections of the Internal Analysis.)

2.1. Human Resources (Only a heading, i.e., no information is required for 2.1 Human Resources. The HR information is included in the following sub-sections, such as 2.1.1, and so forth.)

2.1.1. Planning

2.1.2. Values, morale, and motivation

2.1.3. Compensation, benefits, and incentives

2.1.4. Employment laws

2.1.5. Job creation process

2.1.6. Recruiting

2.1.7. Selection

2.1.8. Orientation

2.1.9. Training

2.1.10. Performance appraisals and discipline

[For the non-human resource internal factors (marketing, operations, etc.), you only need to give a very brief analysis of performance.]

2.2. Marketing (Heading only)

2.2.1. Products offered

2.2.2. Prices

2.2.3. Place (location factors)

2.2.4. Promotions

2.2.5. Marketing management (overall performance of Marketing Dept.)

2.3. Operations (The production of the product or service. See the Internal Analysis section.)

2.4. Finance (optional—Is the company making a profit, financial flexibility, etc.)

3. Environmental Analysis (Heading only)

3.1. Operating Factors (For directions, see explanation and examples.)

3.1.1. Human resources

3.1.2. Customers
3.1.3. Competitors
3.1.4. Suppliers
3.2. Remote Factors (Heading only)
3.2.1. Political regulations
3.2.2. The economy
3.2.3. Societal trends
3.2.4. Technology
4. SWOT Analysis (Heading only)
4.1. Strengths
4.2. Weaknesses
4.3. Opportunities
4.4. Threats
5. Key Factor Analysis (The primary SWOT factors that will be dealt with in the strategies.)
6. Objectives (Heading only, as the objectives would be listed after the heading.) (Format – 6.1. to 6.10, Planning through Performance Appraisals and Discipline)
7. Strategies and tactics (Heading only) (You can use numbers, such as 7.1., 7.2. and so forth for the different strategies.)
8. Controls (Heading only) (8.1., 8.2., etc.)
9. References
10. Graphs
11. Grade (You must prepare a grade for your plan. This requires you to review your plan relative to the requirements. Your grade will be taken into consideration, but the instructor's opinion of how well the project followed these guidelines and its quality will determine your final grade.)

The following includes general information on each section of the plan (e.g., Executive Summary), requirements for the section, and samples of what you will do:

Cover Page

Human Resources Plan
Company Name
Date

Blank Space >
Bottom of page >

Prepared by: Your Name
Human Resources Consultant
The name of your school or college
for:
Course name
Instructor's name

1. Executive Summary

This is a short introduction and summary of the Human Resources Plan, detailing the key factors focused on in the plan, main objectives, or other important information. The executive summary should have its own page and, if less than one page, be centered on the page. Few are longer than one page, unless accompanying a lengthy or highly technical report. Because a company's executives must be sold on it or convinced of the plan's merits, it should create a feeling of confidence that what you are doing is the best choice for the company. Generally, the executive summary is the last section to be written.

••••••••••••••••••••••••••••••Executive Summary Requirement••••••••••••••••••••••••••••••

One or two paragraphs.

Example:

During the past year, the HR department has achieved the majority of 20XX objectives, with the exception of customer satisfaction scores. For the coming year our primary focus will be on improvements in hiring, training manuals, and the training process for every position within the firm. The overall goal being to raise our customer satisfaction scores above those of each of our major competitors.

2. Internal Analysis

The Internal Analysis is a narrative (i.e., paragraph form) of the company's performance in critical areas. In other words, you simply record what is going on in each area. For example, are employees happy with the quality of management, the physical environment, morale, training, and so forth? Are company policies effective and efficient for the firm? How do they compare to competitors' efforts? The simplest way to conceptualize this is to rate a firm's performance in any area on a 5-point scale (1 = poor, 2 = fair, 3 = average, 4 = above average, 5 = excellent). Ratings will vary between highly objective (unbiased) and highly subjective (opinionated) based on how they are determined. A customer survey prepared according to the scientific method (simplistically, research that is unbiased, randomly administered, valid, and reliable) may be highly objective. A Director of Human Resources saying that his/her training process is excellent would be considered a highly subjective rating. This opinion may be accurate, but may also represent an attempt at covering up problems.

All major factors from other functional areas that affect HR are normally included in the plan. For example, sales have declined (marketing), slow service times (operations), profits are down (finance) will all have an impact on the HR department. In the operations example above (slow service times), the following HR actions may be necessary: (a) review of the present job descriptions to see if there are too many tasks assigned; (b) employees with more experience or certain skills could be recruited and hired; (c) training could be increased or a new training program may need to be developed; and/or (d) some form of motivation could be added.

The idea is that you include all major and, within reason, minor performance issues for the company in the Internal Analysis. Later, as you read each paragraph (and sentence) you will note whether the information represents/infers a strength or weakness. This information will then be summarized in the SWOT Analysis. **Generally, you do not label any factor(s) in the internal analysis as strengths or weaknesses.** The reason for this is that you will not know if it is truly a strength or weakness until you compare it to what you find in your Environmental Analysis (e.g., you think your performance on morale is a strength, but then learn in the competitor analysis—in the Environmental Analysis—that it is actually a weakness—because of the excellent performance of your competitor in this area).

Strengths are any advantage—primarily assets and skills that a company has, relative to competitors and the demands of the various stakeholders—employees, management, owners, current or potential market, etc. (Examples: Great food or service, excellent locations, thorough training system, competent management and employees, many regular customers, and high sales.) Weaknesses are the opposite of the strengths.

Access to Information

As a student, you will have limited access to information. The easiest solution is to select a business that you currently work for or have worked for in the past. If you have not worked for the business, you should visit it to see what you can learn. If you are observant as a customer in a restaurant, you can learn a lot about their performance in various areas. You could also ask employees that work there, managers, looking on web sites, and browser searches (Yahoo and Google). For information that you cannot get, you can make *inferences* based on what you know or have found out. For example, if servers seem not to care, you could assume that morale is low and that managers are not talking to them about the problem. If the restaurant is not clean, perhaps there is no information in a job description or position manual that details who is supposed to do it, when it is supposed to be done, and how specific things are supposed to be cleaned. Essentially, what you are doing is identifying the *symptom* of a problem, and then attempting to identify the *cause*. In this particular situation, you may or may not be identifying the exact cause, however, the experience you get from this will be the same as if you had more information. That is, you identified a problem and prepared a solution for it.

Planning Focus

For Human Resources, the planning focus for the Internal Analysis will be to maximize strengths and minimize or correct weaknesses. A company cannot attempt to take advantage of a certain environmental opportunity and achieve corresponding objectives without having the appropriate skills or strengths. For example, if customers want better service or employees expect better training and your firm is weak in those areas, then something should be done to improve the weak areas—turn the weaknesses into strengths. Also, the company cannot defend itself against threats when it is weak in a related area. For example, if employee morale of a major competitor is higher than your firm's, then something should be done to turn your weakness into a strength, which would subsequently lessen or remove the threat of the competitor's morale being higher. In the HR department, the first focus of planning is to turn weaknesses into strengths.

Planning Focus

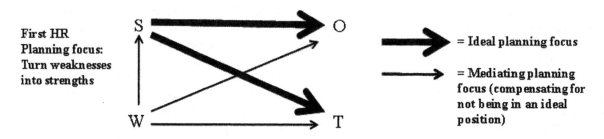

First HR Planning focus: Turn weaknesses into strengths

= Ideal planning focus

= Mediating planning focus (compensating for not being in an ideal position)

Functional Areas for the Internal Analysis
The following is a menu of possible topics that could be discussed. As you are assessing your firm's performance, you should record specifics and details rather than simply stating that morale or other factors are very good. For example, rather than simply stating that morale is good, fair, and so forth, specifics such as the following would be better: Our recent employee survey showed that employees are happy with benefits (4.5 on a 5-point scale), wages (4.4), and personal development (4.7), but are not pleased with our orientation program (2.8). In preparing a Human Resources plan, HR will be your main focus, but as previously mentioned, you must be aware of other functional areas of the business that may have an impact on HR.

Topics for the Internal Analysis

You Do Not Need To Include Every Detail That Follows In Your HR Plan. Quality is more important than quantity, but a reasonable quantity is necessary. Sometimes information that you thought was not important, may be found to be important when considered with other information that has been gathered. Because of your limited access to information, you will normally be limited to general descriptions of the company's performance in each major area. As your access increases, so should the accuracy and quality of assessments.

Human Resource Management
These HR topics are what we are focusing on in the course:
1. Planning related to human resources; 2. Values, morale, and motivation of employees and management; 3. Compensation, benefits, and incentive programs; 4. Upholds federal and state employment laws; 5. Job creation process; 6. Recruitment efforts; 7. Hiring; 8. Orientation and socialization, effective general policies (employee handbook); 9. Training procedures, level of employee skills; 10. Performance evaluation/appraisal and discipline policies. Additional details from each topic, such as the following, can be added:
11. General performance of human resources activities
12. Management skills (leadership and supervisory ability of managers)
13. Management morale and motivation
14. Management empowerment, initiative, intrapreneurship (ability of management to think and act like an entrepreneur)
15. Incentives, rewards and benefits for management
16. Management turnover percentage
17. Employee empowerment, initiative, intrapreneurship (ability of employees to think and act like an entrepreneur)
18. Employee turnover percentage
19. Quality and improvement are rewarded
20. Procedures for trainers

21. Training manuals for each position
22. Leaders' ability to sell their vision
23. Open channels of communication for all levels of the company
24. Opportunities for promotions and personal growth within the firm
25. Working conditions conducive to peak performance
26. Recruitment procedures/available pool of employees and managers

Operations
1. Product quality—For a restaurant, this would mainly focus on food, but could also include atmosphere, curb appeal, etc. For a hotel, this could include the quality of the room, lobby, curb appeal, etc. Customer satisfaction index (CSI) and relative perceived product/service quality (RPPQ) are often used as indicators of performance (i.e., relative to competitors).
2. Service quality—all services performed by employees for customers
3. Cleanliness—internal and external
4. Sanitation
5. Sales maximized by food and beverage servers and front desk employees
6. Effectiveness of controls (scheduling, purchasing, quality, operations)
7. Equipment—cleanliness, in working order, and serves its purpose
8. Labor cost percentage
9. Functional layout of restaurant or hotel
10. Safety and Security
11. Economies of scale (able to purchase large quantities at reduced prices)
12. Purchasing and inventory systems in use
13. Specifications written for all recurrent purchases
14. Employee scheduling
15. Written policies covering all tasks
16. Communication and enforcement of policies
17. Employees' performance according to policies/company standards

Marketing
Here you include a description of the Four Ps of marketing, plus the effectiveness with which it has been carried out—termed "marketing management."
1. Product
• Restaurants—Menu mix (type of foods offered and number of items of each food category offered—appetizers, entrees, desserts, and so forth), individual product sales, day part sales, sales by day, week, month, and seasonal fluctuations; the type of service and its compatibility with the restaurant's concept, etc.
• Hotels—Offerings such as the category of service for the hotel (budget, midscale, full-service, luxury, resort, etc.), the number and types of rooms, meeting facilities, catering services, room service menu, workout facilities, concierge, types of restaurants, menus, meals offered—breakfast, Sunday brunch, etc.
• Atmosphere and furnishings for both restaurants and hotels (meets customer's expectations and state of repair):
　　• Interior—dining room, hotel rooms, lobby, bar, meeting space, restrooms, hallways, elevators, recreational areas, etc.
　　• Exterior—building, parking lot, landscaping, etc.
2. Price
• Relative perceived value (RPV), price/value relationship, fairness
• Pricing strategies—how set, and flexibility—ability to raise or lower prices
3. Place/distribution
• The physical or geographic location—adequacy of location, accessibility, parking, recognized dining area, area stability, traffic generators, and any distribution or marketing channel factors such as delivery or vertical integration (e.g., buying your produce from growers)
4. Promotions
• Effectiveness of promotions—advertising, public relations, sales promotions, personal selling, merchandising
• Creativity of promotions

• An analysis of the effectiveness of present and past promotional efforts focused on employees, such as recruiting brochures, employee newsletters, and other employee communications (This would actually be a recruitment factor, but marketing could help with HR's recruitment efforts.)

5. Marketing Management (overall performance of the marketing department)

• Marketing department's general planning efforts

• Creativity of promotions—An analysis of the effectiveness of present and past promotional efforts focused on employees, such as recruiting brochures, employee newsletters, and other employee communications.

• Research and development of new products, services, and other strategies

• Market share or REVPAR compared to primary competitors

• Marketing information system—Keeping track of and utilization of information from internal records, and the Environmental Analysis. Ability to determine consumer needs, wants, demands.

• Brand loyalty and image

• Image as a socially responsible member of the community

• Market position

Financial

As a student, the amount of financial information accessible will be limited or nonexistent. You can make inferences based on whether the business appears to be busy at various key times (e.g., lunch or dinner for a restaurant or weekdays for most hotels). The most important financial figure is the company's profit relative to major competitors and to its debt. Is the company is making a profit, why, if not, why not and how much was the loss? Other financial indicators and factors will be helpful, such as working capital position—excess of current assets over current liabilities, and having an efficient/effective accounting system.

The following are examples of financial information that would be beneficial if obtainable:

1. General performance of finance/accounting activities
2. Profitability—What are the reasons for the company's current ROS—return on sales?
3. Sales/revenues
4. Financial strength—applicable financial ratios
5. Ability and cost of borrowing—relative to competition
6. Effective cost controls
7. Total cost of sales percentage
8. Food and beverage cost percentage
9. Labor cost percentage
10. Working capital position
11. Management's knowledge of cost control principles
12. Overhead compared to industry averages
13. Effective and efficient accounting system—DSR, monthly statements
14. Internal cash control
15. Computerized accounting/management system

Administrative Management (general managers up through corporate management)

1. Overall performance of top management
2. Organizational structure—chart available, technically correct and followed
3. Record of accurately recognizing internal abilities
4. Record of anticipating environmental trends
5. Record of setting and achieving appropriate objectives
6. Record of setting strategies, policies, and action plans that achieve stated objectives
7. Ability to recognize the need to change course, and the ability and willingness to change the firm's course
8. Aware of latest technologies and makes use of appropriate technologies
9. Overall success and growth of business
10. Vision for company and communication of the vision
11. Corporate culture compatible with goals of business
12. Sensitivity to diversity of local community
13. Systematic procedures for decision-making

14. Top management's leadership ability
15. Management and marketing information system—effective and easily accessible
16. Strategic planning system in place
17. Strategic plan followed

•••••••••••••••••••••••••••••Internal Analysis Requirement•••••••••••••••••••••••••••••••••••

You must include at least **Human Resources, Operational, and Marketing factors** in the Internal Analysis (see the Outline of the Human Resources Plan for specific topics). Since you will need to address each of the ten HR chapter topics throughout the project, you will want to identify areas for each where either performance is below what employees or customers expect, or determine that even though performance is good, it could be better. For example, our training program is perceived by employees to be excellent (a strength), but we have determined that it is important that we improve it (key factor). We will therefore set an objective related to the desire to improve the training program (Improve the employee's perception of the training program from 4.3 to 4.6 by June, 20XX) and the appropriate strategy and tactics detailing how the objective will be accomplished. A control mechanism will be created to monitor the implementation of the strategy and tactics.

The examples of factors listed under each of the functional areas above are only examples of what you can analyze. If you were preparing a Human Resources Plan for a company, you would probably analyze these factors and maybe more. For this project, you will only need the ten HR factors or Chapters from the book, five for marketing and an overview of operations. You should have about one paragraph for each section (i.e., one paragraph for each of the ten HR factors, five paragraphs for marketing and one or more for operations).

Examples: (You should have more information than what is shown below.)

2.1 Human Resources

Here you simply list the ten major Human Resources strategies, then comment on them. Only four of the strategies are listed below as examples. You should have more information than what follows.

2.1.2. Morale. The morale problem is probably associated with the training problem and a manager who does not relate well to employees (poor interpersonal skills). Morale was measured at 2.1 on a 5-point scale.

2.1.3. Compensation. The compensation package is barely adequate. Our pay is about what competitors are offering and we only have mandated benefits, such as social security, workers' compensation, and unemployment. It should be reassessed after finding out what competitors are offering.

2.1.9. Training. Poor customer service scores appear to be caused by a weak training program and low morale.

2.1.10. Performance Appraisals. There has not been a formal performance appraisal program in place for five years.

Continue with the balance of your HR strategies and information.

2.2. Marketing

2.2.1. Product. Customer satisfaction with service quality is lower than it should be. Currently, the Customer Satisfaction Index is at 3.2 on a 5-point scale. There are too many menu items for a limited staff.

2.2.2.Price………………………

2.2.3.Place/distribution……………………………

2.2.4.Promotion………………………

2.2.5. Marketing Management…………………

2.3. Operations (Operations is the production of the product or service.)

Servers are waiting on too many customers during their shift. Most other restaurants give servers one less table. The menu has too many items and is causing a slowdown in the kitchen. Managers are mostly doing a good job; however, some lower level supervisors appear to need additional training. Frequently, there are not enough employees to take care of customers.

3. Environmental Analysis

The purpose here is to gather information from the environment that can later be analyzed to help identify **Opportunities** to take advantage of, or **Threats** to defend against. In other words, you simply record information about a certain topic (e.g., competitors) that can be analyzed for its potential impact on the business.

• Opportunities are factors in the environment that represent a chance to increase sales and/or improve the business's image.

• Threats are anything in the environment that represents an obstacle to success or could reduce sales.

The decision on whether to refer to something as an opportunity or a threat can be abstract and based on your preference. For example, if potential employees expect flexible schedules and your firm is not currently as flexible as employees would like, is this an opportunity for your firm or a threat that could hurt your firm? It might depend on whether your firm has developed a reputation for *being* or *not being* flexible. In the end, it matters more that you are considering the fact that potential employees want more flexible hours, than referring to it as an opportunity or a threat. **The actual opportunities and threats are generally not listed in the Environmental Analysis. They are listed later in the SWOT Analysis.**

The Environmental Analysis, like the Internal Analysis, is generally in paragraph form and is often accompanied by pertinent supportive information (e.g., articles from magazines, printed material from the Internet, accounting reports, etc.). It is divided up into two areas, the **Operating Environment**, where you have some control, and the **Remote Environment**, where you have very little control. Each area is subdivided into specific topics.

The following topics addressed in the Environmental Analysis:

Operating Environment

(Human Resources/personnel (potential employees), Customers, Competitors, Suppliers—acronym HCCS— pronounced HECCS)

Human resources—Since this is the Environmental Analysis, the focus here is on **potential** employees—those not yet working for the business (i.e., not a description of your current employees). The simplest way of viewing this is by looking at the following four areas:

1. Potential Employee Expectations

These are the expectations of potential employees in applicable strategy areas of HR. In the real world you would ideally survey potential employees (informally or formally) to get this information. This way, you would be dealing with reasonably objective information, rather than your opinion. For this project you could use some of the ten major topics covered in the course. Some would be more important to potential employees (e.g., morale) than others (e.g., planning). Obviously one of the most important factors would be compensation. Most employees if asked would like the company they are considering going to work for to have the best possible training program. If you feel that this is a critical expectation of employees, you could include it. Other factors could include company values, high morale, obeying employment laws, diversity, clear directions (position manuals that describe how things should be done), a thorough orientation, effective training, and fair performance appraisals. For additional possible topics, see the list of morale and motivation factors in Chapter Two, Values, Morale, and Motivation.

Later in the SWOT Analysis, if the company *can* or *is* satisfying employee expectations, the applicable factor (e.g., compensation or training) could be included as an *opportunity*. If the company cannot satisfy employee expectations, it may be a *threat*. As in the Internal Analysis, you simply state the facts, without labeling it as an *opportunity* or *threat*.

2. Potential Employee Perceptions (Individual Perceptions and Overall Image/Perception)

There are two ways to look at this, applicants' overall image of the firm and the image/perceptions for specific areas. In the General Employee Expectations above, what potential employees want or would like was considered. Here, it is what they think a firm has to offer. Theoretically, the overall image would be based on the cumulative perceptions of the firm by potential employees. For example, if there were ten perception areas that were rated on a 5-point scale (1 = poor to 5 = excellent) and the average was 4.2, this would be the overall company image. If potential employees' perception of competitors individual factors and overall image were surveyed, the firm would have better information to help determine how to recruit these potential employees and for making decisions of what perceptions need to be changed.

For the same items noted in General Employee Expectations, you could simply state what you feel are potential employees' perceptions of your company's performance. You could also add other items if you thought potential employees perception of them had an impact on whether or not they would want to work for your firm. If potential employees had a poor perception of your firm in certain areas (threat), you could attempt to change it. If potential employees had an excellent perception (opportunity), you could use it to attract employees. The goal here is to become the *Employer-of-Choice*.

3. Employee Performance

You could make one overall judgment of the performance of potential employees or divide it by positions (i.e., servers, front desk agents) or skill categories (cleanliness, customer service skills). You could also discuss the characteristics of potential employees and their ability relative to your HR strategies. For example, do they have similar values to those espoused by our firm? Can employees be recruited and hired who can be trained to perform up to the standards in the firm's job descriptions/position manuals? Later in the SWOT Analysis, if the performance of employees who are available to work for your business, relative to your policies (e.g., job descriptions), is good, then this would be an opportunity. If not, then it would be a threat.

4. Availability

Are quality employees available within a reasonable distance from your business? If not, you will need to develop strategies to deal with the situation.

Competitors—An analysis of HR strategies for primary competitors (similar product and compete for the same type of employee and to a lesser degree, the same target customer). For example, if your HR Plan is for a casual-dining restaurant, then Chili's and other casual-dining restaurants in the trade area should be considered as primary competitors. Another important concept for the Human Resources competitor analysis is other places where employees can find jobs. For example, a bookstore, theater, or other businesses may be competing with your firm for employees.

      If this were a marketing plan, your primary concerns would be with the primary competitors' performance or quality in their products, prices, place (location), promotional activities, and marketing management (i.e., the 4 Ps of marketing plus marketing management). Since this is a Human Resources plan, your primary focus is on factors that impact potential employees' decision to work for those firms. While this can include some marketing factors, HR factors should be the primary focus for an HR plan. The analysis of HR factors for competitors is the same as those considered in the Internal Analysis for HR (i.e., you want to know about morale, pay, training, performance appraisals process, etc.). You could also try to find competitor performance information on the various factors that were considered in the Human Resources section of this Environmental Analysis (e.g., expectations and perceptions). Are there any HR strategies, or any strategies that impact employees, that a competitor has that your business could beneficially adopt (an opportunity)? Because of lack of access, this will obviously not be as complete as the company's Internal Analysis, but the more information, the better.

Customers—You should have a reasonable idea of customers' expectations before you can determine what type of employees you will need to hire and how those employees can best serve the customers (policies). The justification is that it is the employees who will attempt to meet customers' expectations. A common means of analyzing customers' characteristics is by what is know as the *Four Bases of Segmentation.*

1. Geographics—Where do actual and potential customers live or work?

2. Demographics—A statistical representation of a population by age, race, religion, education, income, value and type of home or car, life cycle—single, married, married with no children, married with a certain number of children, age of children, and so forth.

3. Psychographics—This is information about the general or inherent way people think or act, what they like to do, and how they occupy their time. These characteristics allow the firm to identify propensities of narrowly or broadly defined market groups to purchase various products or services. For example, someone who bowls will probably have different wants than someone that plays tennis. It includes, lifestyle analysis (activities, interests, and opinions), personality characteristics, and social class.

4. Buyer behavior—What are the benefits or attributes customers are seeking (quality service, fast service, relaxation, status, nutrition, location, atmosphere and so on), their price sensitivity (How much do they spend? They may want the Ruth's Chris, but demand/go to Chili's.), loyalty to one's business or a competitor's (Do they go to a variety of restaurants or do they have only a few favorites?), frequency of use (How often do they dine away from the home in general, and especially at your restaurant or your hotel, or competitors' businesses?).

Suppliers—Is an appropriate and consistent quality of supplies available at a reasonable price? Justification: A cook cannot serve good food if the suppliers are not delivering the appropriate quality. Of course, it may be management that is responsible for requesting and purchasing poor quality ingredients.

Remote Environment

(Politics, the Economy, Societal trends, Technology; acronym—PEST)

Politics/government—Are there any current or future political activities (local, state, or national) that may affect the business, such as taxes, healthcare, minimum wage laws, pollution, spending on infrastructure, change in political parties or philosophy (liberal to conservative). The government may also be a major customer.

Economy—What is the nature and direction of the economy, including inflation, recession, interest rates, available credit, disposable income (what is left after taxes) and discretionary income (what is left after basic needs are covered), and propensity of people to spend, especially at restaurants and hotels.

Societal trends—Are there any current or possible future lifestyle, employment choice, product or service trends, or demographic shifts that could affect human resources?

For example:

- There are fewer young people to work in restaurants and hotels;
- There are more elderly people available to work in restaurants and hotels;
- There are more minorities employed at restaurants and hotels;
- People are focused on having a better quality-of-life;
- People are eating foods lower in fat, salt/sodium, and sugar;
- People want spicier foods;
- People are trying more ethnic foods;
- With the increased consumer awareness about foods, people's tastes are becoming more discerning;
- Consumption of alcoholic beverages is decreasing;
- Travelers are more concerned about exercise;
- Families are taking more short vacations and weekend trips;
- Middle-income families are desiring of nicer hotels and facilities; and
- Woman are traveling more on their own.

Technology—Are there new methods or equipment that will make operating the restaurant or hotel simpler, less expensive, more productive, or speed delivery of products or services? For example, newer generation property management systems for hotels or point-of-sale terminals for restaurants, energy control devices, robotics, less labor intensive hotel laundry equipment, kitchen equipment that reduces labor cost, and so forth.

•••••••••••••••••••••••• **Environmental Analysis Requirements** ••••••••••••••••••••••••••••

1. You must include **a minimum of one paragraph** for each of the eight components of the Environmental Analysis (Operating environment—HCCS and Remote environment—PEST); **except** for numbers 2 and 3 below:

2. For *human resources* you must include data on at least **eight factors** (opportunities and/or threats) that could impact your business. The HR section of the Environmental Analysis has plenty of options. See the format below for one method of presenting this information.

3. For the Competitor Analysis you must record at least **eight factors** that represent opportunities or threats to your business. These could include your assessment of a competitor on the ten topics covered in the course (i.e., Planning through Performance Appraisals and Discipline). You can include non-HR factors that would have an impact on competitors' ability to attract potential employees, such as sales, location, decor, cleanliness, product quality, service quality, and so forth, however, most need to from HR.

<u>**Examples:**</u>

3.1. Operating Environment

3.1.1. Human Resources. Employees are readily available (1), however their ability is questionable (2). The firm's reputation amongst potential employees is only slightly better than most primary competitors (3). Expectations for pay (4) and training programs (5) are higher than what can currently be met by our firm……………

3.1.2. Customers…………………

3.1.3. Competitors. Our main competitor, Courtyard by Marriott, pays 50¢ more per hour (1), has a better training program than ours (2), but their morale is lower because…………………………(3).

3.1.4. Suppliers…………………

3.2. Remote Environment

3.2.1. Politics…………………

3.2.2. The Economy………………

3.2.3. Societal Trends. Because people are taking more short vacations, the leisure segment of the hotel industry is increasing.

   (This environmental factor might lead us to set strategies for hiring people who are family-oriented and those enthused about working with children.)

3.2.4. Technology…………………

4. SWOT Factors

A *listing* of the strengths, weaknesses, opportunities, and threats derived from the Situational Analysis (i.e., strengths and weaknesses from the Internal Analysis and opportunities and threats from the Environmental Analysis). The basic goal is to locate, within a Situational Analysis, the variables that will affect the choice of strategy. The process is to carefully review information from the Internal and Environmental Analyses, and then determine whether each sentence or section is important enough to be included in your SWOT Analysis. (Note: Most information should be included because you may not know what is important until you view the entire SWOT.) The SWOT Analysis serves as a framework to guide the selection of key factors—what you will focus on. The first consideration for HR management is to attempt to turn weaknesses into strengths. The second is to take advantage of strengths by going after environmental opportunities or using the strength to defend against threats.

You could quantify the SWOT factors, for example, "service quality is a 2.5 on a 5-point scale." The list could be prioritized, that is, each factor listed in order of potential importance to a company's strategy selection. One effective means of prioritization is to designate factors as Major Strengths, Minor Strengths, Neutral Internal Factors, Minor Weaknesses, and Major Weaknesses. For the environment, you would have Major Opportunities, Minor Opportunities, Neutral Environmental Factors, Minor Threats, and Major Threats.

Sample SWOT Analysis
(Examples of possible SWOT factors)

Strengths	**Weaknesses**
Experienced management team	Low profit/poor cost control
Most employees doing a good job	Last year's recruiting efforts were not effective
Customers highly satisfied	Few employee policies
with food and service	Potential employees in trade area
Excellent training program	have not answered newspaper ads
Corporate group business up 10%	Some employees have attitude problem
Fast service times	Management is not assertive
Ready access to capital	Unsuccessful ad campaigns
Good HR information system	High food or labor cost
Excellent sales	Problem with cleanliness
Great atmosphere	
Good image/position with customers	

Opportunities	**Threats**
Recession coming	Recession coming
(for fast-food and	(for casual-dining and midscale properties)
budget properties)	People are traveling less
No strong competitors	Chain competitor is advertising heavily
in trade area	Competitors have good employee policies
Weak competition	Competitors pay higher wages than we do
College nearby	Target customers limiting travel
Company with 300 employees	Demographic profile of customers
opening soon	does not fit product offering
Target customers in trade	Strong competitors doing poorly
area need a fast lunch	(sales are down)
Research identified that employees	Airline strike, or fare increases
want flexible schedules	
Research identified that employees	
want a stable work environment	
Many elderly in trade area	

•••••••••••••••••••••••••••• SWOT Analysis Requirement ••••••••••••••••••••••••••••

At least six factors for each SWOT section

Since you will be required to write strategies for each of the ten topics/chapters (e.g., Planning through Performance Appraisals and Discipline), you could begin here by listing them and identifying areas for improvement.

Examples: (The following provides a different format option for the SWOT Analysis from the one on the prior page. Both formats are commonly used in business.)

Strengths

> **Training:** Excellent cooks training manual
>
> **Morale:** Cooks' morale is high
>
> **Employment Laws:** Managers are vigorous in enforcing EEO laws
>
> **Recruiting:** The hotel has an excellent applicant pool from which to select excellent employees
>
> ....

Weaknesses

> **Performance Appraisals and Discipline:** Employee Performance is below that of competitors
>
> **Training:** No organized server training
>
> **Orientation:** The orientation takes 20 minutes
>
> **Morale:** Morale of servers
>
> **Selective Hiring:** Lower level supervisors' interpersonal skills
>
> **Planning:** Management has meetings, but many problems still persist
>
> ....

Opportunities

> ....

Threats

> ....

5. Key Factor Analysis

The business must now select those factors from the SWOT Analysis that have the greatest possibility for impacting the firm in a positive or negative manner. For example, in a firm's SWOT Analysis, there could be 40 weakness for human resources and 60 or more potential opportunities listed. It would not be economically or logistically feasible to try to focus on each. Therefore, only those with the greatest potential to help further the firm's competitive position will be selected.

If a skill that is needed to take advantage of an attractive opportunity does not exist—a weakness, then management must decide whether it is worth the effort to make appropriate changes. Weaknesses are generally the first focus of HR managers.

Also, if there are threats that pose an eminent risk, the company may need to make plans to defend against them. If the firm has a weakness in the area necessary to defend against the threat, management must determine whether the improvement is worth the effort or financial cost.

•••••••••••••••••••••••••••••••••••••Key Factor Requirement••••••••••••••••••••••••••••••••

You must select at least ten key factors related to your HR strategies from the Internal Analysis (strengths or weaknesses). You could also include areas that represent opportunities or threats from your Environmental Analysis (e.g. employees expect better pay, a competitor's morale is higher, customers expect better service, etc.). Since you will need objectives, strategies, and tactics for the 10 HR topics in the book, an environmental factor such as employees expect $9.00 per hour to work at the front desk could serve as the basis for an objective to raise front desk pay to $9.00. These will generally be directly related to the objectives you select and your strategies. They could also be indirectly related. For example, since the business's *image* impacts recruiting, almost any situational factor could be included to support the need for a new recruiting strategy (e.g., the perception that there is little advancement potential with your firm, low morale of the business's employees, few benefits, etc.).

Examples:
Strengths:
Selective Hiring and/or Planning: Experienced management team.
Marketing or Operations: Superior meeting space
Morale: Employee and Management morale is very high
Weaknesses:
Recruiting: Recruiting efforts have been marginal
Operations: Poor or slow service
Selection and/or Training: Inexperienced managers
Finance: Lack of capital
Operations: Low product or service quality
Training: No organized server training.
Orientation: The orientation is 20 minutes long and grossly inadequate
Morale: Morale of servers is low
Selective Hiring: Lower-level supervisors' interpersonal skills
Planning: Management has planning meetings, but nothing seems to improve
Performance Appraisals: Management has been too lenient with appraisals
Employment Laws: None of the 40+ year old applicants have been hired
Opportunities:
Human Resources: front desk agents expect $9.50 per hour to start
Human Resources: the perception of our restaurant's overall image is high
Competitors: Competing hotels have few employee benefits
Customers: Target customers in trade area want seafood.
Customers: Customers want more nutritious foods.
Customers: Target customers in trade area want a fast lunch
Economy: Recession coming (people will seek good values, tips may be lower)
Customers: Customers 40% more likely to go out on Friday and Saturday night
Human Resources and/or Customers: Large population of elderly in trade area
Societal Trends: People are seeking a better quality-of-life in everything
Threats:
Human Resources: Employees expect excellent training program
Human Resources: There are very few employees in the area with fine-dining experience
Customers: Trade area customers think our menu is out of date
Competitors: Trade area saturated with similar restaurants
Competitors: Competitors have lower overhead
Economy: because of recession, low occupancy for the area relative to other areas

6. Objectives

The objectives are desired outcomes that will be pursued, based on the key factors selected. The objectives should in most cases be quantified/measurable as a dollar amount, a percentage, a certain number of something, *and* have a specified time for completion. This helps establish clear goals and allows for the measurement of results. A new training program is essentially quantified because it represents one training program. The objective could be improved by adding a measurement such as, "Develop a new training program that will increase customer satisfaction by 20% (or employee satisfaction by 30%) by January 20XX."

In the following examples, the key factors are placed here only to show how the objectives were derived. If desired, the Key Factor Analysis could be combined with the objectives section (as in this example).
Three Components of a Good/Proper Objective:
1. What will be accomplished;
2. How it will be measured; and
3. When it will be accomplished.

•••••••••••••••••••••••••••• Objectives Requirement ••••••••••••••••••••••••••••••••

At least ten objectives, one for each main strategy (the ten covered in the course, Planning through Performance Appraisals and Discipline) that support the related key factors. You will later set strategies and tactics designed to help you achieve your objectives.

Examples:

Key Factor: Recruiting: Recruiting efforts have been marginal.
Objective: Increase number of qualified recruits (the applicant pool) by 40% by 9/1/20XX.
Key Factor: Morale: Morale is low for both employees (2.8 on 5-point scale) and managers (3.3)
Objective: Increase employee morale from 2.8 to 3.8 by March, 20XX; and management morale from 3.3 to 4.0 by February, 20XX.
Key Factor: Training: Managers need to constantly correct employees
Objective: Create new training program by 4/20/20XX; Implement the program by 5/20/20XX.
Key Factor: Customers: Travelers are taking more short trips.
Objective: Train staff to take better care of weekend leisure guests by January 15, 20XX (this segment includes: weekend vacationers, shoppers, those seeking entertainment, etc.).
Key Factor: Customers: The target customer wants a fast lunch.
Objective: Reduce kitchen time from 15 minutes to 10 minutes within the next 3 months.

Additional Examples: Unless otherwise stated, all objectives below are for one year. Normally, interim objectives—quarterly or monthly—would be set so employees and managers would know whether or not they were on track to meet the annual goal. While some of these objectives directly relate to HR, they all relate in one way or another to HR. For example, an objective of a 97% customer satisfaction index may require finding new employees to handle an increase in customer traffic, additional training, and perhaps better pay, etc.
• Have new recruitment plan ready within one month.
• Prepare new employee policy manual by February 20XX.
• Review and update training manuals by March 20XX
• Create a new compensation and benefits package by January 20XX.
• Improve customer satisfaction scores from their current 3.5 (5-pt. scale) to 4.0 by January 20XX.
• $1,600,000 sales for the coming year. (Last year's sales were $1,525,000.)
• 35% food cost for the next year. (Last year FC was 37%) (Food cost can be included because without its being controlled, pricing and profit could not be controlled.)
• Increase daily customer count to 400—250 for lunch, 150 for dinner.
• Increase overall occupancy by 10% by June 20XX.
• Increase corporate group segment by 15% by June 20XX.
• Increase number of elderly customers by 25% by March 20XX.
• Increase take-out business by 15% by January 20XX.
• Add a bakery to the restaurant by January 20XX.
• Lower service time for lunch to 15 minutes by February 15, 20XX.

Note: If desired, you can immediately follow a key factor with its related objective, strategy, tactics, and controls. Alternatively, you can include all key factors together in one section, doing the same for objectives, strategies, tactics, and controls.

7. Strategies and Tactics

Strategies are brief statements of how the human resources department will achieve its stated objectives. The strategies you include should be based on the key factors selected and the objectives that were set. For example, if you had a key factor of morale being low and an objective to improve it from 2.8 to 3.8 by a certain date, the strategy would be a brief and general statement about how you will achieve that objective. For example, Increase morale through better incentives programs.

The strategies listed should follow the chapter topics from the course. You could add other HR topics or divide up topics (e.g., values, morale, and motivation could be separated into (a) values and (b) morale and motivation; compensation could be divided up into (a) pay, (b) benefits, and (c) incentives. An effective presentation method for both strategies and tactics follows in the next section.

Tactics are the specifics of what is necessary to accomplish the human resource strategies. **Action Plans** are relatively temporary tactics, while **Policies** are relatively permanent tactics. For most HR tactics, you will need to prepare both action plans and policies, the reason being that you will generally need additional information before you attempt to prepare a policy (e.g., someone may need to do more research on a topic, such as training programs). Additionally, because most HR tactics do not change very frequently, the outcome of most tactics for HR are policies. Marketing tactics, on the other hand, are mostly action plans, because they are subject to change on a moment's notice.

There should be enough information for anyone reading it to understand: *what* will be done (server training program) and what the *focus* will be (personality and relaxed/positive customer interaction), *who* is responsible, the *time frame* for its accomplishment, any *costs* involved, *where* the policies will be recorded (e.g., human resources policies, employee manual, operations manual, etc.) can also be included. It is not mandatory to include each of these factors, but they are the most common.

•••••••••••••••••••••••••••••••••••Strategies and Tactics Requirement••••••••••••••••••••••••••••••

1. You are required to have strategies and tactics for each of the ten topics covered in the course (i.e., Planning through Performance Appraisals and Discipline).

2. Except for recruitment, where only action plans are the norm, you must include *at least* one action plan and one policy for each set of tactics and they must be labeled as such. *Including just the minimum would get you a minimum grade.*

3. For the job creation process (JCP), you must include an example of how you would apply the four components of the JCP on the position of your choice. See the 7.5. Job Creation Process for Servers below for an example. Please select a position other than server.

3. A minimum of about four pages is required. You do not need to write the complete tactics for every strategy you select. The Job Analysis (the policies) for a server in a restaurant could take ten pages or more. Just include a portion of the tactics, as in the "very brief/minimum" examples below.

The strategies and tactics selected should solve the problems or address the issues you have noted in your key factor (based on the Situational Analysis and SWOT Analysis) and help the company achieve its objectives.

Examples:
The following three examples provide the format you should follow:
7.5. Job Creation Process for Servers
Strategy
Prepare a new job analysis, design, description, and specifications for servers. The focus should be on personality and relaxed verbal interaction with guests and with fellow employees.
Tactics
Action Plans
Job Creation Process:
1. John Doe will be responsible for preparing the server's job analysis, design, description, and specifications.
2. Research for new job descriptions and specifications must be gathered that highlight the latest developments concerning personality and effective verbal interaction in services.
3. The job descriptions and specifications should be completed and ready for testing by December 15, 20XX.
Policies
Job Analysis
Position: Server
Duties (number) and Tasks (letter):
1. ORDER-TAKING
A. If you cannot take an order immediately, acknowledge the party by saying, "I'm your server. I'll be right with you."
B. Write the date, table number, number of covers (number of customers ordering from the table), and your name on the guest check.
C...................

2. SERVING FOOD AND BEVERAGES

A. Hot food is the server's number one priority. Make sure all food is served as soon as it is ready. (If a food runner system is used, where each server delivers any orders that are ready, each server should deliver his or her share.)

B. Check the order for problems such as spills, an unappetizing appearance, or improper portions before taking the order into the dining room. When necessary, politely ask the cook to correct the order. If the cook refuses, or if the problem persists, tell the manager.

C...............

3. SERVICE DURING THE MEAL

A. After delivering the food, ask customers whether there is anything else they might want.

B. Return to each table approximately two minutes after serving the customers or after they have sampled their food or drinks, to make sure that the customers are satisfied. Ask such questions as "How is everything?" or, if possible, be more specific, "Is the steak cooked to your liking?" If there is a problem, solve it immediately and inform the manager.

C......................

4. DELIVERING THE CHECK

A. Make sure the customer does not wait too long for the check. At breakfast, the check is normally delivered with the meal. For lunch and dinner, deliver the check after everyone at the table has finished their meal, their plates have been removed, and they have turned down your offer of dessert. If they are having dessert, deliver the check after the customers have finished it.

B. Make sure the guest check is complete (all items rung up) and correctly totaled. Write the total on the back in one-inch-tall numbers and circle it to avoid any misunderstandings.

C.......................

Job Design

> **Job Simplification**:
> Servers will no longer need to cut and prepare desserts.
>
> **Job Enlargement**
> Servers will begin polishing silverware to remove water spots before rolling in napkins.

Job Description

> **Position**: Server
> **Reports to**: Manager on duty
> **Works closely with**: Hostperson, bussers, and cooks
> **Rate of pay**: Current rate authorized by the U.S. tax code or established by the business
> **Job Summary**: Efficiently and courteously serves guests, while.........................
> **Duties**: (The duties are transferred from the Job Analysis.)

Job Specifications

1. Must be 21 years of age
2. Must be able to stand on feet for 3 or more hours at a time
3. Well mannered
4. Well groomed, effective personal hygiene
5. Outgoing, pleasant personality
6. Above average interpersonal skills, patience, and teamwork-oriented
7.........................

7.6. Recruitment

Strategy

Develop a new recruiting program focused on college graduates.

Tactics

Action Plans

1. Visit NAU and UNLV twice each during 20XX during their career fairs.
2. Visit the Human Resources classes in Hotel and Restaurant Programs in our region.
3. Interview graduating seniors on each trip.
4. Hire four graduates from our new university contacts.

Note: In recruitment, if the action plan includes everything necessary to accomplish the strategy, then nothing more is necessary (i.e., no policies). For example, since recruiting tasks are frequently modified based on need (not permanent policies), the majority of recruiting tasks will likely be action plans.

7.9. Training

Strategy

Prepare a new training program for servers. The current training program has been in place for four years and needs to be updated. Also, primary competitors are receiving higher customer satisfaction scores than us.

Tactics

Action Plan

1. John Doe is responsible for the preparing the training program.
2. Research must be implemented to gather data on effective training programs.
3. The new training program must begin by December 15, 20XX.
4. After researching theoretically sound methods of services training, meet with servers to get their input.
5. Hold a training meeting for all servers.

       A. Announce the new incentive program.

       B. Review changes in job descriptions.

       C. Utilize role playing to show servers how the restaurant can improve its service quality.

       D.....................

Policies

1. Have all present servers go through new training program.

[The core of the training program is the Position Manual (derived from the Job Analysis—Duties and Tasks). The balance includes tests and other evaluation techniques, means of training employees to perform the duties and tasks, training trainers, and so forth.]

2. The training methods for servers will include ... The justification for these methods includes ...
3. The training manual will include ... (See training topic for ideas.)
4. The training schedule for servers follows:

Day 1 ...

       1. The day will begin with ...

       2. Each trainee will ...

Day 2 ..., etc.

5. During and after training, trainers will evaluate each trainee's progress (Form XXX). The trainee will likewise evaluate their own progress (Form XXX)
6. Have monthly meetings to update servers on the progress of their efforts (e.g., improvements in service quality scores, increases in sales, etc.)
7. Managers are to coach servers who are having problems completing all of their require tasks according to the company standards.

       8. ....

8. Controls

Controls denote how the company will monitor the plan during its implementation to make sure it is achieving its potential relative to its strengths and weaknesses and the opportunities and threats in the environment. Progressing from the beginning of the plan:

- Have there been changes in the environment that require a change in objectives and/or strategies and tactics?
- Were the right objectives set? Perhaps they were too high, too low, or they need to be changed because of a change in the environment.
- Were the right strategies and tactics set and implemented?
- Were the strategies and tactics effectively implemented?
- Are contingency plans needed and ready in case any portions of the plan are falling short of their target?
- After the period of time the plan covers, the Human Resources department must decide what was successful and why it was successful. Unsuccessful strategies and tactics must also be analyzed.

•••••••••••••••••••••••••••••• **Controls Requirement** ••••••••••••••••••••••••••••••

You are required to have controls for two of your strategies.

Example:
    "We will monitor our progress towards our objective of an increase in our customer satisfaction index from 3.5 (5-pt. scale) to 4.0. If we are not meeting our objective, we will increase training and possibly incentives."

9. References and Citations

Each time you use information from a source other than your own memory, you must *reference* and *cite* the author's work.

The reference is at the end of the plan. <u>You will need a minimum of ten references from books, periodicals, or from the Internet</u>. Additional references from personal interviews can and should be included, but they cannot be counted as your ten from publications. The citation is the recognition in the text of where the information came from (see example below).

•••••••••••••••••••••••••••••**References and Citations Requirement**••••••••••••••••••••••••••••

Ten references. Each reference must be cited in the text of your plan. For this project, please **put all citations in bold print** (see below). This will make it easier for me to find them. You would generally not do this in a real-world project.

Usually, most references are for your Environmental Analysis (e.g., The economy is in a slow recovery (**Chen, 2008**). Those of you who select larger firms, like Hilton, should be able to locate information on current employee strategies/tactics (e.g., The majority of Hilton's new training program is web-based (**Hart, 2008**).

Examples:

<u>All references used must be cited (see example below).</u>
The format for the references are as follows:
Book:
Luck, D. J., & Rubin, R. S. (1997). *Human resources research* (7th ed.). New Jersey: Prentice Hall.
Periodical:
Costen, W. M., Johanson, M. M., & Poisson, D. K. (2010). The development of quality managers in the
        hospitality industry: Do employee development programs make cents? *Journal of Human
        Resources in Hospitality & Tourism, 9*(2), 131-141.

                        Volume = 9   Number = (2)
Internet:
Barsky, J. (2010). Luxury Hotels and recession: A view from around the world. www.lhw.com/download_s/230.pdf

Personal Interview: (These <u>do not</u> count as part of your ten published references.)
Williams, John (2003). A general discussion of human resources management for hotels. Flagstaff, Arizona:
<u>Comfort Inn.</u>

Citation Examples (citing in text):
The main problem is a lack of planning **(Luck & Rubin, 1987)**. Another problem area is having the appropriate leadership skills to carry the plan out **(Makridakis, 1996)**.
If this were a quote, add the page number(s):
"The main problem is a lack of planning" **(Luck & Rubin, 1987, p. 243)**.

10. Supportive Data/Graphs

You must make tables from actual information or information as you perceive it, then create Excel graphs from the information in the tables. Supportive data could be related to the particular firm or to its industry (e.g., monthly or quarterly sales, unit growth, employee turnover rate, guest counts, customer survey data, employee benefits offered by companies, morale for each quarter, strengths and weaknesses, opportunities and threats, and other supportive information. Basically any information directly or indirectly related to employees in the hospitality industry.)

•••••••••••••••••••••••••**Supportive Date/Graphs Requirement**••••••••••••••••••••••••••

You must create two graphs as specified above. Include the tables from which the graphs were created. They can be any kind of graph, circle, bar, trend line (x and y axis), etc..

11. Grade

Each plan will be graded by the student(s) that prepared according to how well it followed the directions, quality of content, insight (degree of understanding of the project) thoroughness (covers each section adequately), effort, and appearance of the plan (not the cover, but the organization and neatness). The instructor will also examine how well directions were followed, especially your identification of situational factors (SWOT and Key Factor Analysis) and how you developed objectives, strategies, and tactics that support your findings (solved weaknesses, defended against threats, etc.).

••••••••••••••••••••••••••••••**Grading Requirement**••••••••••••••••••••••••••••••••••••

1. You must grade your own project according to the requirements for each section. Full credit can be given for excellent work; in the average range for meeting basic requirements; and no credit if directions for the section were not followed.
The total potential points for each section are included below.
2. Submit the following grading outline with your project.

Grading Outline for your Project (to be submitted with your project).

1. Cover page—2 points   _____

2. Grammar—5 pts.   _____

3. References—5 pts.   _____

4. Citations—5 pts   _____

5. Executive summary—3 pts.   _____

6. Internal Analysis—10 pts.   _____

7. Environmental Analysis—10 pts. _____

8. SWOT Analysis—5 pts.   _____

9. Key Factor Analysis—5 pts.   _____

10. Objectives (#s and dates)
          —10 pts.   _____

11. Strategies, tactics, and
implementation of tactics
(policies and action plans)—15 pts. _____

12. Controls—5 pts.   _____

13. Charts/graphs—5 pts.   _____

14. Overall quality—10 pts.
format followed (2.1., etc.),
professionalism, detail, etc.   _____

15. Grade sheet completed in an objective manner and by comparing the requirements in the project to the work in the project. 5 pts.   _____

Total Grade _____ (out of 100)

References

Altinay, L., Altinay, E., & Gannon, J. (2008). Exploring the relationship between the human resource management practices and growth in small service firms. *Service Industries Journal, 28*, 919-937.

Americans with Disabilities Act (1992). A technical assistance manual of the employment provisions (Title I) of the Americans with disabilities act. Equal Employment Opportunity Commission.

Bernhardt, K. L., Donthu, N., & Kennett, P. A. (2000). A longitudinal analysis of satisfaction and profitability. *Journal of Business Research, 47*, 161-171.

Berry, C. M., Sackett, P. R., & Johnson, J. W. (2009) Faking in personnel selection: Tradeoffs in performance versus fairness resulting from two cut-score strategies. *Personnel Psychology, 62*, 833-863.

Brenner, B. K. (2010). Instituting employee volunteer programs as part of employee benefit plans yields tangible business benefits. *Journal of Financial Service Professionals, 64*(1), 32-35.

Brewer, T. Virtues we can share: Friendship and Aristotelian ethical theory. *Ethics, 115*, 721-758.

Byars, L. L. (1984). Strategic management: Planning and implementation. New York: Harper & Row.

Collins, A. B. (2007). Human resources: A hidden advantage? *International of Contemporary Hospitality Management, 19*(1), 78-84.

Costen, W. M., Johanson, M. M., & Poisson, D. K. (2010). The development of quality managers in the hospitality industry: Do employee development programs make cents? *Journal of Human Resources in Hospitality & Tourism, 9*(2), 131-141.

Craig, E., & Silverstone, Y. (2010). Tapping the power of collective engagement. *Strategic HR Review, 9*(3), 5-10.

De Cenzo, D. A. & Robbins, S. P. (1996). Human resource management (5th ed.). New York; Wiley.

Dewhurst, M., Guthridge, M., & Mohr, E. (2010). Motivating people: Getting beyond money. *McKinsey Quarterly, 1*, 12-15.

Dressler, B. (1997). Human resource management (7th ed.). Upper Saddle River, New Jersey: Prentice Hall.

Drucker, P. (1974). Management: task, responsibilities, practices. New York: Harper & Row, Publishers, Inc. p. 75.

Dunlap, M. (2010). Create a successful incentive program. *Journal of Financial Planning, May*, 12-13.

Enz, C. (2009). Human Resource Management. *Cornell Hospitality Quarterly, 50*, 578-583.

Gibbons, F. X., & Kleijner, B. H. (1994). Factors that bias employee performance appraisals. Work Study, 43, 10-13

Gomez-Mejua, L. R., Balkin, D. B., & Cardy, R. L. (1998). Managing human resources (2nd ed.). Upper Saddle River, New Jersey: Prentice Hall.

Jerris, L. A. (1999). Human resources management for hospitality. Upper Saddle River, New Jersey: Prentice Hall.

Jung, C.G. (1969). The archetypes and the collective unconscious. (RF.C. Hull, Trans.) 2nd ed. New York: Princeton University Press.

Juran, J. M. (1992). Juran on quality by design. New York: The Free Press.

Kale, S. H. (2007). Internal marketing: An antidote for Macau's labor shortage. *UNLV Gaming Research & Review Journal, 11*(1), 1-11.

Kanji, G. K., & Chopra, P. K., (2010). Corporate social responsibility in a global economy. *Total Quality Management & Business Excellence, 21*(2), 119-143.

Kontoghiorghes, C. & Frangou, K. (2009). The association between talent retention, antecedent factors, and consequent organizational performance. *Advanced Management Journal, 74*(1), 29-58.

Kuo, T. H., & Ho, L. A. (2010). Individual difference and job performance: The relationships among personal factors, job characteristics, flow experience, and service quality. *Social Behavior & Peronality: An international Journal, 38*, 531-552.

LBJ Library, University of Texas, (2010). President Lyndon B. Johnson's Commencement Address at Howard University: "To Fulfill These Rights", June 4, 1965. (www.lbjlib.utexas.edu/Johnson/archives.hom/speeches.hom/650604.asp)

Liddle, A. J. (2008). Operators: Technology improves training, save time and money. *Nation's Restaurant News, 42*(31), 18-20.

Lindner, J., & Zoller, C. (2010). Selecting employees for small businesses: Doing it right the first time. Ohio State University, ohioline.ag.okio-state.edu

Luthans, F., Avey, J. B., Avolio, B. J., & Peterson, S. J. (2010). The development and resulting performance impact of positive psychological capital. *Human Resource Development Quarterly, 21*(1), 41-67.

Malik, F. McKie, L., Beatie, r., & Hogg, G. (2010). A toolkit to support human resource practice. *Personnel Review 39*, 287-307.

Mathis, R. L. & Jackson, J. H. (1997). Human resource management (8th ed.). New York: West Publishing Company.

Millar, M. (2010). Internet recruiting in the cruise industry. Journal of Human Resourses in Hospitality & Tourism, 9(1), 17-32.

Milliman Medical Index (2009). Milliman.com

Momeni, N. (2009). The relationship between managers' emotional intelligence and the organizational climate they create. *Public Personnel Management, 38*(2), 3-48.

Murphy, K. S., Dipietro, R. B., Rivera, M., & Muller, C. C. (2009). An exploratory case study of factors that impact the turnover intentions and job satisfaction of multi-unit managers in the casual theme segment of the U.S. Restaurant industry. *Journal of Foodservice Business Research, 12*, 200-218.

National Restaurant Association (1977). NRA Seminar on supervision.

Noland, J., & Phillips, R. (2010). Stakeholder engagement, discourse ethics and strategic management. *International Journal of Management Reviews, 12*(1), 39-49.

Oh, I. S., & Berry, C. M. (2009). The five-factor model of personality and managerial performance: Validity gains through the use of 360 degree performance ratings. *Journal of Applied Psychology, 94*, 1498-1513.

Paul, A. K., & Anatharaman, R. N. (2003). Impact of people management practices on organizational performance: analysis of a causal model. *International Journal of Human Resource Management, 14*, 1246-1266.

Parker, L. D., & Ritson, P. (2005). Fads, stereotypes and management gurus: Fayol and today. *Management Decision 43*, 1335-1357.

Pearce, J. II, & Robinson, R. B., Jr. (2009). *Formulation, implementation, and control of competitive strategy* (11th ed.). New York: McGraw Hill.

Pope, H. H. (1972). Guidelines for foodservice managers.

Raub, S., & Streit, E. M. (2006). Realistic recruitment: An empirical study of the cruise industry. *International Journal of Contemporary Hospitality Management, 18*, 278-289.

Reich, A. Z. (1997). *Marketing management for the hospitality industry: A strategic approach.* New York: John Wiley.

Reich, A. Z. (2000). A good battle cry is half the battle: mission statements with a sense of mission. *Journal of Hospitality and Tourism Education, 12*(3), 32-39.

Reich, A. Z. (2000). Improving the strategy selection process: The strategic analysis questioning sequence. *Journal of Hospitality & Leisure Marketing, 7*(1).

Reich, A. Z., Xu, Y., & McCleary, K. W. (2010). The influence of social responsibility image relative to product and service quality on brand loyalty. *Florida International University Review, 28*(1), 20-51.

Reich, A. Z. (in-press) Relative Perceived Product Quality: Achieving a better understanding of the competitive environment. *Journal of Foodservice Business Research.*

Schmidt, F. L., Shaffer, J. A., & Oh, I. S. (2008). Increased accuracy for range restriction corrections: Implications for the role of personality and general mental ability in job and training performance. *Personnel Psychology, 61*, 827-868.

Schneier, C. E., Shaw, D. G., & Beatty, R. (1992). Companies' attempts to improve performance while containing costs: Quick fix versus lasting change. *Human Resource Planning, 15*(3), 1-25.

Somaya, D., & Williamson, I. O. (2008). Rethinking the 'Ward for Talent.' *MIT Sloan Management Review, 49*(4), 29-34.

Small Business Majority. (March 29, 2010) What's in healthcare reform for small businesses?

Staff (2005). The competitive advantage of embracing diversity. *Leader to Leader, 36*, 61-62.

Sturman, M. C., & Sherwyn, D. (2009) The utility of integrity testing for controlling worker's compensation costs. *Cornell Hospitality Quarterly, 50*, 432-445.

Sutton, C. D., & Woodman, R. W. (1989). Pygmalion goes to work: The effects of supervisor expectations in a retail setting. *Journal of Applied Psychology, 74*(6), 943-950.

Tews, M. J., Michel, J. W., & Lyons, B. D. Beyond personality: The impact of GMA on performance for entry-level service employees. (2010). *Journal of Service Management, 21*, 344-362.

Thompson, A. A., & Strickland, A. J. III (1992). *Strategic management: Concepts and Cases.* Illinois: Richard D. Irwin, Inc.

Tracey, J. B., Sturman, M. C., & Tews, M. J. (2007). Ability versus Personality. *Cornell Hotel & Restaurant Administration Quarterly, 48*, 313-322.

U.S. Commission on Civil Rights. 2010. www.usccr.gov/

U.S. Department of Labor. 2010. Fair Labor Standards Act (FLSA). www.dol.gov/compliance/laws/comp-flsa.htm

U.S. Equal Employment Opportunity Commission. 2010. www.eeoc.gov.

US.gov (The primary U.S. federal government web site).

Vitell, S. J., Ramos, E., & Nishihara, C. M. (2009). The role of ethics and social responsibility in organizational success: A Spanish perspective. *Journal of business Ethics, 91*, 467-483.

Wang, S., & He, Y. (2008). Compensating non-dedicated cross-functional teams. *Organization Science, 19*, 753-765.

Wiesner, W. H., & Cronshaw, S. F. (1988). A meta-analytic investigation of the impact of interview format and degree of structure on the validity of the interview. *Journal of Occupational Psychology, 61*, 275-290.

Williams, C., & Thwaites, E. (2007). Adding value to toursim and leisure organizations through frontline staff. *Tourism Recreation Research, 32*(1), 95-105.

Woods, R. (2002). Managing hospitality human resources (3rd ed.). Lansing, Michigan: American Hotel and Lodging Association.